Bloom's Modern Critical Interpretations

Bloom's Modern Critical Interpretations

Emily Brontë's
Wuthering Heights
Updated Edition

Edited and with an introduction by
Harold Bloom
Sterling Professor of the Humanities
Yale University

BLOOM'S
LITERARY CRITICISM
An imprint of Infobase Publishing

Bloom's Modern Critical Interpretations: Wuthering Heights, Updated Edition

Copyright ©2007 Infobase Publishing
Introduction © 2007 by Harold Bloom

Bloom's Literary Criticism
An imprint of Infobase Publishing
132 West 31st Street
New York NY 10001

ISBN-10: 0-7910-9364-6
ISBN-13: 978-0-7910-9364-1

Library of Congress Cataloging-in-Publication Data
Emily Brontë's Wuthering Heights / Harold Bloom, editor. — Updated ed.
   p. cm. — (Bloom's modern critical interpretations)
  Includes bibliographical references and index.
  ISBN 0-7910-9364-6 (hardcover)
  1. Brontë, Emily, 1818-1848. Wuthering Heights. I. Bloom, Harold. II. Title.
  PR4172.W73E45 2007
  823'.8--dc22
                                        2006031148

Contributing Editor: Amy Sickels
Cover design by Ben Peterson
Cover photo: Victoria & Albert Museum, London/Art Resource, New York

Printed in the United States of America
Bang EJB 10 9 8 7 6 5 4 3 2 1

This book is printed on acid-free paper.

Contents

Editor's Note

My introduction meditates upon the *strangeness* of Emily Brontë's Byronic "northern romance," which I judge to be essentially Gnostic in its very original spiritual orientation.

Virginia Woolf, major novelist-critic, considers *Wuthering Heights* in conjunction with *Jane Eyre*, both of which she finds to be prose-poems.

In Dorothy Van Ghent's visionary interpretation, Heathcliff is more daemonic than human, while the founding mothers of Feminist literary criticism, Sandra Gilbert and Susan Gubar, read the novel as Emily Brontë's proto-feminist critique of John Milton's *Paradise Lost*.

For Nancy Armstrong, *Wuthering Heights* deliberately evades all literary genres, after which Stevie Davies gives us an account of the novel as a singular myth of rebirth, in which every new life entails the sacrifice of a previous one.

Joseph Allen Boone sees the book as a profound critique of societal-approved sexual unions, while Regina Barreca emphasizes the feminist dominance of the relations between sex and death in Emily Brontë.

This volumes final essay is a politicized treatment in which Susan Meyer traces a mode of reverse colonialism (which I admit my inability to locate).

HAROLD BLOOM

Introduction

The three Brontë sisters—Charlotte, Emily Jane, and Anne—are unique literary artists whose works resemble one another's far more than they do the works of writers before or since. Charlotte's compelling novel *Jane Eyre* and her three lesser yet strong narratives—*The Professor, Shirley, Villette*—form the most extensive achievement of the sisters, but critics and common readers alike set even higher the one novel of Emily Jane's, *Wuthering Heights*, and a handful of her lyrical poems. Anne's two novels—*Agnes Grey* and *The Tenant of Wildfell Hall*—remain highly readable, although dwarfed by *Jane Eyre* and the authentically sublime *Wuthering Heights*.

Between them, the Brontës can be said to have invented a relatively new genre, a kind of northern romance, deeply influenced both by Byron's poetry and by his myth and personality, but going back also, more remotely yet as definitely, to the Gothic novel and to the Elizabethan drama. In a definite, if difficult to establish sense, the heirs of the Brontës include Thomas Hardy and D. H. Lawrence. There is a harsh vitalism in the Brontës that finds its match in the Lawrence of *The Rainbow* and *Women in Love*, though the comparison is rendered problematic by Lawrence's moral zeal, enchantingly absent from the Brontës' literary cosmos.

The aesthetic puzzle of the Brontës has less to do with the mature transformations of their vision of Byron into Rochester and Heathcliff, than with their earlier fantasy-life and its literature, and the relation of that life and literature to its hero and precursor, George Gordon, Lord Byron. At his rare worst and silliest, Byron has nothing like this scene from Charlotte

Brontë's "Caroline Vernon," where Caroline confronts the Byronic Duke of Zamorna:

> The Duke spoke again in a single blunt and almost coarse sentence, compressing what remained to be said, "If I were a bearded Turk, Caroline, I would take you to my harem." His deep voice as he uttered this, his high featured face, and dark, large eye burning bright with a spark from the depths of Gehenna, struck Caroline Vernon with a thrill of nameless dread. Here he was, the man Montmorency had described to her. All at once she knew him. Her guardian was gone, something terrible sat in his place.

Byron died his more-or-less heroic death at Missolonghi in Greece on April 19, 1824, aged thirty-six years and three months, after having set an impossible paradigm for authors that has become what the late Nelson Algren called "Hemingway all the way," in a mode still being exploited by Norman Mailer, Gore Vidal, and some of their younger peers. Charlotte was eight, Emily Jane six, and Anne four when the Noble Lord died and when his cult gorgeously flowered, dominating their girlhood and their young womanhood. Byron's passive-aggressive sexuality—at once sadomasochistic, homoerotic, incestuous, and ambivalently narcissistic—clearly sets the pattern for the ambiguously erotic universes of *Jane Eyre* and *Wuthering Heights*. What Schopenhauer named (and deplored) as the Will to Live, and Freud subsequently posited as the domain of the drives, is the cosmos of the Brontës, as it would come to be of Hardy and Lawrence. Byron rather than Schopenhauer is the source of the Brontës' vision of the Will to Live, but the Brontës add to Byron what his inverted Calvinism only partly accepted, the Protestant will proper, a heroic zest to assert one's own election, one's place in the hierarchy of souls.

Jane Eyre and Catherine Earnshaw do not fit into the grand array of heroines of the Protestant will that commences with Richardson's Clarissa Harlowe and goes through Austen's Emma Woodhouse and Fanny Price to triumph in George Eliot's Dorothea Brooke and Henry James's Isabel Archer. They are simply too wild and Byronic, too High Romantic, to keep such company. But we can see them with Hardy's Tess and, even more, his Eustacia Vye, and with Lawrence's Gudrun and Ursula. Their version of the Protestant will stems from the Romantic reading of Milton, but largely in its Byronic dramatization, rather than its more dialectical and subtle analyses in Blake and Shelley, and its more normative condemnation in Coleridge and in the Wordsworth of *The Borderers*.

II

Wuthering Heights is as unique and idiosyncratic a narrative as *Moby-Dick*, and like Melville's masterwork breaks all the confines of genre. Its sources, like the writings of the other Brontës, are in the fantasy literature of a very young woman, in the poems that made up Emily Brontë's Gondal saga or cycle. Many of those poems, while deeply felt, simply string together Byronic commonplaces. A few of them are extraordinarily strong and match *Wuthering Heights* in sublimity, as in the famous lyric dated January 2, 1846:

No coward soul is mine
No trembler in the world's storm-troubled sphere
I see Heaven's glories shine
And Faith shines equal arming me from Fear

O God within my breast
Almighty ever-present Deity
Life, that in me hast rest
As I Undying Life, have power in Thee

Vain are the thousand creeds
That move men's hearts, unutterably vain,
Worthless as withered weeds
Or idlest froth amid the boundless main

To waken doubt in one
Holding so fast by thy infinity
So surely anchored on
The steadfast rock of Immortality

With wide-embracing love
Thy spirit animates eternal years
Pervades and broods above,
Changes, sustains, dissolves, creates and rears

Though Earth and moon were gone
And suns and universes ceased to be
And thou wert left alone
Every Existence would exist in thee

There is not room for Death
Nor atom that his might could render void
Since thou art Being and Breath
And what thou art may never be destroyed.

We could hardly envision Catherine Earnshaw, let alone Heathcliff, chanting these stanzas. The voice is that of Emily Jane Brontë addressing the God within her own breast, a God who certainly has nothing in common with the one worshipped by the Reverend Patrick Brontë. I do not hear in this poem, despite all its Protestant resonances, any nuance of Byron's inverted Miltonisms. *Wuthering Heights* seems to me a triumphant revision of Byron's *Manfred*, with the revisionary swerve taking Emily Brontë into what I would call an original gnosis, a kind of poetic faith, like Blake's or Emerson's, that resembles some aspects (but not others) of ancient Gnosticism without in any way actually deriving from Gnostic texts. "No coward soul is mine" also emerges from an original gnosis, from the poet's knowing that her *pneuma* or breath-soul, as compared to her less ontological psyche, is no part of the created world, since that world fell even as it was created. Indeed the creation, whether heights or valley, appears in *Wuthering Heights* as what the ancient Gnostics called the *kenoma*, a cosmological emptiness into which *we have been thrown*, a trope that Catherine Earnshaw originates for herself. A more overt Victorian Gnostic, Dante Gabriel Rossetti, made the best (if anti-feminist) observation on the setting of *Wuthering Heights*, a book whose "power and sound style" he greatly admired:

> It is a fiend of a book, an incredible monster, combining all
> the stronger female tendencies from Mrs. Browning to Mrs.
> Brownrigg. The action is laid in Hell,—only it seems places and
> people have English names there.

Mrs. Brownrigg was a notorious eighteenth-century sadistic and murderous midwife, and Rossetti rather nastily imputed to *Wuthering Heights* a considerable female sadism. The book's violence is astonishing but appropriate, and appealed darkly both to Rossetti and to his close friend, the even more sadomasochistic Swinburne. Certainly the psychodynamics of the relationship between Heathcliff and Catherine go well beyond the domain of the pleasure principle. Gilbert and Gubar may stress too much that Heathcliff is Catherine's whip, the answer to her most profound fantasies, but the suggestion was Emily Brontë's before it became so fully developed by her best feminist critics.

Walter Pater remarked that the precise use of the term *romantic* did not apply to Sir Walter Scott, but rather:

> Much later, in a Yorkshire village, the spirit of romanticism bore a more really characteristic fruit in the work of a young girl, Emily Brontë, the romance of *Wuthering Heights*; the figures of Hareton Earnshaw, of Catherine Linton, and of Heathcliff—tearing open Catherine's grave, removing one side of her coffin, that he may really lie beside her in death—figures so passionate, yet woven on a background of delicately beautiful, moorland scenery, being typical examples of that spirit.

I always have wondered why Pater found the Romantic spirit more in Hareton and the younger Catherine than in Catherine Earnshaw, but I think now that Pater's implicit judgment was characteristically shrewd. The elder Catherine is the problematical figure in the book; she alone belongs to both orders of representation, that of social reality and that of otherness, of the Romantic Sublime. After she and the Lintons, Edgar and Isabella, are dead, then we are wholly in Heathcliff's world for the last half-year of his life, and it is in that world that Hareton and the younger Catherine are portrayed for us. They are—as Heathcliff obscurely senses—the true heirs to whatever societally possible relationship Heathcliff and the first Catherine could have had.

Emily Brontë died less than half a year after her thirtieth birthday, having finished *Wuthering Heights* when she was twenty-eight. Even Charlotte, the family survivor, died before she turned thirty-nine, and the world of *Wuthering Heights* reflects the Brontë reality: the first Catherine dies at eighteen, Hindley at twenty-seven, Heathcliff's son Linton at seventeen, Isabella at thirty-one, Edgar at thirty-nine, and Heathcliff at thirty-seven or thirty-eight. It is a world where you marry early, because you will not live long. Hindley is twenty when he marries Frances, while Catherine Earnshaw is seventeen when she marries the twenty-one-year-old Edgar Linton. Heathcliff is nineteen when he makes his hellish marriage to poor Isabella, who is eighteen at the time. The only happy lovers, Hareton and the second Catherine, are twenty-four and eighteen, respectively, when they marry. Both patterns—early marriage and early death—are thoroughly High Romantic, and emerge from the legacy of Shelley, dead at twenty-nine, and of Byron, martyred to the cause of Greek independence at thirty-six.

The passions of Gondal are scarcely moderated in *Wuthering Heights*, nor could they be; Emily Brontë's religion is essentially erotic, and her vision of triumphant sexuality is so mingled with death that we can imagine no consummation for the love of Heathcliff and Catherine Earnshaw except death. I find it difficult therefore to accept Gilbert and Gubar's reading in which *Wuthering Heights* becomes a Romantic feminist critique of *Paradise Lost*, akin to Mary Shelley's *Frankenstein*. Emily Brontë is no more interested in refuting Milton than in sustaining him. What Gilbert and Gubar uncover in *Wuthering Heights* that is antithetical to *Paradise Lost* comes directly from Byron's *Manfred*, which certainly is a Romantic critique of *Paradise Lost*. *Wuthering Heights* is *Manfred* converted to prose romance, and Heathcliff is more like Manfred, Lara, and Byron himself than is Charlotte Brontë's Rochester.

Byronic incest—the crime of Manfred and Astarte—is no crime for Emily Brontë, since Heathcliff and Catherine Earnshaw are more truly brother and sister than are Hindley and Catherine. Whatever inverted morality—a curious blend of Catholicism and Calvinism—Byron enjoyed, Emily Brontë herself repudiates, so that *Wuthering Heights* becomes a critique of *Manfred*, though hardly from a conventional feminist perspective. The furious energy that is loosed in *Wuthering Heights* is precisely Gnostic; its aim is to get back to the original Abyss, before the creation-fall. Like Blake, Emily Brontë identifies her imagination with the Abyss, and her *pneuma* or breath-soul with the Alien God, who is antithetical to the God of the creeds. The heroic rhetoric of Catherine Earnshaw is beyond every ideology, every merely social formulation, beyond even the dream of justice or of a better life, because it is beyond this cosmos, "this shattered prison":

> "Oh, you see, Nelly! he would not relent a moment, to keep me out of the grave! *That* is how I'm loved! Well, never mind! That is not my Heathcliff. I shall love mine yet; and take him with me—he's in my soul. And," added she, musingly, "the thing that irks me most is this shattered prison, after all. I'm tired, tired of being enclosed here. I'm wearying to escape into that glorious world, and to be always there; not seeing it dimly through tears, and yearning for it through the walls of an aching heart; but really with it, and in it. Nelly, you think you are better and more fortunate than I; in full health and strength. You are sorry for me—very soon that will be altered. I shall be sorry for *you*. I shall be incomparably beyond and above you all. I *wonder* he won't be near me!" She went on to herself. "I thought he wished it. Heathcliff, dear! you should not be sullen now. Do come to me, Heathcliff."

Whatever we are to call the mutual passion of Catherine and Heathcliff, it has no societal aspect and neither seeks nor needs societal sanction. Romantic love has no fiercer representation in all of literature. But "love" seems an inadequate term for the connection between Catherine and Heathcliff. There are no elements of transference in that relation, nor can we call the attachment involved either narcissistic or anaclitic. If Freud is not applicable, then neither is Plato. These extraordinary vitalists, Catherine and Heathcliff, do not desire in one another that which each does not possess, do not lean themselves against one another, and do not even find and thus augment their own selves. They *are* one another, which is neither sane nor possible, and which does not support any doctrine of liberation whatsoever. Only that most extreme of visions, Gnosticism, could accommodate them, for, like the Gnostic adepts, Catherine and Heathcliff can only enter the *pleroma* or fullness together, as presumably they have done after Heathcliff's self-induced death by starvation.

Blake may have promised us the Bible of Hell; Emily Brontë seems to have disdained Heaven and Hell alike. Her finest poem (for which we have no manuscript, but it is inconceivable that it could have been written by Charlotte) rejects every feeling save her own inborn "first feelings" and every world except a vision of earth consonant with those inaugural emotions:

Often rebuked, yet always back returning
    To those first feelings that were born with me,
And leaving busy chase of wealth and learning
    For idle dreams of things which cannot be:

To-day, I will seek not the shadowy region;
    Its unsustaining vastness waxes drear;
And visions rising, legion after legion,
    Bring the unreal world too strangely near.

I'll walk, but not in old heroic traces,
    And not in paths of high morality,
And not among the half-distinguished faces,
    The clouded forms of long-past history.

I'll walk where any own nature would be leading:
    It vexes me to choose another guide:
Where the gray flocks in ferny glens are feeding;
    Where the wild wind blows on the mountain side.

What have those lonely mountains worth revealing?
    More glory and more grief than I can tell:

The earth that wakes *one* human heart to feeling
  Can centre both the worlds of Heaven and Hell.

Whatever that centering is, it is purely individual, and as beyond gender as it is beyond creed or "high morality." It is the voice of Catherine Earnshaw, celebrating her awakening from the dream of heaven:

> "I was only going to say that heaven did not seem to be my home; and I broke my heart with weeping to come back to earth; and the angels were so angry that they flung me out, into the middle of the heath on the top of Wuthering Heights; where I woke sobbing for joy."

VIRGINIA WOOLF

Jane Eyre and Wuthering Heights

Of the hundred years that have passed since Charlotte Brontë was born, she, the centre now of so much legend, devotion, and literature, lived but thirty-nine. It is strange to reflect how different those legends might have been had her life reached the ordinary human span. She might have become, like some of her famous contemporaries, a figure familiarly met with in London and elsewhere, the subject of pictures and anecdotes innumerable, the writer of many novels, of memoirs possibly, removed from us well within the memory of the middle-aged in all the splendour of established fame. She might have been wealthy, she might have been prosperous. But it is not so. When we think of her we have to imagine some one who had no lot in our modern world; we have to cast our minds back to the 'fifties of the last century, to a remote parsonage upon the wild Yorkshire moors. In that parsonage, and on those moors, unhappy and lonely, in her poverty and her exaltation, she remains for ever.

These circumstances, as they affected her character, may have left their traces on her work. A novelist, we reflect, is bound to build up his structure with much very perishable material which begins by lending it reality and ends by cumbering it with rubbish. As we open *Jane Eyre* once more we cannot stifle the suspicion that we shall find her world of imagination as antiquated, mid-Victorian, and out of date as the parsonage on the moor, a place only to

From *The Common Reader*, 196–204. © 1925 by The Hogarth Press be visited by the curious, only preserved by the pious. So we open *Jane Eyre*; and in two pages every doubt is swept clean from our minds.

> Folds of scarlet drapery shut in my view to the right hand; to the left were the clear panes of glass, protecting, but not separating me from the drear November day. At intervals, while turning over the leaves of my book, I studied the aspect of that winter afternoon. Afar, it offered a pale blank of mist and cloud; near, a scene of wet lawn and storm-beat shrub, with ceaseless rain sweeping away wildly before a long and lamentable blast.

There is nothing there more perishable than the moor itself, or more subject to the sway of fashion than the "long and lamentable blast". Nor is this exhilaration short-lived. It rushes us through the entire volume, without giving us time to think, without letting us lift our eyes from the page. So intense is our absorption that if some one moves in the room the movement seems to take place not there but up in Yorkshire. The writer has us by the hand, forces us along her road, makes us see what she sees, never leaves us for a moment or allows us to forget her. At the end we are steeped through and through with the genius, the vehemence, the indignation of Charlotte Brontë. Remarkable faces, figures of strong outline and gnarled feature have flashed upon us in passing; but it is through her eyes that we have seen them. Once she is gone, we seek for them in vain. Think of Rochester and we have to think of Jane Eyre. Think of the moor, and again there is Jane Eyre. Think of the drawing-room,[1] even, those "white carpets on which seemed laid brilliant garlands of flowers", that "pale Parian mantelpiece" with its Bohemia glass of "ruby red" and the "general blending of snow and fire"—what is all that except Jane Eyre?

The drawbacks of being Jane Eyre are not far to seek. Always to be a governess and always to be in love is a serious limitation in a world which is full, after all, of people who are neither one nor the other. The characters of a Jane Austen or of a Tolstoi have a million facets compared with these. They live and are complex by means of their effect upon many different people who serve to mirror them in the round. They move hither and thither whether their creators watch them or not, and the world in which they live seems to us an independent world which we can visit, now that they have created it, by ourselves. Thomas Hardy is more akin to Charlotte Brontë in the power of his personality and the narrowness of his vision. But the differences are vast. As we read *Jude the Obscure* we are not rushed to a finish; we brood and ponder and drift away from the text in plethoric trains of thought which build up round the characters an atmosphere of question and suggestion of which they are themselves, as often as not, unconscious. Simple peasants as they are, we are forced to confront them with destinies and questionings of the hugest import, so that often it seems as if the most important characters in a Hardy novel are those which have no names. Of this power, of this speculative curiosity, Charlotte Brontë has no trace. She does not attempt to solve the problems of human life; she is even unaware that such problems exist; all her force, and it is the more tremendous for being constricted, goes into the assertion, "I love", "I hate", "I suffer".

For the self-centred and self-limited writers have a power denied the more catholic and broad-minded. Their impressions are close packed and strongly stamped between their narrow walls. Nothing issues from their minds which has not been marked with their own impress. They learn little from other writers, and what they adopt they cannot assimilate. Both Hardy and Charlotte Brontë appear to have founded their styles upon a stiff and decorous journalism. The staple of their prose is awkward and unyielding. But both with labour and the most obstinate integrity, by thinking every thought until it has subdued words to itself, have forged for themselves a prose which takes the mould of their minds entire; which has, into the bargain, a beauty, a power, a swiftness of its own. Charlotte Brontë, at least, owed nothing to the reading of many books. She never learnt the smoothness of the professional writer, or acquired his ability to stuff and sway his language as he chooses. "I could never rest in communication with strong, discreet, and refined minds, whether male or female", she writes, as any leader-writer in a provincial journal might have written; but gathering fire and speed goes on in her own authentic voice "till I had passed the outworks of conventional reserve and crossed the threshold of confidence, and won a place by their hearts' very hearthstone". It is there that she takes her seat; it is the red and fitful glow of the heart's fire which illumines her page. In other words, we read Charlotte Brontë not for exquisite observation of character—her characters are vigorous and elementary; not for comedy—hers is grim and crude; not for a philosophic view of life—hers is that of a country parson's daughter; but for her poetry. Probably that is so with all writers who have, as she has, an overpowering personality, so that, as we say in real life, they have only to open the door to make themselves felt. There is in them some untamed ferocity perpetually at war with the accepted order of things which makes them desire to create instantly rather than to observe patiently. This very ardour, rejecting half shades and other minor impediments, wings its way past the daily conduct of ordinary people and allies itself with their more inarticulate passions. It makes them poets, or, if they choose to write in prose, intolerant of its restrictions. Hence it is that both Emily and Charlotte are always invoking the help of nature. They both feel the need of some more powerful symbol of the vast and slumbering passions in human nature than words or actions can convey. It is with a description of a storm that Charlotte ends her finest novel *Villette*. "The skies hang full and dark—a wrack sails from the west; the clouds cast themselves into strange forms." So she calls in nature to describe a state of mind which could not otherwise be expressed. But neither of the sisters observed nature accurately as Dorothy Wordsworth observed it, or painted it minutely as Tennyson painted it. They seized those aspects of the earth which were most akin to what they themselves felt or imputed to their characters, and so their storms, their moors, their lovely spaces of summer weather are not ornaments applied to decorate a dull page or display the writer's powers of observation—they carry on the emotion and light up the meaning of the book.

The meaning of a book, which lies so often apart from what happens and what is said and consists rather in some connection which things in themselves different have had for the writer, is necessarily hard to grasp. Especially this is so when, like the Brontës, the writer is poetic, and his meaning inseparable from his language, and itself rather a mood than a particular observation. *Wuthering Heights* is a more difficult book to understand than *Jane Eyre*, because Emily was a greater poet than Charlotte. When Charlotte wrote she said with eloquence and splendour and passion "I love", "I hate", "I suffer". Her experience, though more intense, is on a level with our own. But there is no "I" in *Wuthering Heights*. There are no governesses. There are no employers. There is love, but it is not the love of men and women. Emily was inspired by some more general conception. The impulse which urged her to create was not her own suffering or her own injuries. She looked out upon a world cleft into gigantic disorder and felt within her the power to unite it in a book. That gigantic ambition is to be felt throughout the novel—a struggle, half thwarted but of superb conviction, to say something through the mouths of her characters which is not merely "I love" or "I hate", but "we, the whole human race" and "you, the eternal powers ..." the sentence remains unfinished. It is not strange that it should be so; rather it is astonishing that she can make us feel what she had it in her to say at all. It surges up in the half-articulate words of Catherine Earnshaw, "If all else perished and *he* remained, I should still continue to be; and if all else remained and he were annihilated, the universe would turn to a mighty stranger; I should not seem part of it". It breaks out again in the presence of the dead. "I see a repose that neither earth nor hell can break, and I feel an assurance of the endless and shadowless hereafter—the eternity they have entered—where life is boundless in its duration, and love in its sympathy and joy in its fulness." It is this suggestion of power underlying the apparitions of human nature and lifting them up into the presence of greatness that gives the book its huge stature among other novels. But it was not enough for Emily Brontë to write a few lyrics, to utter a cry, to express a creed. In her poems she did this once and for all, and her poems will perhaps outlast her novel. But she was novelist as well as poet. She must take upon herself a more laborious and a more ungrateful task. She must face the fact of other existences, grapple with the mechanism of external things, build up, in recognisable shape, farms and houses and report the speeches of men and women who existed independently of herself. And so we reach these summits of emotion not by rant or rhapsody but by hearing a girl sing old songs to herself as she rocks in the branches of a tree; by watching the moor sheep crop the turf; by listening to the soft wind breathing through the grass. The life at the farm with all its absurdities and its improbability is laid open to us. We are given every opportunity of comparing *Wuthering Heights* with a real farm and Heathcliff with a real man. How, we are allowed to ask, can there be truth or insight or the finer shades of emotion in men and women who so little resemble what we have seen ourselves? But even as we ask it we see in Heathcliff the brother that a sister of genius might have seen; he is impossible we say, but nevertheless no boy in literature has a more vivid existence than his. So it is with the two Catherines; never could women feel as they do or act in their manner, we say. All the same, they are the most lovable women in English fiction. It is as if she could tear up all that we know human beings by, and fill these unrecognisable transparences with such a gust of life that they transcend reality. Hers, then, is the rarest of all powers. She could free life from its dependence on facts; with a few touches indicate the spirit of a face so that it needs no body; by speaking of the moor make the wind blow and the thunder roar.

NOTES

1. Charlotte and Emily Brontë had much the same sense of colour. "... we saw—ah! it was beautiful—a splendid place carpeted with crimson, and crimson-covered chairs and tables, and a pure white ceiling bordered by gold, a shower of glass drops hanging in silver chains from the centre, and shimmering with little soft tapers" (*Wuthering Heights*). "Yet it was merely a very pretty drawing-room, and within it a boudoir, both spread with white carpets, on which seemed laid brilliant garlands of flowers; both ceiled with snowy mouldings of white grapes and vine leaves, beneath which glowed in rich contrast crimson couches and ottomans; while the ornaments on the pale Parian mantelpiece were of sparkling Bohemia glass, ruby red; and between the windows large mirrors repeated the general blending of snow and fire" (*Jane Eyre*).

DOROTHY VAN GHENT

On Wuthering Heights

Emily Brontë's single novel is, of all English novels, the most treacherous
for the analytical understanding to approach. It is treacherous not because
of failure in its own formal controls on its meaning—for the book is highly
wrought in form—but because it works as a level of experience that is
unsympathetic to, or rather, simply irrelevant to the social and moral reason.
One critic has spoken of the quality of feeling in this book as "a quality of
suffering":

> It has anonymity. It is not complete. Perhaps some ballads rep-
> resent it in English, but it seldom appears in the main stream,
> and few writers are in touch with it. It is a quality of experience
> the expression of which is at once an act of despair and an act
> of recognition or of worship. It is the recognition of an abso-
> lute hierarchy. This is also the feeling in Aeschylus. It is found
> amongst genuine peasants and is a great strength. Developing in
> places which yield only the permanent essentials of existence, it
> is undistracted and universal.[1]

We feel the lack of "completeness," which this critic refers to, in the nature
of the dramatic figures that Emily Brontë uses: they are figures that arise on

---

From *The English Novel: Form and Function*, 153–170. © 1953 by Dorothy Van Ghent and enact their drama on some ground of the psychic life where ethical ideas are not at home, at least such ethical ideas as those that inform our ordinary experience of the manners of men. They have the "anonymity" of figures in dreams or in religious ritual. The attitude toward life that they suggest is rather one of awed contemplation of an unregenerate universe than a feeling for values or disvalues in types of human intercourse. It is an attitude that is expressed in some of the great Chinese paintings of the Middle Ages, where the fall of a torrent from an enormous height, or a single huge wave breaking under the moon, or a barely indicated chain of distant mountains lost among mists, seems to be animated by some mysterious, universal, half-divine life which can only be "recognized," not understood.

The strangeness that sets *Wuthering Heights* apart from other English novels does not lie alone in the attitude that it expresses and the level of experience that it defines, for something of the same quality of feeling exists, for instance, in Conrad's work. Its strangeness is the perfect simplicity with which it presents its elemental figures almost naked of the web of civilized habits, ways of thinking, forms of intercourse, that provides the familiar background of other fiction. Even Conrad's adventurers, no matter how far they may go into the "heart of darkness," carry with them enough threads of this web to orient them socially and morally. We can illustrate what we mean by this simplicity, this almost nakedness, if we compare Emily Brontë's handling of her materials with Richardson's handling of materials that, in some respects, are similar in kind. For example, the daemonic character of Heathcliff, associated as it is with the wildness of heath and moors, has a recognizable kinship with that of Lovelace, daemonic also, though associated with town life and sophisticated manners. Both are, essentially, an anthropomorphized primitive energy, concentrated in activity, terrible in effect. But Emily Brontë insists on Heathcliff's gypsy lack of origins, his lack of orientation and determination in the social world, his equivocal status on the edge of the human. When Mr. Earnshaw first brings the child home, the child is an "it," not a "he," and "dark almost as if it came from the devil"; and one of Nelly Dean's last reflections is, "Is he a ghoul or a vampire?" But Richardson's Lovelace has all sorts of social relationships and determinations, an ample family economic orientation, college acquaintances, a position in a clique of young rakes; and Richardson is careful, through Lovelace's own pen, to offer various rationalizations of his behavior, each in some degree cogent. So with the whole multifold *Clarissa*-myth: on all sides it is supported for the understanding by historically familiar morality and manners. But *Wuthering Heights* is almost bare of such supports in social rationalization. Heathcliff might *really* be a demon. The passion of Catherine and Heathcliff is too simple and undeviating in its intensity, too uncomplex, for us to find in it any echo of practical social reality. To say that the motivation of this passion is "simple" is not to say that it is easy to define: much easier to define are the motivations that are somewhat complex and devious, for this is the familiar nature of human motivations. We might associate perfectly "simple" motivations with animal nature or extrahuman nature, but by the same token the quality of feeling involved would resist analysis.

But this nakedness from the web of familiar morality and manners is not quite complete. There is the framework formed by the convention of narration (the "point of view"): we see the drama through the eyes of Lockwood and Nelly Dean, who belong firmly to the world of practical reality. Sifted through the idiom of their commonplace vision, the drama taking place among the major characters finds contact with the temporal and the secular. Because Lockwood and Nelly Dean have witnessed the incredible violence of the life at the Heights, or rather, because Nelly Dean has witnessed the full span and capacity of that violence and because Lockwood credits her witness, the drama is oriented in the context of the psychologically familiar. There is also another technical bulwark that supports this uneasy tale in the social and moral imagination, and that is its extension over the lives of two generations and into a time of ameliorated and respectable manners. At the end, we see young Cathy teaching Hareton his letters and correcting his boorishness (which, after all, is only the natural boorishness consequent on neglect, and has none of the cannibal unregeneracy of Heathcliff in it); the prospect is one of decent, socially responsible domesticity. For this part of the tale, Lockwood alone is sufficient witness; and the fact that now Nelly Dean's experienced old eyes and memory can be dispensed with assures us of the present reasonableness and objectivity of events, and even infects retrospection on what has happened earlier—making it possible for the dream-rejecting reason to settle complacently for the "naturalness" of the entire story. If ghosts have been mentioned, if the country people swear that Heathcliff "walks," we can, with Lockwood at the end, affirm our skepticism as to "how anyone could ever imagine unquiet slumbers for the sleepers in that quiet earth."

Let us try to diagram these technical aspects of the work, for the compositional soundness of *Wuthering Heights* is owing to them. We may divide the action of the book into two parts, following each other chronologically, the one associated with the earlier generation (Hindley and Catherine and Heathcliff, Edgar and Isabella Linton), the other with the later generation (young Cathy and Linton and Hareton). The first of these actions is centered in what we shall call a "mythological romance"—for the astonishingly ravenous and possessive, perfectly amoral love of Catherine and Heathcliff belongs to that realm of the imagination where myths are created. The second action, centered in the protracted effects of Heathcliff's revenge, involves two sets of young lives and two small "romances": the childish romance of Cathy and Linton, which Heathcliff manages to pervert utterly; and the successful assertion of a healthy, culturally viable kind of love between Cathy and Hareton, asserted as Heathcliff's cruel energies flag and decay. Binding the two "actions" is the perduring figure of Heathcliff himself, demon-lover in the first, paternal ogre in the second. Binding them also is the framing narrational convention or "point of view": the voices of Nelly Dean and Lockwood are always in our ears; one or the other of them is always present at a scene, or is the confidant of someone who was present; through Lockwood we encounter Heathcliff at the beginning of the book, and through his eyes we look on Heathcliff's grave at the end. Still another pattern that binds the two actions is the repetition of what we shall call the "two children" figure—two children raised virtually as brother and sister, in a vibrant relationship of charity and passion and real or possible metamorphosis. The figure is repeated, with variation, three times, in the relationships of the main characters. Of this we shall speak again later. The technical continuities or patterning of the book could, then, be simplified in this way:

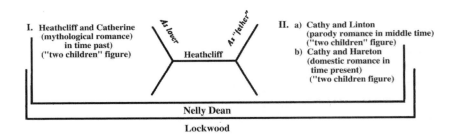

What, concretely, is the effect of this strict patterning and binding? What does it "mean"? The design of the book is drawn in the spirit of intense compositional rigor, of *limitation*; the characters act in the spirit of passionate immoderacy, of *excess*. Let us consider this contrast a little more closely. Essentially, *Wuthering Heights* exists for the mind as a tension between two kinds of reality: the raw, inhuman reality of anonymous natural energies, and the restrictive reality of civilized habits, manners, and codes. The first kind of reality is given to the imagination in the violent figures of Catherine and Heathcliff, portions of the flux of nature, children of rock and heath and tempest, striving to identify themselves as human, but disrupting all around them with their monstrous appetite for an inhuman kind of intercourse, and finally disintegrated from within by the very energies out of which they are made. It is this vision of a reality radically alien from the human that the ancient Chinese landscape paintings offer also. But in those ancient paintings there is often a tiny human figure, a figure that is obviously that of a philosopher, for instance, or that of a peasant—in other words, a human figure decisively belonging to and representing a culture—who is placed in diminutive perspective beside the enormously cascading torrent, or who is seen driving his water buffalo through the overwhelming mists or faceless snows; and this figure is outlined sharply, so that, though it is extremely tiny, it is very definite in the giant surrounding indefiniteness. The effect is one of contrast between finite and infinite, between the limitation of the known and human, and the unlimitedness of the unknown and the nonhuman. So also in *Wuthering Heights*: set over against the wilderness of inhuman reality is the quietly secular, voluntarily limited, safely human reality that we find in the gossipy concourse of Nelly Dean and Lockwood, the one an old family servant with a strong grip on the necessary emotional economies that make life endurable, the other a city visitor in the country, a man whose very disinterestedness and facility of feeling and attention indicate the manifold emotional economies by which city people particularly protect themselves from any disturbing note of the ironic discord between civilized life and the insentient wild flux of nature in which it is islanded. This second kind of reality is given also in the romance of Cathy and Hareton, where book learning and gentled manners and domestic charities form a little island of complacence. The tension between these two kinds reality, their inveterate opposition and at the same time their *continuity* one with another, provides at once the content and the form of *Wuthering Heights*. We see the tension graphically in the diagram given above. The inhuman excess of Heathcliff's and Catherine's passion, an excess that is carried over into the second half of the book by Heathcliff's revenge, an excess everywhere present in language[2]—in verbs and modifiers and metaphors that seethe with a brute fury—this excess is held within a most rigorous pattern of repeated motifs and of what someone has called the "Chinese box" of Nelly Dean's and Lockwood's interlocution. The form of the book, then—a form that may be expressed as a tension between the impulse to excess and the impulse to limitation or economy—*is* the content. The form, in short, is the book itself. Only in the fully wrought, fully realized, work of art does form so exhaust the possibilities of the material that it identifies itself with these possibilities.

If there has been any cogency in what we have said above, we should ask now how it is that the book is able to represent dramatically, in terms of human "character," its vision of the inhuman. After all, Catherine and Heathcliff *are* "characters," and not merely molecular vibrations in the primordial surge of things; indeed, they are so credibly characterized that

Hollywood has been able to costume and cosmeticize them. As "characters," what are they? As lovers, what kind of love is theirs? They gnash and foam at each other. One could borrow for them a line from a poem by John Crowe Ransom describing lovers in hell: "Stuprate, they rend each other when they kiss." This is not "romantic love," as that term has popular meaning; and it is not even sexual love, naturalistically considered—the impulse to destruction is too pure in it, too simple and direct. Catherine says she *is* Heathcliff, and the implication is not of the possibility of a "mating," for one does not "mate" with oneself. Similarly, after her death, when Heathcliff howls that he cannot live without his *life*, he cannot live without his *soul* (and Nellie says that he "howled, not like a man, but like a savage beast"), the relationship and the destiny suggested are not those of adult human lovers, because the complex attendant motivations of adult life are lacking. But the emotional implications of Catherine's and Heathcliff's passion are never "adult," in the sense of there being in that passion any recognition of the domestic and social responsibilities, and the spiritual complexities, of adult life. Whatever could happen to these two, if they could be happily together, would be something altogether asocial, amoral, savagely irresponsible, wildly impulsive: it would be the enthusiastic, experimental, quite random activity of childhood, occult to the socialized adult. But since no conceivable *human* male and female, not brutish, not anthropologically rudimentary, could be together in this way as adults, all that we can really imagine for the grown-up Catherine and Heathcliff, as "characters" on the human plane, is what the book gives of them—their mutual destruction by tooth and nail in an effort, through death, to get back to the lost state of gypsy freedom in childhood.

Caught in the economical forms of adult life—concepts of social and intellectual "betterment" (such as lead Catherine to marry Edgar Linton), the frames of wealth and property ownership (which Heathcliff at first exploits in order to "raise" himself to Catherine's standard, and then as an engine of revenge against both the Earnshaws and the Lintons), marital relationships, and parenthood—they are, for the imagination, "humanized," endowed with "character," at least to the extent that we see their explosive confusions, resistances, and misery convulsing the forms usual to human adulthood. Their obsession, their prime passion, is also "human" although it is utterly destructive of the values signified by that word: the passion to lose the self in some "otherness," whether in complete identification with another person (an identification for which "mating" is a surrogate only of a temporary and lapsing kind), or by absorption into "nature"—but it is a passion that is tabooed for the socialized adult, disguised, held in check by the complex cultural economies, safely stabled in the unconscious, at best put to work in that darkness to turn the mill of other objectives. This regressive passion is seen in uncompromised purity in Catherine and Heathcliff, and it opens the prospect of disintegration—disintegration into the unconsciousness of childhood and the molecular fluidity of death—in a word, into anonymous natural energy.

If the story of Catherine and Heathcliff had not been a story told by an old woman as something that had had its inception many years ago, if the old woman who tells the story had not been limited in imagination and provincial in her sympathies, if the story had been dramatized immediately in the here-and-now and not at a temporal remove and through a dispassioned intermediator, it is doubtful that it would resonate emotionally for us or carry any conviction—even any "meaning." Because of the very fact that the impulses it represents are taboo, they can conveniently be observed only at a remove, as someone else's, as of the past, and from the judicial point of view of conventional manners. The "someone else's" and the "long ago" are the mind's saving convention for making a distance with itself such as will allow it perspective. Thus the technical *displacement* of Heathcliff's and Catherine's story into past time and into the memory of an old woman functions in the same way as dream displacements: it both censors and indulges, protects and liberates.

Significantly, our first real contact with the Catherine–Heathcliff drama is established through a dream—Lockwood's dream of the ghost-child at the window. Lockwood is motivated to dream the dream by the most easily convincing circumstances; he has fallen asleep while reading Catherine's diary, and during his sleep a tempest-blown branch is scratching on the windowpane. But why should Lockwood, the well-mannered urbanite, dream *this*?

> I pulled its wrist on to the broken pane, and rubbed it to and fro till the blood ran down and soaked the bedclothes.

The image is probably the most cruel one in the book. Hareton's hanging puppies, Heathcliff's hanging the springer spaniel, Hindley's forcing a knife between Nelly's teeth or throwing his baby over the staircase, Catherine's leaving the blue print of her nails on Isabella's arm, Heathcliff stamping on Hindley's face—these images and others like them imply savagery or revengefulness or drunkenness or hysteria, but always a motivating set of emotional circumstances. But this is the punctilious Lockwood—whose antecedents and psychology are so insipid that we care little about them—who scrapes the dream-waif's wrist back and forth on broken glass till the blood runs down and soaks the bedclothes. The cruelty of the dream is the gratuitousness of the violence wrought on a child by an emotionally unmotivated vacationer from the city, dreaming in a strange bed. The bed is an old-fashioned closet bed ("a large oak case ... it formed a little closet" with a window set in it): its paneled sides Lockwood has "pulled together" before going to sleep. The bed is like a coffin (at the end of the book, Heathcliff dies in it, behind its closed panels); it had been Catherine's bed, and the movable panels themselves suggest the coffin in which she is laid, whose "panels" Heathcliff bribes the sexton to remove at one side. Psychologically, Lockwood's dream has only the most perfunctory determinations, and nothing at all of result for the dreamer himself, except to put him uncomfortably out of bed. But poetically the dream has its reasons, compacted into the image of the daemonic child scratching at the pane, trying to get from the "outside" "in," and of the dreamer in a bed like a coffin, released by that deathly privacy to indiscriminate violence. The coffin-like bed shuts off any interference with the wild deterioration of the psyche. Had the dream used any other agent then the effete, almost epicene Lockwood, it would have lost this symbolic force; for Lockwood, more successfully than anyone else in the book, has shut out the powers of darkness (the pun in his name is obvious in this context); and his lack of any dramatically thorough motivation for dreaming the cruel dream suggests those powers as existing autonomously, not only in the "outsideness" of external nature, beyond the physical windowpane, but also within, even in the soul least prone to passionate excursion.

The windowpane is the medium, treacherously transparent, separating the "inside" from the "outside," the "human" from the alien and terrible "other." Immediately after the incident of the dream, the time of the narrative is displaced into the childhood of Heathcliff and Catherine, and we see the two children looking through the window of the Linton's drawing room.

> "Both of us were able to look in by standing on the basement, and clinging to the ledge, and we saw—ah! it was beautiful—a splendid place carpeted with crimson, and crimson-covered chairs and tables, and a pure white ceiling bordered by gold, a shower of glass-drops hanging in silver chains from the centre, and shimmering with little soft tapers. Old Mr. and Mrs. Linton were not there; Edgar and his sister had it entirely to themselves. Shouldn't they have been happy? We should have thought ourselves in heaven!"

Here the two unregenerate waifs look *in* from the night on the heavenly vision of the refinements and securities of the most privileged human estate. But Heathcliff rejects the vision: seeing the Linton children blubbering and bored there (*they* cannot get *out!*), he senses the menace of its limitations;

while Catherine is fatally tempted. She is taken in by the Lintons, and now it is Heathcliff alone outside looking through the window.

"The curtains were still looped up at one corner, and I resumed my station as a spy; because Catherine had wished to return, I intended shattering their great glass panes to a million of fragments, unless they let her out. She sat on the sofa quietly ... the woman-servant brought a basin of warm water, and washed her feet; and Mr. Linton mixed a tumbler of negus, and Isabella emptied a plateful of cakes into her lap ... Afterwards, they dried and combed her beautiful hair."

Thus the first snare is laid by which Catherine will be held for a human destiny—her feet washed, cakes and wine for her delectation, her beautiful hair combed (the motifs here are limpid as those of fairy tale, where the changeling in the "otherworld" is held there mysteriously by bathing and by the strange new food he has been given to eat). By her marriage to Edgar Linton, Catherine yields to that destiny; later she resists it tormentedly and finds her way out of it by death. Literally she "catches her death" by throwing open the window.

"Open the window again wide: fasten it open! Quick, why don't you move?" [she says to Nelly].
"Because I won't give you your death of cold," I answered.
"You won't give me a chance of life, you mean," she said.

In her delirium, she opens the window, leans out into the winter wind, and calls across the moors to Heathcliff,

" Heathcliff, if I dare you now, will you venture ... Find a way, then! ... You are slow! ... you always followed me!"

On the night after her burial, unable to follow her (though he digs up her grave in order to lie beside her in the coffin from which the side panels have been removed), he returns to the Heights *through the window*—for Hindley has barred the door—to wreak on the living the fury of his frustration. It is years later that Lockwood arrives at the Heights and spends his uncomfortable night there. Lockwood's outcry in his dream brings Heathcliff *to the window*, Heathcliff who has been caught ineluctably in the human to grapple with its interdictions long after Catherine has broken through them. The treachery of the window is that Catherine, lost now in the "other," can look through the transparent membrane that separates her from humanity, can scratch on the pane, but cannot get "in," while Heathcliff, though he forces the window open and howls into the night, cannot get "out." When he dies, Nelly Dean discovers the window swinging open, the window of that old-fashioned coffin-like bed where Lockwood had had the dream. Rain has been pouring in during the night, drenching the dead man. Nelly says,

> I hasped the window; I combed his black long hair from his forehead; I tried to close his eyes: to extinguish, if possible, that frightful, lifelike gaze of exultation before any one else beheld it. They would not shut: they seemed to sneer at my attempts.

Earlier, Heathcliff's eyes have been spoken of as "the clouded windows of hell" from which a "fiend" looks out. All the other uses of the "window" that we have spoken of here are not figurative but perfectly naturalistic uses, though their symbolic value is inescapable. But the fact that Heathcliff's eyes refuse to close in death suggests the symbol in a metaphorical form (the "fiend" has now got "out," leaving the window open), elucidating with simplicity the meaning of the "window" as a separation between the daemonic depths of the soul and the limited and limiting lucidities of consciousness, a separation between the soul's "otherness" and its humanness.

There is still the difficulty of defining, with any precision, the quality of the daemonic that is realized most vividly in the conception of Heathcliff, a difficulty that is mainly due to our tendency always to give the "daemonic" some ethical status—that is, to relate it to an ethical hierarchy. Heathcliff's is an archetypal figure, untraceably ancient in mythological thought—an imaged recognition of that part of nature which is "other" than the human soul (the world of the elements and the animals) and of that part of the soul itself which is "other" than the conscious part. But since Martin Luther's revival of this archetype for modern mythology, it has tended to forget its relationship with the elemental "otherness" of the outer world and to identify itself solely with the dark functions of the soul. As an image of soul work, it is ethically relevant, since everything that the soul does—even unconsciously, even "ignorantly" (as in the case of Oedipus)—offers itself for ethical judgment, whereas the elements and the animals do not. Puritanism perpetuated the figure for the imagination; Milton give it its greatest aesthetic splendor, in the fallen angel through whom the divine beauty still shone; Richardson introduced it, in the person of Lovelace, to an infatuated middle class; and always the figure was ethically relevant through the conception of "sin" and "guilt." (Let us note here, however, the ambivalence of the figure, an ambivalence that the medieval devil does not have. The medieval devil is a really ugly customer, so ugly that he can even become a comedy figure—as in the medieval moralities. The daemonic archetype of which we are speaking here is deeply serious in quality because of his ambivalence: he is a fertilizing energy and profoundly attractive, and at the same time horribly destructive to civilized institutionalism. It is because of his ambivalence that, though he is the "enemy," ethically speaking, he so easily takes on the stature and beauty of a hero, as he does in the Satan of *Paradise Lost.*) In Byron's Manfred, the archetype underwent a rather confusing sea-change, for Manfred's crime is, presumably, so frightful that it cannot be mentioned, and the indefinable nature of the crime blurs the edges of the figure and cuts down its resonance in the imagination (when we guess that the crime might be incest, we are disposed to find this a rather paltry equation for the Byronic incantation of guilt); nevertheless, the ethical relevancy of the figure remains. Let us follow it a little further, before returning to Emily Brontë's Heathcliff. In the later nineteenth century, in the novels of Dostoyevski, it reappears with an enormous development of psychological subtlety, and also with a great strengthening and clarification of its ethical significance. In the work of André Gide, it undergoes another sea-change: the archetypal daemonic figure now becomes the principle of progress, the spirit of free investigation and creative experience; with this reorientation, it becomes positively ethical rather than negatively so. In Thomas Mann's Doctor Faustus, it reverts to its earlier and more constant significance, as the type of the instinctive part of the soul, a great and fertilizing power, but ethically unregenerate and therefore a great danger to ethical man.

Our interest in sketching some phases of the history of this archetype has been to show that it has had, in modern mythology, constantly a status in relation to ethical thought. The exception is Heathcliff. Heathcliff is no more ethically relevant than is flood or earthquake or whirlwind. It is as impossible to speak of him in terms of "sin" and "guilt" as it is to speak in this way of the natural elements or the creatures of the animal world. In him, the type reverts to a more ancient mythology and to an earlier symbolism. Wuthering Heights so baffles and confounds the ethical sense because it is not informed with that sense at all: it is profoundly informed with the attitudes of "animism," by which the natural world—that world which is "other" than and "outside of" the consciously individualized human—*appears* to act with an energy similar to the energies of the soul; to be permeated with soul energy but of a mysterious and alien kind that the conscious human soul, bent on securing itself through civilization, cannot identify itself with as to purpose; an energy that can be propitiated, that can at times be canalized into humanly purposeful channels, that *must* be given religious recognition both for its enormous fertility and its enormous potential destructiveness. But Heathcliff does have human shape and human relationships; he is, so to speak, "caught in" the human; two kinds of reality intersect in him—as they do, with a somewhat different balance, in Catherine; as they do, indeed, in the other characters. Each entertains, in some degree, the powers of darkness—from Hindley, with his passion for self-destruction (he, too, wants to get "out"), to Nelly Dean, who in a sense "propitiates" those powers with the casuistry of her actions, and even to Lockwood, with his sadistic dream. Even in the weakest of these souls there is an intimation of the dark Otherness, by which the soul is related psychologically to the inhuman world of pure energy, for it carries within itself an "otherness" of its own, that inhabits below consciousness.

The imagery of the windowpane is metamorphic, suggesting a total change of mode of being by the breaking-through of a separating medium that exists between consciousness and the "other." The strangest and boldest and most radiant figuration that Emily Brontë has given to her subject is the "two children" figure, also a metamorphic figure of breakthrough and transformation. The *type* or classic form of this figure is a girl with golden hair and a boy with dark hair and shadowed brow, bound in kinship and in a relationship of charity and passion, and with a metamorphosis of some kind potential in the relationship. The beautiful dark boy will be brightened, made angelic and happy, by the beautiful golden girl: this, apparently, is what *should* happen. But the dynamics of the change are not perfectly trustworthy. In one of Emily Brontë's poems, describing a child who might be the child Heathcliff, the ambivalent dark boy will evidently sink further into his darkness.

> I love thee, boy; for all divine,
> All full of God thy features shine.
> Darling enthusiast, holy child,
> Too good for this world's warring wild,
> Too heavenly now but doomed to be
> Hell-like in heart and misery.[3]

In the 1850 printing of the Brontë poems (the printing supervised by the Brontë sisters) two companion pieces appear under the title "The Two Children," in the first of which the dark boy is still unchanged.

> Frowning on the infant,
> Shadowing childhood's joy,
> Guardian angel knows not
> That melancholy boy...[4]

In the second of these companion pieces, the golden child is evoked, and now the change in the dark one is promised.

> Child of Delight! with sunbright hair,
> And seablue, seadeep eyes;
> Spirit of Bliss, what brings thee here,
> Beneath these sullen skies?
>
> Though shouldest live in eternal spring,
> Where endless day is never dim;
> Why, Seraph, has thy erring wing
> Borne thee down to weep with him?

She answers that she is "not from heaven descended," but that she has seen and pities "that mournful boy."

> And I swore to take his gloomy sadness,
> And give to him my beamy joy.[5]

Here, with the change of the dark child, the golden child will be changed also, for she will take his "gloomy sadness." In another set of verses, the light–dark contrast is turned around bewilderingly.

> And only *he* had locks of light,
> And *she* had raven hair;
> While now, his curls are dark as night,
> And hers as morning fair.[6]

What really seems to be implied by all these shifts is not a mere exchange of characteristics but a radical identification of the two children, so that each can appear in the mode of the other, the bright one in the mode of darkness and the dark one in the mode of light.

In still another of those poems that dramatize affairs in the kingdom of Gondal that occupied Emily Brontë's youthful fantasy, a brooding phantom figure haunts the moonlit grounds of a castle. Its face is "divinely fair," but on its "angel brow"

> Rests such a shade of deep despair
> As nought divine could ever know.

Apparently the cause of his death was adoration of another man's wife ("Lord Alfred's idol queen"), and it is for this reason that his spirit is "shut from heaven—an outcast for eternity." The woman for whom he died is represented as an "infant fair," looking from a golden frame in a portrait gallery.

> And just like his its ringlets bright,
> Its large dark eye of shadowy light,
> Its cheeks' pure hue, its forehead white,
> And like its noble name.

A deliberate confusion of the planes of reality—a sifting into the life inside the picture frame (like the shifts "through the window" in *Wuthering Heights*), and with it a shifting from despairing adulthood into childhood—is suggested with the following questions:

> And did he never smile to see
> Himself restored to infancy?
>
> Never part back that golden flow
> Of curls, and kiss that pearly brow,
> And feel no other earthly bliss
> Was equal to that parent's kiss?[7]

The suggestions are those of metamorphic changes, but all under the aspect of frustration: the despairing lover cannot get through the picture frame where the child is. Other motifs here are reminiscent of those of *Wuthering Heights*. The spectral lover is an ambivalent figure, of divine beauty, but an outcast from heaven. Kinship is suggested between him and the child in the picture ("And just like his its ringlets bright ... And like its noble name"), and one is left to imagine that "Lord Alfred's idol queen" was his sister, wherefore the frustration of their love. The last stanza quoted above remarks ambiguously on the parental feeling involved in the relationship: is it not the infant who is the "parent" here? Parental charity is the feeling of the golden "guardian angel" for her dark charge in "The Two Children" poems, as it is, in a degree, of Catherine for Heathcliff during their childhood, and of young Cathy first for Linton and then for Hareton. The fact that, in the poem, both the infant and the spectral lover have golden hair seems, in this elusive fantasy, to be a mark of perversion of the metamorphic sequence, at least of its having gone awry (as in the case, too, of young Cathy and Linton, who is not dark but fair).

In the relationship of Catherine and Heathcliff, the fantasy has its typical form. She is golden, he is dark. His daemonic origin is always kept open, by reiterations of the likelihood that he is really a ghoul, a fiend, an offspring of hell, and not merely so in behavior. And Catherine also, like the guardian child in "The Two Children" poems, is "not from heaven descended": she has furious tantrums, she lies, she bites, her chosen toy is a whip. They are raised as brother and sister; there are three references to their sleeping in the same bed as infants. She scolds and orders and mothers and cherishes him ("much too fond of him" as a child, Nelly says). The notions of somatic change and discovery of noble birth, as in fairy tale, are deliberately played with; as, when Catherine returns from her first sojourn at the Lintons' and Heathcliff asks Nelly to "make him decent," he says, comparing himself with Edgar,

> "I wish I had light hair and a fair skin, and was dressed and behaved as well, and had a chance of being as rich as he will be!"

and Nelly answers,
> "You're fit for a prince in disguise ... Were I in your place, I would frame high notions of my birth."

(If Heathcliff is really of daemonic origin, he is, in a sense, indeed of "high birth," a "prince in disguise," and might be expected, like the princes of fairy tale, to drop his "disguise" at the crisis of the tale and be revealed in original splendor: the dynamics of the "two children" figure also points to the potential transformation.) Some alluring and astonishing destiny seems possible for the two. *What* that phenomenon might be or mean, we cannot know, for it is frustrated by Catherine's marriage to Edgar, which dooms Heathcliff to be "hell-like in heart and misery." Catherine's decision dooms her also, for she is of the same daemonic substance as Heathcliff, and a civilized marriage and domesticity are not sympathetic to the daemonic quality.

With the second generation, the "two children" figure is distorted and parodied in the relationship of Catherine's daughter and Heathcliff's son. Young Cathy, another "child of delight, with sunbright hair," has still some of the original daemonic energy, but her "erring wing" has brought her down to "weep with" a *pale-haired* and pallid little boy whose only talents are for sucking sugar candy and torturing cats. She does her best, as infant mother, to metamorphose him, but he is an ungrateful and impossible subject. Her passionate charity finally finds her "married" to his corpse in a locked bedroom. With Cathy and Hareton Earnshaw, her cousin on her mother's side, the "two children" are again in their right relationship of golden and dark, and now the pathos of the dark child cures the daemon out of the golden one, and the maternal care of the golden child raises the dark one to civilized humanity and makes of him a proper husband.

In these several pairs, the relation of kinship has various resonances. Between Catherine and Heathcliff, identity of "kind" is greatest, although they are foster brother and sister only. The foster kinship provides an imaginative implicit reason for the unnaturalness and impossibility of their mating. Impassioned by their brother-and-sister-like identity of kind, they can only destroy each other, for it is impossible for two persons to be each other (as Catherine says she "is" Heathcliff) without destruction of the physical limitations that individualize and separate. In Emily Brontë's use of the symbolism of the incest motive, the incestual impulse appears as an attempt to make what is "outside" oneself identical with what is "inside" oneself—a performance that can be construed in physical and human terms only by violent destruction of personality bounds, by rending of flesh and at last by death.

With Catherine's daughter and young Linton, who are cousins, the implicit incestuousness of the "two children" figure is suggested morbidly by Linton's disease and by his finally becoming a husband only as a corpse. With Cathy and Hareton Earnshaw, also cousins, Victorian "ameliorism" finds a way to sanction the relationship by symbolic emasculation; Cathy literally teaches the devil out of Hareton, and "esteem" between the two takes the place of the old passion for identification. With this successful metamorphosis and mating, the daemonic quality has been completely suppressed, and, though humanity and civilization have been secured for the "two children," one feels that some magnificent bounty is now irrecoverable. The great magic, the wild power, of the original two has been lost.

We are led to speculate on what the bounty might have been,[8] had the windowpane not stood between the original pair, had the golden child and the dark child not been secularized by a spelling book. Perhaps, had the ideal and impossible eventuality taken place, had the "inside" and the "outside," the bright child and the dark one, become identified in such a way that they could freely assume each other's modes, then perhaps the world of the animals and the elements—the world of wild moor and barren rock, of fierce wind and attacking beast, that is the strongest palpability in *Wuthering Heights*— would have offered itself completely to human understanding and creative intercourse. Perhaps the dark powers that exist within the soul, as well as in the outer elemental world, would have assumed the language of consciousness, or consciousness would have bravely entered into companionship with those dark powers and transliterated their language into its own. Emily Brontë's book has been said to be nonphilosophical—as it is certainly nonethical; but all philosophy is not ethics, and the book seizes, at the point where the soul feels itself cleft within and in cleavage from the universe, the first germs of philosophic thought, the thought of the duality of human and nonhuman existence, and the thought of the cognate duality of the psyche.

NOTES

1. G. D. Klingopulos, "The Novel as Dramatic Poem (II): 'Wuthering Heights,'" in *Scrutiny* XIV:4 (1946–1947).

2. Mark Schorer examines this aspect of *Wuthering Heights* in his essay "Fiction and the 'Analogical Matrix,'" in *Critiques and Essays on Modern Fiction* (New York: The Ronald Press Company, 1952).

3. *The Complete Poems of Emily Jane Brontë*, edited by C. W. Hatfield (New York: Columbia University Press, 1941), p. 121.

4. *Ibid.*, p. 229.

5. *Ibid.*, p. 230.

6. *Ibid.*, p. 174.

7. *Ibid.*, pp. 177–178.

8. A stimulating and enlightening interpretation of the book is to be found in Richard Chase's "The Brontës, or Myth Domesticated," in *Forms of Modern Fiction*, edited by William Van O'Connor (Minneapolis: University of Minnesota Press, 1948).

SANDRA GILBERT AND SUSAN GUBAR

Looking Oppositely:
Emily Brontë's Bible of Hell

Down from the waist they are Centaurs,
Though women all above:
But to the girdle do the Gods inherit,
Beneath is all the fiend's: there's hell, there's darkness,
There is the sulphurous pit...

—*King Lear*

It indeed appear'd to Reason as if Desire was cast out, but the Devils account is, that the Messiah fell. & formed a heaven of what he stole from the Abyss

—William Blake

A loss of something ever felt I—
The first that I could recollect
Bereft I was—of what I knew not
Too young that any should suspect

A Mourner walked among the children
I notwithstanding went about
As one bemoaning a Dominion
Itself the only Prince cast out—

From *The Madwoman in the Attic: The Woman Writer and the Nineteenth-Century Imagination*, 248–308. © 1979 by Yale University Press.

Elder, Today, a session wiser
And fainter, too, as Wiseness is—
I find myself still softly searching
For my Delinquent Palaces—

And a Suspicion, like a Finger
Touches my Forehead now and then
That I am looking oppositely
For the site of the Kingdom of Heaven—
                                        —Emily Dickinson

*F*rankenstein and *Wuthering Heights* (1847) are not usually seen as related works, except insofar as both are famous nineteenth-century literary puzzles, with Shelley's plaintive speculation about where she got so "hideous an idea" finding its counterpart in the position of Heathcliff's creator as a sort of mystery woman of literature. Still, if both Brontë and Shelley wrote enigmatic, curiously unprecedented novels, their works are puzzling in different ways: Shelley's is an enigmatic fantasy of metaphysical horror, Brontë's an enigmatic romance of metaphysical passion. Shelley produced an allusive, Romantic, and "masculine" text in which the fates of subordinate female characters seem entirely dependent upon the actions of ostensibly male heroes or anti-heroes. Brontë produced a more realistic narrative in which "the perdurable voice of the country," as Mark Schorer describes Nelly Dean, introduces us to a world where men battle for the favors of apparently high-spirited and independent women.[1]

Despite these dissimilarities, however, *Frankenstein* and *Wuthering Heights* are alike in a number of crucial ways. For one thing, both works *are* enigmatic, puzzling, even in some sense generically problematical. Moreover, in each case the mystery of the novel is associated with what seem to be its metaphysical intentions, intentions around which much critical controversy has collected. For these two "popular" novels—one a thriller, the other a romance—have convinced many readers that their charismatic surfaces conceal (far more than they reveal) complex ontological depths, elaborate structures of allusion, fierce though shadowy moral ambitions. And this point in particular is demonstrated by a simpler characteristic both works have in common. Both make use of what in connection with *Frankenstein* we called an evidentiary narrative technique, a Romantic story-telling method that emphasizes the ironic disjunctions between different perspectives on the same events as well as the ironic tensions that inhere in the relationship between surface drama and concealed authorial intention. In fact, in its use of such a technique, *Wuthering Heights* might be a deliberate copy of *Frankenstein*.

Not only do the stories of both novels emerge through concentric circles of narration, both works contain significant digressions. Catherine Earnshaw's diary, Isabella's letter, Zillah's narrative, and Heathcliff's confidences to Nelly function in *Wuthering Heights* much as Alphonse Frankenstein's letter, Justine's narrative, and Safie's history do in *Frankenstein*.

Their common concern with evidence, especially with written evidence, suggests still another way in which *Wuthering Heights* and *Frankenstein* are alike: more than most novels, both are consciously literary works, at times almost obsessively concerned with books and with reading as not only a symbolic but a dramatic—plot-forwarding—activity. Can this be because, like Shelley, Brontë was something of a literary heiress? The idea is an odd one to consider, because the four Brontë children, scribbling in Yorkshire's remote West Riding, seem as trapped on the periphery of nineteenth-century literary culture as Mary Shelley was embedded in its Godwinian and Byronic center. Nevertheless, peripheral though they were, the Brontës had literary parents just as Mary Shelley did: the Reverend Patrick Brontë was in his youth the author of several books of poetry, a novel, and a collection of sermons, and Maria Branwell, the girl he married, apparently also had some literary abilities.[2] And of course, besides having obscure literary parents Emily Brontë had literary siblings, though they too were in most of her own lifetime almost as unknown as their parents.

Is it coincidental that the author of *Wuthering Heights* was the sister of the authors of *Jane Eyre* and *Agnes Grey*? Did the parents, especially the father, bequeath a frustrated drive toward literary success to their children? These are interesting though unanswerable questions, but they imply a point that is crucial in any consideration of the Brontës, just as it was important in thinking about Mary Shelley: it was the habit in the Brontë family, as in the Wollstonecraft-Godwin-Shelley family, to approach reality through the mediating agency of books, to read one's relatives, and to feel related to one's reading. Thus the transformation of three lonely yet ambitious Yorkshire governesses into the magisterially androgynous trio of Currer, Ellis, and Acton Bell was a communal act, an assertion of family identity. And significantly, even the games these writers played as children prepared them for such a literary mode of self-definition. As most Brontë admirers know, the four young inhabitants of Haworth Parsonage began producing extended narratives at an early age, and these eventually led to the authorship of a large library of miniature books which constitutes perhaps the most famous juvenilia in English. Though in subject matter these works are divided into two groups—one, the history of the imaginary kingdom of Gondal, written by Emily and Anne, and the other, stories of the equally imaginary land of Angria, written by Charlotte and Branwell—all four children read and discussed all the tales, and even served as models for characters in many. Thus the Brontës' deepest feelings of kinship appear to have been expressed first in literary collaboration and private childish attempts at fictionalizing each other, and then, later, in the public collaboration the sisters undertook with the ill-fated collection of poetry that was their first "real" publication. Finally Charlotte, the last survivor of these prodigious siblings, memorialized her lost sisters in print, both in fiction and in non-fiction (*Shirley*, for instance, mythologizes Emily). Given the traditions of her family, it was no doubt inevitable that, for her, writing—not only novel-writing but the writing of prefaces to "family" works—would replace tombstone-raising, hymn-singing, maybe even weeping.[3]

That both literary activity and literary evidence were so important to the Brontës may be traced to another problem they shared with Mary Shelley. Like the anxious creator of *Frankenstein*, the authors of *Wuthering Heights*, *Jane Eyre*, and *The Tenant of Wildfell Hall* lost their mother when they were very young. Like Shelley, indeed, Emily and Anne Brontë were too young when their mother died even to know much about her except through the evidence of older survivors and perhaps through some documents. Just as *Frankenstein*, with its emphasis on orphans and beggars, is a motherless book, so all the Brontë novels betray intense feelings of motherlessness, orphanhood, destitution. And in particular the problems of literary orphanhood seem to lead in *Wuthering Heights*, as in *Frankenstein*, not only to a concern with surviving evidence but also to a fascination with the question of origins. Thus if all women writers, metaphorical orphans in patriarchal culture, seek literary answers to the questions "How are we fal'n, / Fal'n by mistaken rules ...?" motherless orphans like Mary Shelley and Emily Brontë almost seem to seek literal answers to that question, so passionately do their novels enact distinctive female literary obsessions.

Finally, that such a psychodramatic enactment is going on in both *Wuthering Heights* and *Frankenstein* suggests a similarity between the two novels which brings us back to the tension between dramatic surfaces and metaphysical depths with which we began this discussion. For just as one of *Frankenstein*'s most puzzling traits is the symbolic ambiguity or fluidity its characters display when they are studied closely, so one of *Wuthering Heights*'s key elements is what Leo Bersani calls its "ontological slipperiness."[4] In fact, because it is a *metaphysical* romance (just as *Frankenstein* is a *metaphysical* thriller) *Wuthering Heights* seems at times to be about forces or beings rather than people, which is no doubt one reason why some critics have thought it generically problematical, maybe not a novel at all but instead an extended exemplum, or a "prosified" verse drama. And just as all the characters in *Frankenstein* are in a sense the same two characters, so "everyone [in *Wuthering Heights*] is finally related to everyone else and, in a sense, repeated in everyone else," as if the novel, like an illustration of Freud's "Das Unheimlische," were about "the danger of being haunted by alien versions of the self."[5] But when it is created by a woman in the misogynistic context of Western literary culture, this sort of anxiously philosophical, problem-solving, myth-making narrative must—so it seems—inevitably come to grips with the countervailing stories told by patriarchal poetry, and specifically by Milton's patriarchal poetry.

* * *

Milton, Winifred Gérin tells us, was one of Patrick Brontë's favorite writers, so if Shelley was Milton's critic's daughter, Brontë was Milton's admirer's daughter.[6] By the Hegelian law of thesis/antithesis, then, it seems appropriate that Shelley chose to repeat and restate Milton's misogynistic story while Brontë chose to correct it. In fact the most serious matter *Wuthering Heights* and *Frankenstein* share is the matter of *Paradise Lost*, and their profoundest difference is in their attitude toward Milton's myth. Where Shelley was Milton's dutiful daughter, retelling his story to clarify it, Brontë was the poet's rebellious child, radically revising (and even reversing) the terms of his mythic narrative. Given the fact that Brontë never mentions either Milton or *Paradise Lost* in *Wuthering Heights*, any identification of her as Milton's daughter may at first seem eccentric or perverse. Shelley, after all, provided an overtly Miltonic framework in *Frankenstein* to reinforce our sense of her literary intentions. But despite the absence of Milton references, it eventually becomes plain that *Wuthering Heights* is also a novel haunted by Milton's bogey. We may speculate, indeed, that Milton's absence is itself a presence, so painfully does Brontë's story dwell on the places and persons of his imagination.

That *Wuthering Heights* is about heaven and hell, for instance, has long been seen by critics, partly because all the narrative voices, from the beginning of Lockwood's first visit to the Heights, insist upon casting both action and description in religious terms, and partly because one of the first Catherine's major speeches to Nelly Dean raises the questions "What is heaven? Where is hell?" perhaps more urgently than any other speech in an English novel:

> "If I were in heaven, Nelly, I should be extremely miserable.... I dreamt once that I was there [and] that heaven did not seem to be my home, and I broke my heart with weeping to come back to earth; and the angels were so angry that they flung me out into the middle of the heath on the top of Wuthering Heights, where I woke sobbing for joy."[7]

Satan too, however—at least Satan as Milton's prototypical Byronic hero—has long been considered a participant in *Wuthering Heights*, for "that devil Heathcliff," as both demon lover and ferocious natural force, is a phenomenon critics have always studied. Isabella's "Is Mr. Heathcliff a man? If so, is he mad? And if not is he a devil?" (chap. 13) summarizes the traditional Heathcliff problem most succinctly, but Nelly's "I was inclined to believe ... that conscience had turned his heart to an earthly hell" (chap. 33) more obviously echoes *Paradise Lost*.

Again, that *Wuthering Heights* is in some sense about a fall has frequently been suggested, though critics from Charlotte Brontë to Mark Schorer, Q. D. Leavis, and Leo Bersani have always disputed its exact nature and moral implications. Is Catherine's fall the archetypal fall of the *Bildungsroman* protagonist? Is Heathcliff's fall, his perverted "moral teething," a shadow of Catherine's? Which of the two worlds of *Wuthering Heights* (if either) does Brontë mean to represent the truly "fallen" world? These are just some of the controversies that have traditionally attended this issue. Nevertheless, that the story of *Wuthering Heights* is built around a central fall seems indisputable, so that a description of the novel as in part a *Bildungsroman* about a girl's passage from "innocence" to "experience" (leaving aside the precise meaning of those terms) would probably also be widely accepted. And that the fall in *Wuthering Heights* has Miltonic overtones is no doubt culturally inevitable. But even if it weren't, the Miltonic implications of the action would be clear enough from the "mad scene" in which Catherine describes herself as "an exile, and outcast ... from what had been my world," adding "Why am I so changed? Why does my blood rush into a hell of tumult at a few words?" (chap. 12). Given the metaphysical nature of *Wuthering Heights*, Catherine's definition of herself as "an exile and outcast" inevitably suggests those trail-blazing exiles and outcasts Adam, Eve, and Satan. And her Romantic question—"Why am I so changed?"—with its desperate straining after the roots of identity, must ultimately refer back to Satan's hesitant (but equally crucial) speech to Beelzebub, as they lie stunned in the lake of fire: "If thou be'est he; But O ... how chang'd" (*PL* l. 84).

Of course, *Wuthering Heights* has often, also, been seen as a subversively visionary novel. Indeed, Brontë is frequently coupled with Blake as a practitioner of mystical politics. Usually, however, as if her book were written to illustrate the enigmatic religion of "No coward soul is mine," this visionary quality is related to Catherine's assertion that she is tired of "being enclosed" in "this shattered prison" of her body, and "wearying to escape into that glorious world, and to be always there" (chap. 15). Many readers define Brontë, in other words, as a ferocious pantheist/transcendentalist, worshipping the manifestations of the One in rock, tree, cloud, man and woman, while manipulating her story to bring about a Romantic *Liebestod* in which favored characters enter "the endless and shadowless hereafter." And certainly such ideas, like Blake's *Songs of Innocence*, are "something heterodox," to use Lockwood's phrase. At the same time, however, they are soothingly rather than disquietingly neo-Miltonic, like fictionalized visions of *Paradise Lost*'s luminous Father God. They are, in fact, the ideas of "steady, reasonable" Nelly Dean, whose denial of the demonic in life, along with her commitment to the angelic tranquility of death, represents only one of the visionary alternatives in *Wuthering Heights*. And, like Blake's metaphor of the lamb, Nelly's pious alternative has no real meaning for Brontë outside of the context provided by its tigerish opposite.

The tigerish opposite implied by *Wuthering Heights* emerges most dramatically when we bring all the novel's Miltonic elements together with its author's personal concerns in an attempt at a single formulation of Brontë's metaphysical intentions: the sum of this novel's visionary parts is an almost shocking revisionary whole. Heaven (or its rejection), hell, Satan, a fall, mystical politics, metaphysical romance, orphanhood, and the question of origins—disparate as some of these matters may seem, they all cohere in a rebelliously topsy-turvy retelling of Milton's and Western culture's central tale of the fall of woman and her shadow self, Satan. This fall, says Brontë, is not a fall *into* hell. It is a fall from "hell" into "heaven," not a fall from grace (in the religious sense) but a fall into grace (in the cultural sense). Moreover, for the heroine who falls it is the loss of Satan rather than the loss of God that signals the painful passage from innocence to experience. Emily Brontë, in other words, is not just Blakeian in "double" mystical vision, but Blakeian in a tough, radically political commitment to the belief that the state of being patriarchal Christianity calls "hell" is eternally, energetically delightful, whereas the state called "heaven" is rigidly hierarchical, Urizenic, and "kind" as a poison tree. But because she was metaphorically one of Milton's daughters, Brontë differs from Blake, that powerful son of a powerful father, in reversing the terms of Milton's Christian cosmogony for specifically feminist reasons.

Speaking of Jane Lead, a seventeenth-century Protestant mystic who was a significant precursor of Brontë's in visionary sexual politics, Catherine Smith has noted that "to study mysticism and feminism together is to learn more about the links between envisioning power and pursuing it," adding that "Idealist notions of transcendence may shape political notions of sexual equality as much as materialist or rationalist arguments do."[8] Her points are applicable to Brontë, whose revisionary mysticism is inseparable from both politics and feminism, although her emphasis is more on the loss than on the pursuit of power. Nevertheless, the feminist nature of her concern with neo-Miltonic definitions of hell and heaven, power and powerlessness, innocence and experience, has generally been overlooked by critics, many of whom, at their most biographical, tend to ask patronizing questions like "What is the matter with Emily Jane?"[9] Interestingly, however, certain women understood Brontë's feminist mythologies from the first. Speculating on the genesis of A. G. A., the fiery Byronic queen of Gondal with whose life and loves Emily Brontë was always obsessed, Fanny Ratchford noted in 1955 that while Arthur Wellesley, the emperor of Charlotte Brontë's fantasy kingdom of Angria, was "an arch-Byronic hero, for love of whom noble ladies went into romantic decline.... Gondal's queen was of such compelling beauty and charm as to bring all men to her feet, and of such selfish cruelty as to bring tragedy to all who loved her.... It was as if Emily was saying to Charlotte, 'You think the man is the dominant factor in romantic love, I'll show you it is the woman.'"[10] But of course Charlotte herself understood Emily's revisionary tendencies better than anyone. More than one hundred years before Ratchford wrote, the heroine of *Shirley*, that apotheosis of Emily "as she would have been in a happier life," speaks the English novel's first deliberately feminist criticism of Milton—"Milton did not see Eve, it was his cook that he saw"—and proposes as her alternative the Titan woman we discussed earlier, the mate of "Genius" and the potentially Satanic interlocutor of God. Some readers, including most recently the Marxist critic Terence Eagleton, have spoken scornfully of the "maundering rhetoric of *Shirley*'s embarrassing feminist mysticism."[11] But Charlotte, who was intellectually as well as physically akin to Emily, had captured the serious deliberation in her sister's vision. She knew that the author of *Wuthering Heights* was—to quote the Brontës' admirer Emily Dickinson—"looking oppositely / For the site of the Kingdom of Heaven" (J. 959).

* * *

Because Emily Brontë was looking oppositely not only for heaven (and hell) but for her own female origins, *Wuthering Heights* is one of the few authentic instances of novelistic myth-making, myth-making in the functional sense of problem-solving. Where writers from Charlotte Brontë and Henry James to James Joyce and Virginia Woolf have used mythic material to give point and structure to their novels, Emily Brontë uses the novel form to give substance—plausibility, really—to her myth. It is urgent that she do so because, as we shall see, the feminist cogency of this myth derives not only from its daring corrections of Milton but also from the fact that it is a distinctively nineteenth-century answer to the question of origins: it is the myth of how culture came about, and specifically of how nineteenth-century society occurred, the tale of where tea-tables, sofas, crinolines, and parsonages like the one at Haworth came from.

Because it is so ambitious a myth, *Wuthering Heights* has the puzzling self-containment of a *mystery* in the old sense of that word—the sense of mystery plays and Eleusinian mysteries. Locked in by Lockwood's uncomprehending narrative, Nelly Dean's story, with its baffling duplication of names, places, events, seems endlessly to reenact itself, like some ritual that must be cyclically repeated in order to sustain (as well as explain) both nature and culture. At the same time, because it is so prosaic a myth—a myth about crinolines!—*Wuthering Heights* is not in the least portentous or self-consciously "mythic." On the contrary, like all true rituals and myths, Brontë's "cuckoo's tale" turns a practical, casual, humorous face to its audience. For as Lévi-Straus's observations suggest, true believers gossip by the prayer wheel, since that modern reverence which enjoins solemnity is simply the foster child of modern skepticism.[12]

Gossipy but unconventional true believers were rare, even in the pious nineteenth century, as Arnold's anxious meditations and Carlyle's angry sermons note. But Brontë's paradoxically matter-of-fact imaginative strength, her ability to enter a realistically freckled fantasy land, manifested itself early. One of her most famous adolescent diary papers juxtaposes a plea for culinary help from the parsonage housekeeper, Tabby—"Come Anne pilloputate"—with "The Gondals are discovering the interior of Gaaldine" and "Sally Mosely is washing in the back kitchen."[13] Significantly, no distinction is made between the heroic exploits of the fictional Gondals and Sally Mosely's real washday business. The curiously childlike voice of the diarist records all events without commentary, and this reserve suggests an implicit acquiescence in the equal "truth" of all events. Eleven years later, when the sixteen-year-old reporter of "pilloputate" has grown up and is on the edge of *Wuthering Heights*, the naive, uninflected surface of her diary papers is unchanged

> ... Anne and I went our first long journey by ourselves together, leaving home on the 30th of June, Monday, sleeping at York, returning to Keighley Tuesday evening ... during our excursion we were Ronald Mcalgin, Henry Angora, Juliet Angusteena, Rosabella Esmalden, Ella and Julian Egremont, Catharine Navarre, and Cordilia Fitzaphnold, escaping from the palaces of instruction to join the Royalists who are hard driven at present by the victorious Republicans.... I must hurry off now to my turning and ironing. I have plenty of work on hands, and writing, and am altogether full of business.[14]

Psychodramatic "play," this passage suggests, is an activity at once as necessary and as ordinary as housework: ironing and the exploration of alternative lives are the same kind of "business"—a perhaps uniquely female idea of which Anne Bradstreet and Emily Dickinson, those other visionary housekeepers, would have approved.

No doubt, however, it is this deep-seated tendency of Brontë's to live literally with the fantastic that accounts for much of the critical disputation about *Wuthering Heights*, especially the quarrels about the novel's genre and style. Q. D. Leavis and Arnold Kettle, for instance, insist that the work is a "sociological novel," while Mark Schorer thinks it "means to be a work of edification [about] the nature of a grand passion." Leo Bersani sees it as an ontological psychodrama, and Elliot Gose as a sort of expanded fairytale.[15] And strangely there is truth in all these apparently conflicting notions, just as it is also true that (as Robert Kiely has affirmed) "part of the distinction of *Wuthering Heights* [is] that it has no 'literary' aura about it," and true at the same time that (as we have asserted) *Wuthering Heights* is an unusually literary novel because Brontë approached reality chiefly through the mediating agency of literature.[16] In fact, Kiely's comment illuminates not only the uninflected surface of the diary papers but also the controversies about their author's novel, for Brontë is "unliterary" in being without a received sense of what the eighteenth century called literary decorum. As one of her better-known poems declares, she follows "where [her] own nature would be leading," and that nature leads her to an oddly literal—and also, therefore, unliterary—use of extraordinarily various literary works, ideas, and genres, all of which she refers back to herself, since "it vexes [her] to choose another guide."[17]

Thus *Wuthering Heights* is in one sense an elaborate gloss on the Byronic Romanticism and incest fantasy of *Manfred*, written, as Ratchford suggested, from a consciously female perspective. Heathcliff's passionate invocations of Catherine ("Come in! ... hear me" [chap. 3] or "Be with me always—take any form—drive me mad" [chap. 16]) almost exactly echo Manfred's famous speech to Astarte ("Hear me, hear me ... speak to me! Though it be in wrath...").[18] In another way, though, *Wuthering Heights* is a prose redaction of the metaphysical storms and ontological nature/culture conflicts embodied in *King Lear*, with Heathcliff taking the part of Nature's bastard son Edmund, Edgar Linton incarnating the cultivated morality of his namesake Edgar, and the "wuthering" chaos at the Heights repeating the disorder that overwhelms Lear's kingdom when he relinquishes his patriarchal control to his diabolical daughters. But again, both poetic Byronic Romanticism and dramatic Shakespearean metaphysics are filtered through a novelistic sensibility with a surprisingly Austenian grasp of social details, so that *Wuthering Heights* seems also, in its "unliterary" way, to reiterate the feminist psychological concerns of a *Bildungsroman* Brontë may never have read: Jane Austen's *Northanger Abbey*. Catherine Earnshaw's "half savage and hardy and free" girlhood, for example, recalls the tomboy childhood of that other Catherine, Catherine Morland, and Catherine Earnshaw's fall into ladylike "grace" seems to explore the tragic underside of the anxiously comic initiation rites Catherine Morland undergoes at Bath and at Northanger Abbey.[19]

The world of *Wuthering Heights*, in other words, like the world of Brontë's diary papers, is one where what seem to be the most unlikely opposites coexist without, apparently, any consciousness on the author's part that there is anything unlikely in their coexistence. The ghosts of Byron, Shakespeare, and Jane Austen haunt the same ground. People with decent Christian names (Catherine, Nelly, Edgar, Isabella) inhabit a landscape in which also dwell people with strange animal or nature names (Hindley, Hareton, Heathcliff). Fairytale events out of what Mircea Eliade would call "great time" are given a local habitation and a real chronology in just that historical present Eliade defines as great time's opposite.[20] Dogs and gods (or goddesses) turn out to be not opposites but, figuratively speaking, the same words spelled in different ways. Funerals are weddings, weddings funerals. And of course, most important for our purposes here, hell is heaven, heaven hell, though the two are not separated, as Milton and literary decorum would prescribe, by vast eons of space but by a little strip of turf, for Brontë was rebelliously determined to walk

> ... not in old heroic traces
> And not in paths of high morality.
> And not among the half-distinguished faces,
> The clouded forms of long-past history.

On the contrary, surveying that history and its implications, she came to the revisionary conclusion that "the earth that wakes *one* human heart to feeling / Can centre both the worlds of Heaven and Hell."[21]

* * *

If we identify with Lockwood, civilized man at his most genteelly "cooked" and literary, we cannot fail to begin Brontë's novel by deciding that hell is a household very like Wuthering Heights. Lockwood himself, as if wittily predicting the reversal of values that is to be the story's central concern, at first calls the place "a perfect misanthropist's Heaven" (chap. 1). But then what is the traditional Miltonic or Dantesque hell if not a misanthropist's heaven, a site that substitutes hate for love, violence for peace, death for life, and in consequence the material for the spiritual, disorder for order? Certainly Wuthering Heights rings all these changes on Lockwood's first two visits. Heathcliff's first invitation to enter, for instance, is uttered through closed teeth, and appropriately enough it seems to his visitor to express "the sentiment 'Go to the Deuce.'" The house's other inhabitants—Catherine II, Hareton, Joseph, and Zillah, as we later learn—are for the most part equally hostile on both occasions, with Joseph muttering insults, Hareton surly, and Catherine II actually practicing (or pretending to practice) the "black arts."[22] Their energies of hatred, moreover, are directed not only at their uninvited guest but at each other, as Lockwood learns to his sorrow when Catherine II suggests that Hareton should accompany him through the storm and Hareton refuses to do so if it would please *her*.

The general air of sour hatred that blankets the Heights, moreover, manifests itself in a continual, aimless violence, a violence most particularly embodied in the snarling dogs that inhabit the premises. "In an arch under the dresser," Lockwood notes, "reposed a huge, liver-coloured bitch pointer, surrounded by a swarm of squealing puppies; and other dogs haunted other recesses" (chap. 1). His use of *haunted* is apt, for these animals, as he later remarks, are more like "four-footed fiends" than ordinary canines, and in particular Juno, the matriarch of the "hive," seems to be a parody of Milton's grotesquely maternal Sin, with her yapping brood of hellhounds. Significantly, too, the only nonhostile creatures in this fiercely Satanic stronghold are dead: in one of a series of blackly comic blunders, Lockwood compliments Catherine II on what in his decorous way he assumes are her cats, only to learn that the "cats" are just a heap of dead rabbits. In addition, though the kitchen is separate from the central family room, "a vast oak dresser" reaching "to the very roof" of the sitting room is laden with oatcakes, guns, and raw meat: "clusters of legs of beef, mutton, and ham." Dead or raw flesh and the instruments by which living bodies may be converted into more dead flesh are such distinctive features of the room that even the piles of oatcakes and the "immense pewter dishes ... towering row after row" (chap. 1) suggest that, like hell or the land at the top of the beanstalk, Wuthering Heights is the abode of some particularly bloodthirsty giant.

The disorder that quite naturally accompanies the hatred, violence, and death that prevail at Wuthering Heights on Lockwood's first visits leads to more of the city-bred gentleman's blunders, in particular his inability to fathom the relationships among the three principal members of the household's pseudo-family—Catherine II, Hareton, and Heathcliff. First he suggests that the girl is Heathcliff's "amiable lady," then surmises that Hareton is "the favoured possessor of the beneficent fairy" (chap. 2). His phrases, like most of his assumptions, parody the sentimentality of fictions that keep women in their "place" by defining them as beneficent fairies or amiable ladies. Heathcliff, perceiving this, adds a third stereotype to the discussion: "You would intimate that [my wife's] spirit has taken the form of ministering angel," he comments with the "almost diabolical sneer" of a Satanic literary critic. But of course, though Lockwood's thinking is stereotypical, he is right to expect some familial relationship among his tea-table companions, and right too to be daunted by the hellish lack of relationship among them. For though Hareton, Heathcliff, and Catherine II are all in some sense related, the primordial schisms that have overwhelmed the Heights with hatred and violence have divided them from the human orderliness represented by the ties of kinship. Thus just as Milton's hell consists of envious and (in the poet's view) equality-mad devils jostling for position, so these inhabitants of Wuthering Heights seem to live in chaos without the structuring principle of heaven's hierarchical chain of being, and therefore without the heavenly harmony God the Father's ranking of virtues, thrones, and powers makes possible. For this reason Catherine sullenly refuses to do anything "except what I please" (chap. 4), the servant Zillah vociferously rebukes Hareton for laughing, and old Joseph—whose viciously parodic religion seems here to represent a hellish joke at heaven's expense—lets the dogs loose on Linton without consulting his "maister," Heathcliff.

In keeping with this problem of "equality," a final and perhaps definitive sign of the hellishness that has enveloped Wuthering Heights at the time of Lockwood's first visits is the blinding snowfall that temporarily imprisons the by now unwilling guest in the home of his infernal hosts. Pathless as the kingdom of the damned, the "billowy white ocean" of cold that surrounds Wuthering Heights recalls the freezing polar sea on which Frankenstein, Walton; the monster—and the Ancient Mariner—voyaged. It recalls, too, the "deep snow and ice" of Milton's hell, "A gulf profound as that *Serbonian Bog* ... Where Armies whole have sunk" and where "by harpy-footed" and no doubt rather Heathcliff-ish "Furies hal'd / ... all the damn'd / Are brought ... to starve in Ice" (*PL* 2. 592–600). But of course, as *King Lear* implies, hell is simply another word for uncontrolled "nature," and here as elsewhere *Wuthering Heights* follows *Lear's* model.

Engulfing the Earnshaws' ancestral home and the Lintons', too, in a blizzard of destruction, hellish nature traps and freezes everyone in the isolation of a "perfect misanthropist's heaven." And again, as in *Lear* this hellish nature is somehow female or associated with femaleness, like an angry goddess shaking locks of ice and introducing Lockwood (and his readers) to the female rage that will be a central theme in *Wuthering Heights*. The femaleness of this "natural" hell is suggested, too, by its likeness to the "false" material creation Robert Graves analyzed so well in *The White Goddess*. Female nature has risen, it seems, in a storm of protest, just as the Sin-like dog Juno rises in a fury when Lockwood "unfortunately indulge[s] in winking and making faces" at her while musing on his heartless treatment of a "goddess" to whom he never "told" his love (chap. 1). Finally, that the storm is both hellish and female is made clearest of all by Lockwood's second visionary dream. Out of the tapping of branches, out of the wind and swirling snow, like an icy-fingered incarnation of the storm rising in protest against the patriarchal sermon of "Jabes Branderham," appears that ghostly female witch-child the *original* Catherine Earnshaw, who has now been "a waif for twenty years."

* * *

Why is Wuthering Heights so Miltonically hellish? And what happened to Catherine Earnshaw? Why has she become a demonic, storm-driven ghost? The "real" etiological story of *Wuthering Heights* begins, as Lockwood learns from his "human fixture" Nelly Dean, with a random weakening of the fabric of ordinary human society. Once upon a time, somewhere in what mythically speaking qualifies as pre-history or what Eliade calls "illo tempore," there is/ was a primordial family, the Earnshaws, who trace their lineage back at least as far as the paradigmatic Renaissance inscription "1500 Hareton Earnshaw" over their "principal doorway." And one fine summer morning toward the end of the eighteenth century, the "old master" of the house decides to take a walking tour of sixty miles to Liverpool (chap. 4). His decision, like Lear's decision to divide his kingdom, is apparently quite arbitrary, one of those mystifying psychic *données* for which the fictional convention of "once upon a time" was devised. Perhaps it means, like Lear's action, that he is half-consciously beginning to prepare for death. In any case, his ritual questions to his two children—an older son and a younger daughter—and to their servant Nelly are equally stylized and arbitrary, as are the children's answers. "What shall I bring you?" the old master asks, like the fisherman to whom the flounder gave three wishes. And the children reply, as convention dictates, by requesting their heart's desires. In other words, they reveal their true selves, just as a father contemplating his own ultimate absence from their lives might have hoped they would.

Strangely enough, however, only the servant Nelly's heart's desire is sensible and conventional: she asks for (or, rather, accepts the promise of) a pocketful of apples and pears. Hindley, on the other hand, the son who is destined to be next master of the household, does not ask for a particularly masterful gift. His wish, indeed, seems frivolous in the context of the harsh world of the Heights. He asks for a fiddle, betraying both a secret, soft-hearted desire for culture and an almost decadent lack of virile purpose. Stranger still is Catherine's wish for a whip. "She could ride any horse in the stable," says Nelly, but in the fairy-tale context of this narrative that realistic explanation hardly seems to suffice,[23] for, symbolically, the small Catherine's longing for a whip seems like a powerless younger daughter's yearning for power.

Of course, as we might expect from our experience of fairy tales, at least one of the children receives the desired boon. Catherine gets her whip. She gets it figuratively—in the form of a "gypsy brat"—rather than literally, but nevertheless "it" (both whip and brat) functions just as she must unconsciously have hoped it would, smashing her rival-brother's fiddle and making a desirable third among the children in the family so as to insulate her from the pressure of her brother's domination. (That there should always have been three children in the family is clear from the way other fairytale rituals of three are observed, and also from the fact that Heathcliff is given the name of a dead son, perhaps even the true oldest son, as if he were a reincarnation of the lost child.)

Having received her deeply desired whip, Catherine now achieves, as Hillis Miller and Leo Bersani have noticed, an extraordinary fullness of being.[24] The phrase may seem pretentiously metaphysical (certainly critics like Q. D. Leavis have objected to such phrases on those grounds)[25] but in discussing the early paradise from which Catherine and Heathcliff eventually fall we are trying to describe elusive psychic states, just as we would in discussing Wordsworth's visionary childhood, Frankenstein's youth before he "learned" that he was (the creator of) a monster, or even the prelapsarian sexuality of Milton's Adam and Eve. And so, like Freud who was driven to grope among such words as *oceanic* when he tried to explain the heaven that lies about us in our infancy, we are obliged to use the paradoxical and metaphorical language of mysticism: phrases like *wholeness, fullness of being*, and *androgyny* come inevitably to mind.[26] All three, as we shall see, apply, to Catherine, or more precisely to Catherine-Heathcliff.

In part Catherine's new wholeness results from a very practical shift in family dynamics. Heathcliff as a fantasy replacement of the dead oldest brother does in fact supplant Hindley in the old master's affections, and therefore he functions as a tool of the dispossessed younger sister whose "whip" he is. Specifically, he enables her for the first time to get possession of the kingdom of Wuthering Heights, which under her rule threatens to become, like Gondal, a queendom. In addition to this, however, Heathcliff's presence gives the girl a fullness of being that goes beyond power in household politics, because as Catherine's whip he is (and she herself recognizes this) an alternative self or double for her, a complementary addition to her being who fleshes out all her lacks the way a bandage might staunch a wound. Thus in her union with him she becomes, like Manfred in his union with his sister

Astarte, a perfect androgyne. As devoid of sexual awareness as Adam and Eve were in the prelapsarian garden, she sleeps with her whip, her other half, every night in the primordial fashion of the countryside. Gifted with that innocent, unselfconscious sexual energy which Blake saw as eternal delight, she has "ways with her," according to Nelly, "such as I never saw a child take up before" (chap. 5). And if Heathcliff's is the body that does her will—strong, dark, proud, and a native speaker of "gibberish" rather than English—she herself is an "unfeminine" instance of transcendently vital spirit. For she is never docile, never submissive, never ladylike. On the contrary, her joy—and the Coleridgean word is not too strong—is in what Milton's Eve is never allowed: a tongue "always going—singing, laughing, and plaguing everybody who would not do the same," and "ready words turning Joseph's religious curses into ridicule... and doing just what her father hated most" (chap. 5).

Perverse as it may seem, this paradise into which Heathcliff's advent has transformed Wuthering Heights for the young Catherine is as authentic a fantasy for women as Milton's Eden was for men, though Milton's misogynistically cowed daughters have rarely had the revisionary courage to spell out so many of the terms of their dream. Still, that the historical process does yield moments when that feminist dream of wholeness has real consequences is another point Brontë wishes us to consider, just as she wishes to convey her rueful awareness that, given the prior strength of patriarchal misogyny, those consequences may be painful as well as paradisal. Producing Heathcliff from beneath his greatcoat as if enacting a mock birth, old Mr. Earnshaw notes at once the equivocal nature of Catherine's whip: "You must e'en take it as a gift of God, though it's as dark almost as if it came from the devil" (chap. 4). His ambivalence is well-founded: strengthened by Heathcliff, Catherine becomes increasingly rebellious against the parodic patriarchal religion Joseph advocates, and thus, too, increasingly unmindful of her father's discipline. As she gains in rebellious energy, she becomes Satanically "as Gods" in her defiance of such socially constituted authority, and in the end, like a demonic Cordelia (that is, like Cordelia, Goneril, and Regan all in one) she has the last laugh at her father, answering his crucial dying question "Why canst thou not always be a good lass, Cathy?" with a defiantly honest question of her own: "Why cannot you always be a good man, Father?" (chap. 5) and then singing him, rather hostilely, "to sleep"—that is, to death.

Catherine's heaven, in other words, is very much like the place such a representative gentleman as Lockwood would call hell, for it is associated (like the hell of *King Lear*) with an ascendent self-willed female who radiates what, as Blake observed, most people consider "diabolical" energy—the creative energy of Los and Satan, the life energy of fierce, raw, uncultivated being.[27] But the ambiguity Catherine's own father perceives in his "gift of God" to the girl is also manifested in the fact that even some of the authentically hellish qualities Lockwood found at Wuthering Heights on his first two visits, especially the qualities of "hate" (i.e. defiance) and "violence" (i.e. energy), would have seemed to him to characterize the Wuthering Heights of Catherine's heavenly childhood. For Catherine, however, the defiance that might seem like hate was made possible by love (her oneness with Heathcliff) and the energy that seemed like violence was facilitated by the peace (the wholeness) of an undivided self.

Nevertheless, her personal heaven is surrounded, like Milton's Eden, by threats from what she would define as "hell." If, for instance, she had in some part of herself hoped that her father's death would ease the stress of that shadowy patriarchal yoke which was the only cloud on her heaven's horizon, Catherine was mistaken. For paradoxically old Earnshaw's passing brings with it the end to Catherine's Edenic "half savage and hardy and free" girlhood. It brings about a divided world in which the once-androgynous child is to be "laid alone" for the first time. And most important it brings about the accession to power of Hindley, by the patriarchal laws of primogeniture the real heir and thus the new father who is to introduce into the novel the proximate causes of Catherine's (and Heathcliff's) fall and subsequent decline.

* * *

Catherine's sojourn in the earthly paradise of childhood lasts for six years, according to C. P. Sanger's precisely worked-out chronology, but it takes Nelly Dean barely fifteen minutes to relate the episode.[28] Prelapsarian history, as Milton knew, is easy to summarize. Since happiness has few of the variations of despair, to be unfallen is to be static, whereas to fall is to enter the processes of time. Thus Nelly's account of Catherine's fall takes at least several hours, though it also covers six years. And as she describes it, that fall—or process of falling—begins with Hindley's marriage, an event associated for obvious reasons with the young man's inheritance of his father's power and position.

It is odd that Hindley's marriage should precipitate Catherine out of her early heaven because that event installs an adult woman in the small Heights family circle for the first time since the death of Mrs. Earnshaw four years earlier, and as conventional (or even feminist) wisdom would have it, Catherine "needs" a mother-figure to look after her, especially now that she is on the verge of adolescence. But precisely because she and Heathcliff are twelve years old and growing up, the arrival of Frances is the worst thing that could happen to her. For Frances, as Nelly's narrative indicates, is a model young lady, a creature of a species Catherine, safely sequestered in her idiosyncratic Eden, has had as little chance of encountering as Eve had of meeting a talking serpent before the time came for her to fall.

Of course, Frances is no serpent. On the contrary, light-footed and fresh-complexioned, she seems much more like a late eighteenth-century model of the Victorian angel in the house, and certainly her effect upon Hindley has been both to subdue him and to make him more ethereal. "He had grown sparer, and lost his colour, and spoke and dressed quite differently," Nelly notes (chap. 6); he even proposes to convert one room into a parlor, an amenity Wuthering Heights has never had. Hindley has in fact become a cultured man, so that in gaining a ladylike bride he has, as it were, gained the metaphorical fiddle that was his heart's desire when he was a boy.

It is no doubt inevitable that Hindley's fiddle and Catherine's whip cannot peaceably coexist. Certainly the early smashing of the fiddle by the "whip" hinted at such a problem, and so perhaps it would not be entirely frivolous to think of the troubles that now ensue for Catherine and Heathcliff as the fiddle's revenge. But even without pressing this conceit we can see that Hindley's angel/fiddle is a problematical representative of what is now introduced as the "heavenly" realm of culture. For one thing, her ladylike sweetness is only skin-deep. Leo Bersani remarks that the distinction between the children at the Heights and those at the Grange is the difference between "aggressively selfish children" and "whiningly selfish children."[29] If this is so, Frances foreshadows the children at the Grange—the children of genteel culture—since "her affection [toward Catherine] tired very soon [and] she grew peevish," at which point the now gentlemanly Hindley becomes "tyrannical" in just the way his position as the household's new *paterfamilias* encourages him to be. His tyranny consists, among other things, in his attempt to impose what Blake would call a Urizenic heavenly order at the heretofore anti-hierarchical Heights. The servants Nelly and Joseph, he decrees, must know their place—which is "the back kitchen"—and Heathcliff, because he is socially nobody, must be exiled from culture: deprived of "the instruction of the curate" and cast out into "the fields" (chap. 6).

Frances's peevishness, however, is not just a sign that her ladylike ways are inimical to the prelapsarian world of Catherine's childhood; it is also a sign that, as the twelve-year-old girl must perceive it, to be a lady is to be diseased. As Nelly hints, Frances is tubercular, and any mention of death causes her to act "half silly," as if in some part of herself she knows she is doomed, or as if she is already half a ghost. And she is. As a metaphor, Frances's tuberculosis means that she is in an advanced state of just that social "consumption" which will eventually kill Catherine, too, so that the thin and silly bride functions for the younger girl as a sort of premonition or ghost of what she herself will become.

But of course the social disease of ladyhood, with its attendant silliness or madness, is only one of the threats Frances incarnates for twelve-year-old Catherine. Another, perhaps even more sinister because harder to confront, is associated with the fact that though Catherine may well need a mother—in the sense in which Eve or Mary Shelley's monster needed a mother/model—Frances does not and cannot function as a good mother for her. The original Earnshaws were shadowy but mythically grand, like the primordial "true" parents of fairy tales (or like most parents seen through the eyes of preadolescent children). Hindley and Frances, on the other hand, the new Earnshaws, are troublesomely real though as oppressive as the step-parents in fairy tales.[30] To say that they are in some way like step-parents, however, is to say that they seem to Catherine like transformed or alien parents, and since this is as much a function of her own vision as of the older couple's behavior, we must assume that it has something to do with the changes wrought by the girl's entrance into adolescence.

Why do parents begin to seem like step-parents when their children reach puberty? The ubiquitousness of step-parents in fairy tales dealing with the crises of adolescence suggests that the phenomenon is both deep-seated and widespread. One explanation—and the one that surely accounts for Catherine Earnshaw's experience—is that when the child gets old enough to become conscious of her parents as sexual beings they really do begin to seem like fiercer, perhaps even (as in the case of Hindley and Frances) younger versions of their "original" selves. Certainly they begin to be more threatening (that is, more "peevish" and "tyrannical") if only because the child's own sexual awakening disturbs them almost as much as their sexuality, now truly comprehended, bothers the child. Thus the crucial passage from Catherine's diary which Lockwood reads even before Nelly begins her narration is concerned not just with Joseph's pious oppressions but with the cause of those puritanical onslaughts, the fact that she and Heathcliff must shiver in the garret because "Hindley and his wife [are basking] downstairs before a comfortable fire ... kissing and talking nonsense by the hour—foolish palaver we should be ashamed of." Catherine's defensiveness is clear. She (and Heathcliff) are troubled by the billing and cooing of her "step-parents" because she understands, perhaps for the first time, the sexual nature of what a minute later she calls Hindley's "paradise on the hearth" and—worse—understands its relevance to her.

Flung into the kitchen, "where Joseph asseverated, 'owd Nick' would fetch us," Catherine and Heathcliff each seek "a separate nook to await his advent." For Catherine-and-Heathcliff—that is, Catherine and Catherine, or Catherine and her whip—have already been separated from each other, not just by tyrannical Hindley, the *deus* produced by time's *machina*, but by the emergence of Catherine's own sexuality, with all the terrors which attend that phenomenon in a puritanical and patriarchal society. And just as peevish Frances incarnates the social illness of ladyhood, so also she quite literally embodies the fearful as well as the frivolous consequences of sexuality. Her foolish if paradisaical palaver on the hearth, after all, leads straight to the death her earlier ghostliness and silliness had predicted. Her sexuality's destructiveness was even implied by the minor but vicious acts of injustice with which it was associated—arbitrarily pulling Heathcliff's hair, for instance— but the sex–death equation, with which Milton and Mary Shelley were also concerned, really surfaces when Frances's and Hindley's son, Hareton, is born. At that time, Kenneth, the lugubrious physician who functions like a medical Greek chorus throughout *Wuthering Heights*, informs Hindley that the winter will "probably finish" Frances.

To Catherine, however, it must appear that the murderous agent is not winter but sex, for as she is beginning to learn, the Miltonic testaments of her world have told woman that "thy sorrow I will greatly multiply / By thy Conception ..." (*PL* 10. 192–95) and the maternal image of Sin birthing Death reinforces this point. That Frances's decline and death accompany Catherine's fall is metaphysically appropriate, therefore. And it is dramatically appropriate as well, for Frances's fate foreshadows the catastrophes which will follow Catherine's fall into sexuality just as surely as the appearance of Sin and Death on earth followed Eve's fall. That Frances's death also, incidentally, yields Hareton—the truest scion of the Earnshaw clan—is also profoundly appropriate. For Hareton is, after all, a resurrected version of the original patriarch whose name is written over the great main door of the house, amid a "wilderness of shameless little boys." Thus his birth marks the beginning of the historical as well as the psychological decline and fall of that Satanic female principle which has temporarily usurped his "rightful" place at Wuthering Heights.

* * *

Catherine's fall, however, is caused by a patriarchal past and present, besides being associated with a patriarchal future. It is significant, then, that her problems begin—violently enough—when she literally falls down and is bitten by a male bulldog, a sort of guard/god from Thrushcross Grange. Though many readers overlook this point, Catherine does not go to the Grange when she is twelve years old. On the contrary, the Grange seizes her and "holds [her] fast," a metaphoric action which emphasizes the turbulent and inexorable nature of the psychosexual *rites de passage Wuthering Heights* describes, just as the ferociously masculine bull/dog—as a symbolic representative of Thrushcross Grange—contrasts strikingly with the ascendancy at the Heights of the hellish female bitch goddess alternately referred to as "Madam" and "Juno."[31]

Realistically speaking, Catherine and Heathcliff have been driven in the direction of Thrushcross Grange by their own desire to escape not only the pietistic tortures Joseph inflicts but also, more urgently, just that sexual awareness irritatingly imposed by Hindley's romantic paradise. Neither sexuality nor its consequences can be evaded, however, and the farther the children run the closer they come to the very fate they secretly wish to avoid. Racing "from the top of the Heights to the park without stopping," they plunge from the periphery of Hindley's paradise (which was transforming their heaven into a hell) to the boundaries of a place that at first seems authentically heavenly, a place full of light and softness and color, a "splendid place carpeted with crimson ... and [with] a pure white ceiling bordered by gold, a shower of glass-drops hanging in silver chains from the centre, and shimmering with little soft tapers" (chap. 6). Looking in the window, the outcasts speculate that if they were inside such a room "we should have thought ourselves in heaven!" From the outside, at least, the Lintons' elegant haven appears paradisaical. But once the children have experienced its Urizenic interior, they know that in their terms this heaven is hell.

Because the first emissary of this heaven who greets them is the bulldog Skulker, a sort of hellhound posing as a hound of heaven, the wound this almost totemic animal inflicts upon Catherine is as symbolically suggestive as his role in the girl's forced passage from Wuthering Heights to Thrushcross Grange. Barefoot, as if to emphasize her "wild child" innocence, Catherine is exceptionally vulnerable, as a wild child must inevitably be, and when the dog is "throttled off, his huge, purple tongue hanging half a foot out of his mouth ... his pendant lips [are] streaming with bloody slaver." "Look ... how her foot bleeds," Edgar Linton exclaims, and "She may be lamed for life," his mother anxiously notes (chap. 6). Obviously such bleeding has sexual connotations, especially when it occurs in a pubescent girl. Crippling injuries to the feet are equally resonant, moreover, almost always signifying symbolic castration, as in the stories of Oedipus, Achilles, and the Fisher King. Additionally, it hardly needs to be noted that Skulker's equipment for aggression—his huge purple tongue and pendant lips, for instance—sounds extraordinarily phallic. In a Freudian sense, then, the imagery of this brief but violent episode hints that Catherine has been simultaneously catapulted into adult female sexuality *and* castrated.

How can a girl "become a woman" and be castrated (that is, desexed) at the same time? Considering how Freudian its iconographic assumptions are, the question is disingenuous, for not only in Freud's terms but in feminist terms, as Elizabeth Janeway and Juliet Mitchell have both observed, femaleness—implying "penis envy"—quite reasonably *means* castration. "No woman has been deprived of a penis; she never had one to begin with," Janeway notes, commenting on Freud's crucial "Female Sexuality" (1931).

> But she *has* been deprived of something else that men enjoy namely, autonomy, freedom, and the power to control her destiny. By insisting, falsely, on female deprivation of the male organ, Freud is pointing to an actual deprivation and one of which he was clearly aware. In Freud's time the advantages enjoyed by the male sex over the inferior female were, of course, even greater than at present, and they were also accepted to a much larger extent, as being inevitable, inescapable. Women were evident social castrates, and the mutilation of their potentiality as achieving human creatures was quite analogous to the physical wound.[32]

But if such things were true in Freud's time, they were even truer in Emily Brontë's. And certainly the hypothesis that Catherine Earnshaw has become in some sense a "social castrate," that she has been "lamed for life," is borne out by her treatment at Thrushcross Grange—and by the treatment of her alter ego, Heathcliff. For, assuming that she is a "young lady," the entire Linton household cossets the wounded (but still healthy) girl as if she were truly an invalid. Indeed, feeding her their alien rich food—negus and cakes from their own table—washing her feet, combing her hair, dressing her in "enormous slippers," and wheeling her about like a doll, they seem to be enacting some sinister ritual of initiation, the sort of ritual that has traditionally weakened mythic heroines from Persephone to Snow White. And because he is "a little Lascar, or an American or Spanish castaway," the Lintons banish Heathcliff from their parlor, thereby separating Catherine from the lover/brother whom she herself defines as her strongest and most necessary "self." For five weeks now, she will be at the mercy of the Grange's heavenly gentility.

To say that Thrushcross Grange is genteel or cultured and that it therefore seems "heavenly" is to say, of course, that it is the opposite of Wuthering Heights. And certainly at every point the two houses are opposed to each other, as if each in its self-assertion must absolutely deny the other's being. Like Milton and Blake, Emily Brontë thought in polarities. Thus, where Wuthering Heights is essentially a great parlorless room built around a huge central hearth, a furnace of dark energy like the fire of Los, Thrushcross Grange has a parlor notable not for heat but for light, for "a pure white ceiling bordered by gold" with "a shower of glass-drops" in the center that seems to parody the "sovran vital Lamp" (*PL* 3. 22) which illuminates Milton's heaven of Right Reason. Where Wuthering Heights, moreover, is close to being naked or "raw" in Lévi-Strauss' sense—its floors uncarpeted, most of its inhabitants barely literate, even the meat on its shelves open to inspection—Thrushcross Grange is clothed and "cooked": carpeted in crimson, bookish, feeding on cakes and tea and negus.[33] It follows from this, then, that where Wuthering Heights is functional, even its dogs working sheepdogs or hunters, Thrushcross Grange (though guarded by bulldogs) appears to be decorative or aesthetic, the home of lapdogs as well as ladies. And finally, therefore, Wuthering Heights in its stripped functional rawness is essentially anti-hierarchical and egalitarian as the aspirations of Eve and Satan, while Thrushcross Grange reproduces the hierarchical chain of being that Western culture traditionally proposes as heaven's decree.

For all these reasons, Catherine Earnshaw, together with her whip Heathcliff, has at Wuthering Heights what Emily Dickinson would call a "Barefoot-Rank."[34] But at Thrushcross Grange, clad first in enormous, crippling slippers and later in "a long cloth habit which she [is] obliged to hold up with both hands" (chap. 7) in order to walk, she seems on the verge of becoming, again in Dickinson's words, a "Lady [who] dare not lift her Veil / For fear it be dispelled" (J. 421). For in comparison to Wuthering Heights, Thrushcross Grange is, finally, the home of concealment and doubleness, a place where, as we shall see, reflections are separated from their owners like souls from bodies, so that the lady in anxiety "peers beyond her mesh— / And wishes—and denies— /Lest Interview—annul a want /That Image—satisfies." And it is here, therefore, at heaven's mercy, that Catherine Earnshaw learns "to adopt a double character without exactly intending to deceive anyone" (chap. 8).

In fact, for Catherine Earnshaw, Thrushcross Grange in those five fatal weeks becomes a Palace of Instruction, as Brontë ironically called the equivocal schools of life where her adolescent Gondals were often incarcerated. But rather than learning, like A. G. A. and her cohorts, to rule a powerful nation, Catherine must learn to rule herself, or so the Lintons and her brother decree. She must learn to repress her own impulses, must girdle her own energies with the iron stays of "reason." Having fallen into the decorous "heaven" of femaleness, Catherine must become a lady. And just as her entrance into the world of Thrushcross Grange was forced and violent, so this process by which she is obliged to accommodate herself to that world is violent and painful, an unsentimental education recorded by a practiced, almost sadistically accurate observer. For the young Gondals, too, had had a difficult time of it in their Palace of Instruction: far from being wonderful Golden Rule days, their school days were spent mostly in dungeons and torture cells, where their elders starved them into submission or self-knowledge.

That education for Emily Brontë is almost always fearful, even agonizing, may reflect the Brontës' own traumatic experiences at the Clergy Daughters School and elsewhere.[35] But it may also reflect in a more general way the repressiveness with which the nineteenth century educated all its young ladies, strapping them to backboards and forcing them to work for hours at didactic samplers until the more high-spirited girls—the Catherine Earnshaws and Catherine Morlands—must have felt, like the inhabitants of Kafka's penal colony, that the morals and maxims of patriarchy were being embroidered on their own skins. To mention Catherine Morland here is not to digress. As we have seen, Austen did not subject her heroine to education as a gothic/Gondalian torture, except parodically. Yet even Austen's parody suggests that for a girl like Catherine Morland the school of life inevitably inspires an almost instinctive fear, just as it would for A. G. A. "Heavenly" Northanger Abbey may somehow conceal a prison cell, Catherine suspects, and she develops this notion by sensing (as Henry Tilney cannot) that the female romances she is reading are in some sense the disguised histories of her own life.

In Catherine Earnshaw's case, these points are made even more subtly than in the Gondal poems or in *Northanger Abbey*, for Catherine's education in doubleness, in ladylike decorum meaning also ladylike deceit, is marked by an actual doubling or fragmentation of her personality. Thus though it is ostensibly Catherine who is being educated, it is Heathcliff—her rebellious alter ego, her whip, her id—who is exiled to a prison cell, as if to implement delicate Isabella Linton's first horrified reaction to him: "Frightful thing! Put him in the cellar" (chap. 6). Not in the cellar but in the garret, Heathcliff is locked up and, significantly, starved, while Catherine, daintily "cutting up the wing of a goose," practices table manners below. Even more significantly, however, she too is finally unable to eat her dinner and retreats under the table cloth to weep for her imprisoned playmate. To Catherine, Heathcliff is "more myself than I am," as she later famously tells Nelly, and so his literal starvation is symbolic of her more terrible because more dangerous spiritual starvation, just as her literal wound at Thrushcross Grange is also a metaphorical deathblow to *his* health and power. For divided from each other, the once androgynous Heathcliff and Catherine are now conquered by the concerted forces of patriarchy, the Lintons of Thrushcross Grange acting together with Hindley and Frances, their emissaries at the Heights.

It is, appropriately enough, during this period, that Frances gives birth to Hareton, the new patriarch-to-be, and dies, having fulfilled her painful function in the book and in the world. During this period, too, Catherine's education in ladylike self-denial causes her dutifully to deny her self and decide to marry Edgar. For when she says of Heathcliff that "he's more myself than I am," she means that as her exiled self the nameless "gipsy" really does preserve in his body more of her original being than she retains: even in his deprivation he seems whole and sure, while she is now entirely absorbed in the ladylike wishing and denying Dickinson's poem describes. Thus, too, it is during this period of loss and transition that Catherine obsessively inscribes on her windowsill the crucial writing Lockwood finds, writing which announces from the first Emily Brontë's central concern with identity: "a name repeated in all kinds of characters, large and small—Catherine Earnshaw, here and there varied to Catherine Heathcliff, and then again to Catherine Linton" (chap. 3). In the light of this repeated and varied name it is no wonder, finally, that Catherine knows Heathcliff is "more myself than I am," for he has only a single name, while she has so many that she may be said in a sense to have none. Just as triumphant self-discovery is the ultimate goal of the male *Bildungsroman*, anxious self-denial, Brontë suggests, is the ultimate product of a female education. What Catherine, or any girl, must learn is that she does not know her own name, and therefore cannot know either who she is or whom she is destined to be.

It has often been argued that Catherine's anxiety and uncertainty about her own identity represents a moral failing, a fatal flaw in her character which leads to her inability to choose between Edgar and Heathcliff. Heathcliff's reproachful "Why did you betray your own heart, Cathy?" (chap. 15) represents a Blakeian form of this moral criticism, a contemptuous suggestion that "those who restrain desire do so because theirs is weak enough to be restrained."[36] The more vulgar and commonsensical attack of the Leavisites, on the other hand—the censorious notion that "maturity" means being strong enough to choose not to have your cake and eat it too—represents what Mark Kinkead-Weekes calls "the view from the Grange."[37] To talk of morality in connection with Catherine's fall—and specifically in connection with her self-deceptive decision to marry Edgar—seems pointless, however, for morality only becomes a relevant term where there are meaningful choices.

As we have seen, Catherine has no meaningful choices. Driven from Wuthering Heights to Thrushcross Grange by her brother's marriage, seized by Thrushcross Grange and held fast in the jaws of reason, education, decorum, she cannot do otherwise than as she does, must marry Edgar because there is no one else for her to marry and a lady must marry. Indeed, her self-justifying description of her love for Edgar—"I love the ground under his feet, and the air over his head, and everything he touches, and every word he says" (chap. 9)—is a bitter parody of a genteel romantic declaration which shows how effective her education has been in indoctrinating her with the literary romanticism deemed suitable for young ladies, the swooning "femininity" that identifies all energies with the charisma of fathers/lovers/husbands. Her concomitant explanation that it would "degrade" her to marry Heathcliff is an equally inevitable product of her education, for her fall into ladyhood has been accompanied by Heathcliff's reduction to an equivalent position of female powerlessness, and Catherine has learned, correctly, that if it is degrading to be a woman it is even more degrading to be *like* a woman. Just as Milton's Eve, therefore, being already fallen, had no meaningful choice despite Milton's best efforts to prove otherwise, so Catherine has no real choice. Given the patriarchal nature of culture, women must fall—that is, they are already fallen because doomed to fall.

In the shadow of this point, however, moral censorship is merely redundant, a sort of interrogative restatement of the novel's central fact. Heathcliff's Blakeian reproach is equally superfluous, except insofar as it is not moral but etiological, a question one part of Catherine asks another, like her later passionate "Why am I so changed?" For as Catherine herself perceives, social and biological forces have fiercely combined against her. God as—in W. H. Auden's words—a "Victorian papa" has hurled her from the equivocal natural paradise she calls "heaven" and He calls "hell" into His idea of "heaven" where she will break her heart with weeping to come back to the Heights. Her speculative, tentative "mad" speech to Nelly captures, finally, both the urgency and the inexorability of her fall. "Supposing at twelve years old, I had been wrenched from the Heights ... and my all in all, as Heathcliff was at that time, and been converted at a stroke into Mrs. Linton, the lady of Thrushcross Grange, and the wife of a stranger: an exile, and outcast, thenceforth, from what had been my world." In terms of the psychodramatic action of *Wuthering Heights*, only Catherine's use of the word *supposing* is here a rhetorical strategy; the rest of her speech is absolutely accurate, and places her subsequent actions beyond good and evil, just as it suggests, in yet another Blakeian reversal of customary terms, that her madness may really be sanity.

* * *

Catherine Earnshaw Linton's decline follows Catherine Earnshaw's fall. Slow at first, it is eventually as rapid, sickening, and deadly as the course of Brontë's own consumption was to be. And the long slide toward death of the body begins with what appears to be an irreversible death of the soul—with Catherine's fatalistic acceptance of Edgar's offer and her consequent self-imprisonment in the role of "Mrs. Linton, the lady of Thrushcross Grange." It is, of course, her announcement of this decision to Nelly, overheard by

Heathcliff, which leads to Heathcliff's self-exile from the Heights and thus definitively to Catherine's psychic fragmentation. And significantly, her response to the departure of her true self is a lapse into illness which both signals the beginning of her decline and foreshadows its mortal end. Her words to Nelly the morning after Heathcliff's departure are therefore symbolically as well as dramatically resonant "Shut the window, Nelly, I'm starving!" (chap. 9).

As Dorothy van Ghent has shown, windows in *Wuthering Heights* consistently represent openings into possibility, apertures through which subversive otherness can enter, or wounds out of which respectability can escape like flowing blood.[38] It is, after all, on the window ledge that Lockwood finds Catherine's different names obsessively inscribed, as if the girl had been trying to decide which self to let in the window or in which direction she ought to fly after making her own escape down the branches of the neighboring pine. It is through the same window that the ghost of Catherine Linton extends her icy fingers to the horrified visitor. And it is a window at the Grange that Catherine, in her "madness," begs Nelly to open so that she can have one breath of the wind that "comes straight down the moor" (chap. 12). "Open the window again wide, fasten it open!" she cries, then rises and, predicting her own death, seems almost ready to start on her journey homeward up the moor. ("I could not trust her alone by the gaping lattice," Nelly comments wisely.) But besides expressing a general wish to escape from "this shattered prison" of her body, her marriage, her self, her life, Catherine's desire now to *open* the window refers specifically back to that moment three years earlier when she had chosen instead to close it, chosen to inflict on herself the imprisonment and starvation that as part of her education had been inflicted on her double, Heathcliff.

Imprisonment leads to madness, solipsism, paralysis, as Byron's *Prisoner of Chillon*, some of Brontë's Gondal poems, and countless other gothic and neo-gothic tales suggest. Starvation—both in the modern sense of malnutrition and the archaic Miltonic sense of freezing ("to starve in ice")—leads to weakness, immobility, death. During her decline, starting with both starvation and imprisonment, Catherine passes through all these grim stages of mental and physical decay. At first she seems (to Nelly anyway) merely somewhat "headstrong." Powerless without her whip, keenly conscious that she has lost the autonomy of her hardy and free girlhood, she gets her way by indulging in tantrums, wheedling, manipulating, so that Nelly's optimistic belief that she and Edgar "were really in possession of a deep and growing happiness" contrasts ironically with the housekeeper's simultaneous admission that Catherine "was never subject to depression of spirits before" the three interlocking events of Heathcliff's departure, her "perilous illness," and her marriage (chap. 10). But Heathcliff's mysterious reappearance six months after her wedding intensifies rather than cures her symptoms. For his return does not in any way suggest a healing of the wound of femaleness that was inflicted at puberty. Instead, it signals the beginning of "madness," a sort of feverish infection of the wound. Catherine's marriage to Edgar has now inexorably locked her into a social system that denies her autonomy, and thus, as psychic symbolism, Heathcliff's return represents the return of her true self's desires without the rebirth of her former powers. And desire without power, as Freud and Blake both knew, inevitably engenders disease.

If we understand all the action that takes place at Thrushcross Grange between Edgar, Catherine, and Heathcliff from the moment of Heathcliff's reappearance until the time of Catherine's death to be ultimately psychodramatic, a grotesque playing out of Catherine's emotional fragmentation on a "real" stage, then further discussion of her sometimes genteelly Victorian, sometimes fiercely Byronic decline becomes almost unnecessary, its meaning is so obvious. Edgar's autocratic hostility to Heathcliff—that is, to Catherine's desirous self, her independent will— manifests itself first in his attempt to have her entertain the returned "gipsy" or "ploughboy" in the kitchen because he doesn't belong in the parlor. But soon Edgar's hatred results in a determination to expel Heathcliff entirely from his house because he fears the effects of this demonic intruder, with all he signifies, not only upon his wife but upon his sister. His fear is justified because, as we shall see, the Satanic rebellion Heathcliff introduces into the parlors of "heaven" contains the germ of a terrible disease with patriarchy that causes women like Catherine and Isabella to try to escape their imprisonment in roles and houses by running away, by starving themselves, and finally by dying.

Because Edgar is so often described as "soft," "weak," slim, fair-haired, even effeminate-looking, the specifically patriarchal nature of his feelings toward Heathcliff may not be immediately evident. Certainly many readers have been misled by his almost stylized angelic qualities to suppose that the rougher, darker Heathcliff incarnates masculinity in contrast to Linton's effeminacy. The returned Heathcliff, Nelly says, "had grown a tall, athletic, well-formed man, beside whom my master seemed quite slender and youthlike. His upright carriage suggested the idea of his having been in the army" (chap. 10). She even seems to acquiesce in his superior maleness. But her constant, reflexive use of the phrase "my master" for Edgar tells us otherwise, as do some of her other expressions. At this point in the novel, anyway, Heathcliff is always merely "Heathcliff" while Edgar is variously "Mr. Linton," "my master," "Mr. Edgar," and "the master," all phrases conveying the power and status he has independent of his physical strength.

In fact, as Milton also did, Emily Brontë demonstrates that the power of the patriarch, Edgar's power, begins with words, for heaven is populated by "*spirits* Masculine," and as above, so below. Edgar does not need a strong, conventionally masculine body, because his mastery is contained in books, wills, testaments, leases, titles, rent-rolls, documents, languages, all the paraphernalia by which patriarchal culture is transmitted from one generation to the next. Indeed, even without Nelly's designation of him as "the master," his notable bookishness would define him as a patriarch, for he rules his house from his library as if to parody that male education in Latin and Greek, privilege and prerogative, which so infuriated Milton's daughters.[39] As a figure in the psychodrama of Catherine's decline, then, he incarnates the education in young ladyhood that has commanded her to learn her "place." In Freudian terms he would no doubt be described as her superego, the internalized guardian of morality and culture, with Heathcliff, his opposite, functioning as her childish and desirous id.

But at the same time, despite Edgar's superegoistic qualities, Emily Brontë shows that his patriarchal rule, like Thrushcross Grange itself, is based on physical as well as spiritual violence. For her, as for Blake, heaven kills. Thus, at a word from Thrushcross Grange, Skulker is let loose, and Edgar's magistrate father cries "What prey, Robert?" to his manservant, explaining that he fears thieves because "yesterday was my rent day." Similarly, Edgar, having decided that he has "humored" Catherine long enough, calls for two strong men servants to support his authority and descends into the kitchen to evict Heathcliff. The patriarch, Brontë notes, needs words, not muscles, and Heathcliff's derisive language paradoxically suggests understanding of the true male power Edgar's "soft" exterior conceals: "Cathy, this lamb of yours threatens like a bull!" (chap. 11). Even more significant, perhaps, is the fact that when Catherine locks Edgar in alone with her and Heathcliff—once more imprisoning herself while ostensibly imprisoning the hated master—this apparently effeminate, "milk-blooded coward" frees himself by striking Heathcliff a breathtaking blow on the throat "that would have levelled a slighter man."

Edgar's victory once again recapitulates that earlier victory of Thrushcross Grange over Wuthering Heights which also meant the victory of a Urizenic "heaven" over a delightful and energetic "hell." At the same time, it seals Catherine's doom, locking her into her downward spiral of self-starvation. And in doing this it finally explains what is perhaps Nelly's most puzzling remark about the relationship between Edgar and Catherine. In chapter 8, noting that the love-struck sixteen-year-old Edgar is "doomed, and flies to his fate," the housekeeper sardonically declares that "the soft thing [Edgar] ... possessed the power to depart [from Catherine] as much as a cat possesses the power to leave a mouse half killed or a bird half eaten." At that point in the novel her metaphor seems odd. Is not headstrong Catherine the hungry cat, and "soft" Edgar the half-eaten mouse? But in fact, as we now see, Edgar all along represented the devouring force that will gnaw and worry Catherine to death, consuming flesh and spirit together. For having fallen into "heaven," she has ultimately—to quote Sylvia Plath—"fallen / Into the stomach of indifference," a social physiology that urgently needs her not so much for herself as for her function.[40]

When we note the significance of such imagery of devouring, as well as the all-pervasive motif of self-starvation in *Wuthering Heights*, the kitchen setting of this crucial confrontation between Edgar and Heathcliff begins to seem more than coincidental. In any case, the episode is followed closely by what C. P. Sanger calls Catherine's "hunger strike" and by her famous mad scene.[41] Another line of Plath's describes the feelings of selflessness that seem to accompany Catherine's realization that she has been reduced to a role, a function, a sort of walking costume: "I have no face, I have wanted to efface myself."[42] For the weakening of Catherine's grasp on the world is most specifically shown by her inability to recognize her own face in the mirror during the mad scene. Explaining to Nelly that she is not mad, she notes that if she were "I should believe you really *were* [a] withered hag, and I should think I *was* under Penistone Crag; and I'm conscious it's night and there are two candles on the table making the black press shine like jet." Then she adds, "It does appear odd—I see a face in it" (chap. 12). But of course, ironically, there is no "black press" in the room, only a mirror in which Catherine sees and repudiates her own image. Her fragmentation has now gone so far beyond the psychic split betokened by her division from Heathcliff that body and image (or body and soul) have separated. Q. D. Leavis would have us believe that his apparently gothic episode, with its allusion to "dark superstitions about premonitions of death, about ghosts and primitive beliefs about the soul ... is a proof of [Emily Brontë's] immaturity at the time of the original conception of *Wuthering Heights*." Leo Bersani, on the other hand, suggests that the scene hints at "the danger of being haunted by alien versions of the self."[43] In a sense, however, the image Catherine sees in the mirror is neither gothic nor alien—though she is alienated from it—but hideously familiar, and further proof that her madness may really equal sanity. Catherine sees in the mirror an image of who and what she has really become in the world's terms: "Mrs. Linton, the lady of Thrushcross Grange." And oddly enough, this image appears to be stored like an article of clothing, a trousseau-treasure, or again in Plath's words "a featureless, fine / Jew linen,"[44] in one of the cupboards of childhood, the black press from her old room at the Heights.

Because of this connection with childhood, part of the horror of Catherine's vision comes from the question it suggests: was the costume/face always there, waiting in a corner of the little girl's wardrobe? But to ask this question is to ask again, as Frankenstein does, whether Eve was created fallen, whether women are not Education's but "Nature's fools," doomed from the start to be exiles and outcasts despite their illusion that they are hardy and free. When Milton's Eve is for her own good led away from her own image by a superegoistic divine voice which tells her that "What there thou sees fair creature is thyself"—*merely* thyself—does she not in a sense determine Catherine Earnshaw's fall? When, substituting Adam's superior image for her own, she concedes that female "beauty is excell'd by manly grace / And wisdom" (*PL* 4. 490–91) does not her "sane" submission outline the contours of Catherine Earnshaw's rebelliously Blakeian madness? Such questions are only implicit in Catherine's mad mirror vision of herself, but it is important to see that they are implied. Once again, where Shelley clarifies Milton, showing the monster's dutiful disgust with "his" own self-image, Brontë repudiates him, showing how his teachings have doomed her protagonist to what dutiful Nelly considers an insane search for her lost true self. "I'm sure I should be myself were I once more among the heather on those hills," Catherine exclaims, meaning that only a journey back into the androgynous wholeness of childhood could heal the wound her mirror-image symbolizes, the fragmentation that began when she was separated from heather and Heathcliff, and "laid alone" in the first fateful enclosure of her oak-panelled bed. For the mirror-image is one more symbol of the cell in which Catherine has been imprisoned by herself and by society.

To escape from the horrible mirror-enclosure, then, might be to escape from all domestic enclosures, or to begin to try to escape. It is significant that in her madness Catherine tears at her pillow with her teeth, begs Nelly to open the window, and seems "to find childish diversion in pulling the feathers from the rents she [has] just made" (chap. 12). Liberating feathers from the prison where they had been reduced to objects of social utility, she imagines them reborn as the birds they once were, whole and free, and pictures them "wheeling over our heads in the middle of the moor," trying to get back to their nests. A moment later, standing by the window "careless of the frosty air," she imagines her own trip back across the moor to Wuthering Heights, noting that "it's a rough journey, and a sad heart to travel it; and we must pass by Gimmerton Kirk to go that journey! ... But Heathcliff, if I dare you now, will you venture? ... I won't rest till you are with me. I never will!" (chap. 12). For a "fallen" woman, trapped in the distorting mirrors of patriarchy, the journey into death is the only way out, Brontë suggests, and the *Liebestod* is not (as it would be for a male artist, like Keats or Wagner) a mystical but a practical solution. In the presence of death, after all, "The mirrors are sheeted," to quote Plath yet again.[45]

The masochism of this surrender to what A. Alvarez has called the "savage god" of suicide is plain, not only from Catherine's own words and actions but also from the many thematic parallels between her speeches and Plath's poems.[46] But of course, taken together, self-starvation or anorexia nervosa, masochism, and suicide form a complex of psychoneurotic symptoms that is almost classically associated with female feelings of powerlessness and rage. Certainly the "hunger strike" is a traditional tool of the powerless, as the history of the feminist movement (and many other movements of oppressed peoples) will attest. Anorexia nervosa, moreover, is a sort of mad corollary of the self-starvation that may be a sane strategy for survival. Clinically associated with "a distorted concept of body size"—like Catherine Earnshaw's alienated/familiar image in the mirror—it is fed by the "false sense of power that the faster derives from her starvation," and is associated, psychologists speculate, with "a struggle for control, for a sense of identity, competence, and effectiveness."

But then in a more general sense it can surely be argued that all masochistic or even suicidal behavior expresses the furious power hunger of the powerless. Catherine's whip—now meaning Heathcliff, her "love" for Heathcliff, and also, more deeply, her desire for the autonomy her union with Heathcliff represented—turns against Catherine. She whips herself because she cannot whip the world, and she must whip something. Besides, in whipping herself does she not, perhaps, torment the world? Of this she is, in her powerlessness, uncertain, and her uncertainty leads to further madness, reinforcing the vicious cycle. "O let me not be mad," she might cry, like Lear, as she tears off her own socially prescribed costumes so that she can more certainly feel the descent of the whip she herself has raised. In her rebelliousness Catherine has earlier played alternately the parts of Cordelia and of Goneril and Regan to the Lear of her father and her husband. Now, in her powerlessness, she seems to have herself become a figure like Lear, mourning her lost kingdom and suicidally surrendering herself to the blasts that come straight down the moor.

Nevertheless, though her madness and its setting echo Lear's disintegration much more than, say, Ophelia's, Catherine is different from Lear in a number of crucial ways, the most obvious being the fact that her femaleness dooms her to a function as well as a role, and threatens her, therefore, with the death Frances's fate had predicted. Critics never comment on this point, but the truth is that Catherine is pregnant during both the kitchen scene and the mad scene, and her death occurs at the time of (and ostensibly because of) her "confinement." In the light of this, her anorexia, her madness, and her masochism become even more fearsomely meaningful. Certainly, for instance, the distorted body that the anorexic imagines for herself is analogous to the distorted body that the pregnant woman really must confront. Can eating produce such a body? The question, mad as it may seem, must be inevitable. In any case, some psychoanalysts have suggested that anorexia, endemic to pubescent girls, reflects a fear of oral impregnation, to which self-starvation would be one obvious response.[47]

But even if a woman accepts, or rather concedes, that she is pregnant, an impulse toward self-starvation would seem to be an equally obvious response to the pregnant woman's inevitable fear of being monstrously inhabited, as well as to her own horror of being enslaved to the species and reduced to a tool of the life process. Excessive ("pathological") morning sickness has traditionally been interpreted as an attempt to vomit up the alien intruder, the child planted in the belly like an incubus.[48] And indeed, if the child has been fathered—as Catherine's has—by a man the woman defines as a stranger, her desire to rid herself of it seems reasonable enough. But what if she must kill herself in the process? This is another question Catherine's masochistic self-starvation implies, especially if we see it as a disguised form of morning sickness. Yet another question is more general: must motherhood, like ladyhood, kill? Is female sexuality necessarily deadly?

To the extent that she answers yes, Brontë swerves once again from Milton, though rather less radically than usual. For when she was separated from her own reflection, Eve was renamed "mother of human race," a title Milton seems to have considered honorifically life-giving despite the dreadful emblem of maternity Sin provided. Catherine's entrance into motherhood, however, darkly parodies even if it does not subvert this story. Certainly childbirth brings death to her (and eventually to Heathcliff) though at the same time it does revitalize the patriarchal order that began to fail at Wuthering Heights with her early assertions of individuality. Birth is, after all, the ultimate fragmentation the self can undergo, just as "confinement" is, for women, the ultimate pun on imprisonment. As if in recognition of this, Catherine's attempt to escape maternity does, if only unconsciously, subvert Milton. For Milton's Eve "knew not eating Death." But Brontë's does. In her refusal to be enslaved to the species, her refusal to be "mother of human race," she closes her mouth on emptiness as, in Plath's words, "on a communion tablet." It is no use, of course. She breaks apart into two Catherines—the old, mad, dead Catherine fathered by Wuthering Heights, and the new, more docile and acceptable Catherine fathered by Thrushcross Grange. But nevertheless, in her defiance Emily Brontë's Eve, like her creator, is a sort of hunger artist, a point Charlotte Brontë acknowledged when she memorialized her sister in *Shirley*, that other revisionary account of the Genesis of female hunger.[49]

* * *

Catherine's fall and her resulting decline, fragmentation, and death are the obvious subjects of the first half of *Wuthering Heights*. Not quite so obviously, the second half of the novel is concerned with the larger, social consequences of Catherine's fall, which spread out in concentric circles like rings from a stone flung into a river, and which are examined in a number of parallel stories, including some that have already been set in motion at the time of Catherine's death. Isabella, Nelly, Heathcliff, and Catherine II—in one way or another all these characters' lives parallel (or even in a sense contain) Catherine's, as if Brontë were working out a series of alternative versions of the same plot.

Isabella is perhaps the most striking of these parallel figures, for like Catherine she is a headstrong, impulsive "miss" who runs away from home at adolescence. But where Catherine's fall is both fated and unconventional, a fall "upward" from hell to heaven, Isabella's is both willful and conventional. Falling from Thrushcross Grange to Wuthering Heights, from "heaven" to "hell," in exactly the opposite direction from Catherine, Isabella patently chooses her own fate, refusing to listen to Catherine's warnings against Heathcliff and carefully evading her brother's vigilance. But then Isabella has from the first functioned as Catherine's opposite, a model of the stereotypical young lady patriarchal education is designed to produce. Thus where Catherine is a "stout hearty lass" raised in the raw heart of nature at Wuthering Heights, Isabella is slim and pale, a daughter of culture and Thrushcross Grange. Where Catherine's childhood is androgynous, moreover, as her oneness with Heathcliff implies, Isabella has borne the stamp of sexual socialization from the first, or so her early division from her brother Edgar—her future guardian and master—would suggest. When Catherine and Heathcliff first see them, after all, Isabella and Edgar are quarreling over a lapdog, a genteel (though covertly sexual) toy they cannot share. "When would you catch me wishing to have what Catherine wanted? or find us [arguing] divided by the whole room?" Heathcliff muses on the scene (chap. 6). Indeed, so much the opposite of Catherine's is Isabella's life and lineage that it is almost as if Brontë, in contriving it, were saying "Let's see what would happen if I told Catherine's story the 'right' way"—that is, with socially approved characters and situations.

As Isabella's fate suggests, however—and this is surely part of Brontë's point—the "right" beginning of the story seems almost as inevitably to lead to the wrong ending as the wrong or "subversive" beginning. Ironically, Isabella's bookish upbringing has prepared her to fall in love with (of all people) Heathcliff. Precisely because she has been taught to believe in coercive literary conventions, Isabella is victimized by the genre of romance. Mistaking appearance for reality, tall athletic Heathcliff for "an honourable soul" instead of "a fierce, pitiless wolfish man," she runs away from her cultured home in the naive belief that it will simply be replaced by another cultivated setting. But like Claire Clairmont, who enacted a similar drama in real life, she underestimates both the ferocity of the Byronic hero and the powerlessness of all women, even "ladies," in her society. Her experiences at Wuthering Heights teach her that hell really is hellish for the children of heaven: like a parody of Catherine, she starves, pines and sickens, oppressed by that Miltonic grotesque, Joseph, for she is unable to stomach the rough food of nature (or hell) just as Catherine cannot swallow the food of culture (or heaven). She does not literally die of all this, but when she escapes, giggling like a madwoman, from *her* self-imprisonment, she is so effectively banished from the novel by her brother (and Brontë) that she might as well be dead.

Would Isabella's fate have been different if she had fallen in love with someone less problematical than Heathcliff—with a man of culture, for instance, rather than a Satanic nature figure? Would she have prospered with the love of someone like her own brother, or Heathcliff's tenant, Lockwood? Her early relationship with Edgar, together with Edgar's patriarchal rigidity, hint that she would not. Even more grimly suggestive is the story Lockwood tells in chapter 1 about his romantic encounter at the seacoast. Readers will recall that the "fascinating creature" he admired was "a real goddess in my eyes, as long as she took no notice of [me]." But when she "looked a return," her lover "shrunk icily into myself ... till finally the poor innocent was led to doubt her own senses ... " (chap. 1). Since even the most cultivated women are powerless, women are evidently at the mercy of all men, Lockwoods and Heathcliffs alike.

Thus if literary Lockwood makes a woman into a goddess, he can unmake her at whim without suffering himself. If literary Isabella makes a man into a god or hero, however, she must suffer—may even have to die—for her mistake. Lockwood in effect kills his goddess for being human, and would no doubt do the same to Isabella. Heathcliff, on the other hand, literally tries to kill Isabella for trying to be a goddess, an angel, a lady, and for having, therefore, a "mawkish, waxen face." Either way, Isabella must in some sense be killed, for her fate, like Catherine's, illustrates the double binds with which patriarchal society inevitably crushes the feet of runaway girls.[50] Perhaps it is to make this point even more dramatically that Brontë has Heathcliff hang Isabella's genteelly named springer, Fanny, from a "bridle hook" on the night he and Isabella elope. Just as the similarity of Isabella's and Catherine's fates suggests that "to fall" and "to fall in love" are equivalents, so the *bridle* or *bridal hook* is an apt, punning metaphor for the institution of marriage in a world where fallen women, like their general mother Eve, are (as Dickinson says) "Born—Bridalled—Shrouded— / In a Day."[51]

Nelly Dean, of course, seems to many critics to have been put into the novel to help Emily Brontë disavow such uniformly dark intentions. "For a specimen of true benevolence and homely fidelity, look at the character of Nelly Dean," Charlotte Brontë says with what certainly appears to be conviction, trying to soften the picture of "perverse passion and passionate perversity" Victorian readers thought her sister had produced.[52] And Charlotte Brontë "rightly defended her sister against allegations of abnormality by pointing out that ... Emily had created the wholesome, maternal Nelly Dean," comments Q. D. Leavis.[53] How wholesome and maternal is Nelly Dean, however? And if we agree that she is basically benevolent, of what does her benevolence consist? Problematic words like *wholesome* and *benevolent* suggest a point where we can start to trace the relationship between Nelly's history and Catherine's (or Isabella's). To begin with, of course, Nelly is healthy and wholesome because she is a survivor, as the artist-narrator must be. Early in the novel, Lockwood refers to her as his "human fixture," and there is, indeed, a durable thinglike quality about her, as if she had outlasted the Earnshaw/Linton storms of passion like their two houses, or as if she were a wall, a door, an object of furniture meant to begin a narration in response to the conventional sigh of "Ah, if only these old walls could speak, what stories they would tell." Like a wall or fixture, moreover, Nelly has a certain impassivity, a diplomatic immunity to entangling emotions. Though she sometimes expresses strong feelings about the action, she manages to avoid taking sides—or, rather, like a wall, she is related to both sides. Consequently, as the artist must, she can go anywhere and hear everything.

At the same time, Nelly's evasions suggest ways in which her history has paralleled the lives of Catherine and Isabella, though she has rejected their commitments and thus avoided their catastrophes. Hindley, for instance, was evidently once as close to Nelly as Heathcliff was to Catherine. Indeed, like Heathcliff, Nelly seems to have been a sort of stepchild at the Heights. When old Mr. Earnshaw left on his fateful trip to Liverpool, he promised to bring back a gift of apples and pears for Nelly as well as the fiddle and whip Hindley and Catherine had asked for. Because she is only "a poor man's daughter," however, Nelly is excluded from the family, specifically by being defined as its servant. Luckily for her, therefore (or so it seems), she has avoided the incestuous/egalitarian relationship with Hindley that Catherine has with Heathcliff, and at the same time—because she is ineligible for marriage into either family—she has escaped the bridal hook of matrimony that destroys both Isabella and Catherine.

It is for these reasons, finally, that Nelly is able to tell the story of all these characters without herself becoming ensnared in it, or perhaps, more accurately, she is able (like Brontë herself) to use the act of telling the story as a strategy for protecting herself from such entrapment. "I have read more than you would fancy, Mr. Lockwood," Nelly remarks to her new master. "You could not open a book in this library that I have not looked into and got something out of also ... it is as much as you can expect of a poor man's daughter" (59). By this she means, no doubt, that in her detachment she knows about Miltonic fears of falling and Richardsonian dreams of rising, about the anxieties induced by patriarchal education and the hallucinations of genteel romance.[54] And precisely because she has such a keen literary consciousness, she is able ultimately to survive and to triumph over her sometimes unruly story. Even when Heathcliff locks her up, for example, Nelly gets out (unlike Catherine and Isabella, who are never really able to escape), and one by one the deviants who have tried to reform her tale—Catherine, Heathcliff, even Isabella—die, while Nelly survives. She survives and, as Bersani has also noted, she coerces the story into a more docile and therefore more congenial mode.[55]

To speak of coercion in connection with Nelly may seem unduly negative, certainly from the Leavisite perspective. And in support of that perspective we should note that besides being wholesome because she is a survivor, Nelly is benevolent because she is a nurse, a nurturer, a foster-mother. The gift Mr. Earnshaw promises her is as symbolically significant in this respect as Catherine's whip and Hindley's fiddle, although our later experiences of Nelly suggest that she wants the apples and pears not so much for herself as for others. For though Nelly's health suggests that she is a hearty eater, she is most often seen feeding others, carrying baskets of apples, stirring porridge, roasting meats, pouring tea. Wholesomely nurturing, she does appear to be in some sense an ideal woman, a "general mother"—if not from Emily Brontë's point of view, then from, say, Milton's. And indeed, if we look again at the crucial passage in *Shirley* where Charlotte Brontë's Shirley/Emily criticizes Milton, we find an unmistakable version of Nelly Dean. "Milton tried to see the first woman," says Shirley, "but, Cary, he saw her not.... It was his cook that he saw ... puzzled 'what choice to choose for delicacy best....'"

This comment explains a great deal. For if Nelly Dean is Eve as Milton's cook—Eve, that is, as Milton (but not Brontë or Shirley) would have had her—she does not pluck apples to eat them herself; she plucks them to make applesauce. And similarly, she does not tell stories to participate in them herself, to consume the emotional food they offer, but to create a moral meal, a didactic fare that will nourish future generations in docility. As Milton's cook, in fact, Nelly Dean is patriarchy's paradigmatic housekeeper, the man's woman who has traditionally been hired to keep men's houses in order by straightening out their parlors, their daughters, and their stories. "My heart invariably cleaved to the master's, in preference to Catherine's side," she herself declares (chap. 10), and she expresses her preference by acting throughout the novel as a censorious agent of patriarchy.

Catherine's self-starvation, for instance, is notably prolonged by Nelly's failure to tell "the master" what his wife is doing, though in the first place it was induced by tale-bearing on Nelly's part. All her life Catherine has had trouble stomaching the food offered by Milton's cook, and so it is no wonder that in her madness she sees Nelly as a witch "gathering elf-bolts to hurt our heifers." It is not so much that Nelly Dean is "Evil," as Q. D. Leavis scolds "an American critic" for suggesting,[56] but that she is accommodatingly manipulative, a stereotypically benevolent man's woman. As such, she would and does "hurt [the] heifers" that inhabit such an anti-Miltonic heaven of femaleness as Wuthering Heights. In fact, as Catherine's "mad" words acknowledge, there is a sense in which Nelly Dean herself is Milton's bogey, the keeper of the house who closes windows (as Nelly does throughout *Wuthering Heights*) and locks women into the common sitting room. And because Emily Brontë is not writing a revolutionary polemic but a myth of origins, she chooses to tell her story of psychogenesis ironically, through the words of the survivor who helped *make* the story—through "the perdurable voice of the country," in Schorer's apt phrase. Reading Nelly's text, we see what we have lost through the eyes of the cook who has transformed us into what we are.

But if Nelly parallels or comments upon Catherine by representing Eve as Milton's cook, while Isabella represents Catherine/Eve as a bourgeois literary lady, it may at first be hard to see how or why Heathcliff parallels Catherine at all. Though he is Catherine's alter ego, he certainly seems to be, in Bersani's words, "a non-identical double."[57] Not only is he male while she is female—implying many subtle as well as a few obvious differences, in this gender-obsessed book—but he seems to be a triumphant survivor, an insider, a power-usurper throughout most of the novel's second half, while Catherine is not only a dead failure but a wailing, outcast ghost. Heathcliff does love her and mourn her—and finally Catherine does in some sense "kill" him—but beyond such melodramatically romantic connections, what bonds unite these one-time lovers?

Perhaps we can best begin to answer this question by examining the passionate words with which Heathcliff closes his first grief-stricken speech after Catherine's death: "Oh, God! it is unutterable! I cannot live without my life! I cannot live without my soul!" (chap. 16). Like the metaphysical paradox embedded in Catherine's crucial adolescent speech to Nelly about Heathcliff ("He's more myself than I am"), these words have often been thought to be, on the one hand, emptily rhetorical, and on the other, severely mystical. But suppose we try to imagine what they might mean as descriptions of a psychological fact about the relationship between Heathcliff and Catherine. Catherine's assertion that Heathcliff was *herself* quite reasonably summarized, after all, her understanding that she was being transformed into a lady while Heathcliff retained the ferocity of her primordial half-savage self. Similarly, Heathcliff's exclamation that he cannot live without his soul may express, as a corollary of this idea, the "gypsy's" own deep sense of being Catherine's whip, and his perception that he has now become merely the soulless body of a vanished passion. But to be merely a body—a whip without a mistress—is to be a sort of monster, a fleshly thing, an object of pure animal materiality like the abortive being Victor Frankenstein created. And such a monster is indeed what Heathcliff becomes.

From the first, Heathcliff has had undeniable monster potential, as many readers have observed. Isabella's questions to Nelly—"Is Mr. Heathcliff a man? If so, is he mad? And if not is he a devil?" (chap. 13)—indicate among other things Emily Brontë's cool awareness of having created an anomalous being, a sort of "Ghoul" or "Afreet," not (as her sister half hoped) "despite" herself but for good reasons. Uniting human and animal traits, the skills of culture with the energies of nature, Heathcliff's character tests the boundaries between human and animal, nature and culture, and in doing so proposes a new definition of the demonic. What is more important for our purposes here, however, is the fact that, despite his outward masculinity, Heathcliff is somehow female in his monstrosity. Besides in a general way suggesting a set of questions about humanness, his existence therefore summarizes a number of important points about the relationship between maleness and femaleness as, say, Milton representatively defines it.

To say that Heathcliff is "female" may at first sound mad or absurd. As we noted earlier, his outward masculinity seems to be definitively demonstrated by his athletic build and military carriage, as well as by the Byronic sexual charisma that he has for ladylike Isabella. And though we saw that Edgar is truly patriarchal despite his apparent effeminacy, there is no real reason why Heathcliff should not simply represent an alternative version of masculinity, the maleness of the younger son, that paradigmatic outsider in patriarchy. To some extent, of course, this is true: Heathcliff is clearly just as male in his Satanic outcast way as Edgar in his angelically established way. But at the same time, on a deeper associative level, Heathcliff is "female"—on the level where younger sons and bastards and devils unite with women in rebelling against the tyranny of heaven, the level where orphans are female and heirs are male, where flesh is female and spirit is male, earth female, sky male, monsters female, angels male.

The sons of Urizen were born from heaven, Blake declares, but "his daughters from green herbs and cattle, / From monsters and worms of the pit." He might be describing Heathcliff, the "little dark thing" whose enigmatic ferocity suggests vegetation spirits, hell, pits, night—all the "female" irrationality of nature. Nameless as a woman, the gypsy orphan old Earnshaw brings back from the mysterious bowels of Liver/pool is clearly as illegitimate as daughters are in a patrilineal culture. He speaks, moreover, a kind of animal-like gibberish which, together with his foreign swarthiness, causes sensible Nelly to refer to him at first as an "it," implying (despite his apparent maleness) a deep inability to get his gender straight. His "it-ness" or id-ness emphasizes, too, both his snarling animal qualities—his appetites, his brutality—and his thingness. And the fact that he speaks gibberish suggests the profound alienation of the physical/natural/female realm he represents from language, culture's tool and the glory of "spirits Masculine." In even the most literal way, then, he is what Elaine Showalter calls "a woman's man," a male figure into which a female artist projects in disguised form her own anxieties about her sex and its meaning in her society.[58] Indeed, if Nelly Dean is Milton's cook, Heathcliff incarnates that unregenerate natural world which must be metaphorically cooked or spiritualized, and therefore a raw kind of femaleness that, Brontë shows, has to be exorcised if it cannot be controlled.

In most human societies the great literal and figurative chefs, from Brillat-Savarin to Milton, are males, but as Sherry Ortner has noted, everyday "cooking" (meaning such low-level conversions from nature to culture as child-rearing, pot-making, bread-baking) is done by women, who are in effect charged with the task of policing the realm they represent.[59] This point may help explain how and why Catherine Earnshaw becomes Heathcliff's "soul." After Nelly as archetypal house-keeper finishes nursing him, high-spirited Catherine takes over his education because he meets her needs for power. Their relationship works so well, however, because just as he provides her with an extra body to lessen her female vulnerability, so she fills his need for a soul, a voice, a language with which to address cultured men like Edgar. Together they constitute an autonymous and androgynous (or, more accurately, gynandrous) whole: a woman's man and a woman *for herself* in Sartre's sense, making up one complete woman.[60] So complete do they feel, in fact, that as we have seen they define their home at Wuthering Heights as a heaven, and themselves as a sort of Blakeian angel, as if sketching out the definition of an angel D. H. Lawrence would have Tom Brangwen offer seventy-five years later in *The Rainbow*:

> "If we've got to be Angels, and if there is no such thing as a man nor a woman amongst them, then ... a married couple makes one Angel.... For ... an Angel can't be less than a human being. And if it was only the soul of a man *minus* the man, then it would be less than a human being."[61]

That the world—particularly Lockwood, Edgar, and Isabella—sees the heaven of Wuthering Heights as a "hell" is further evidence of the hellish femaleness that characterizes this gynandrous body and soul. It is early evidence, too, that without his "soul" Heathcliff will become an entirely diabolical brute, a "Ghoul" or "Afreet." Speculating seriocomically that women have souls "only to make them capable of *Damnation*," John Donne articulated the traditional complex of ideas underlying this point even before Milton did. "Why hath the common opinion afforded women soules?" Donne asked. After all, he noted, women's only really "spiritual" quality is their power of speech, "for which they are beholding to their *bodily instruments*: For perchance an *Oxes* heart, or a *Goates*, or a *Foxes*, or a *Serpents* would speak just so, if it were in the *breast*, and could move that *tongue* and *jawes*."[62] Though speaking of women, he might have been defining the problem Isabella was to articulate for Emily Brontë: "Is Mr. Heathcliff a *man*? Or what is he?"

As we have already seen, when Catherine is first withdrawn from the adolescent Heathcliff, the boy becomes increasingly brutish, as if to foreshadow his eventual soullessness. Returning in her ladylike costume from Thrushcross Grange, Catherine finds her one-time "counterpart" in old clothes covered with "mire and dirt," his face and hands "dismally beclouded" by dirt that suggests his inescapable connection with the filthiness of nature. Similarly, when Catherine is dying Nelly is especially conscious that Heathcliff "gnashed ... and foamed like a mad dog," so that she does not feel as if he is a creature of her own species (chap. 15). Still later, after his "soul's" death, it seems to her that Heathcliff howls "not like a man, but like a savage beast getting goaded to death with knives and spears" (chap. 16). His subsequent conduct, though not so overtly animal-like, is consistent with such behavior. Bastardly and dastardly, a true son of the bitch goddess Nature, throughout the second half of *Wuthering Heights* Heathcliff pursues a murderous revenge against patriarchy, a revenge most appropriately expressed by *King Lear's* equally outcast Edmund: "Well, then,/ Legitimate Edgar, I must have your land."[63] For Brontë's revisionary genius manifests itself especially in her perception of the deep connections among Shakespeare's Edmund, Milton's Satan, Mary

Shelley's monster, the demon lover/animal groom figure of innumerable folktales—and Eve, the original rebellious female.

Because he unites characteristics of all these figures in a single body, Heathcliff in one way or another acts like all of them throughout the second half of *Wuthering Heights*. His general aim in this part of the novel is to wreak the revenge of nature upon culture by subverting legitimacy. Thus, like Edmund (and Edmund's female counterparts Goneril and Regan) he literally *takes* the *place* of one legitimate heir after another, supplanting both Hindley and Hareton at the Heights, and—eventually—Edgar at the Grange. Moreover, he not only replaces legitimate culture but in his rage strives like Frankenstein's monster to end it. His attempts at killing Isabella and Hindley, as well as the infanticidal tendencies expressed in his merciless abuse of his own son, indicate his desire not only to alter the ways of his world but literally to discontinue them, to get at the heart of patriarchy by stifling the line of descent that ultimately gives culture its legitimacy. Lear's "*hysterica passio*," his sense that he is being smothered by female nature, which has inexplicably risen against all fathers everywhere, is seriously parodied, therefore, by the suffocating womb/room of death where Heathcliff locks up his sickly son and legitimate Edgar's daughter.[64] Like Satan, whose fall was originally inspired by envy of the celestial legitimacy incarnated in the Son of God, Heathcliff steals or perverts birthrights. Like Eve and her double, Sin, he undertakes such crimes against a Urizenic heaven in order to vindicate his own worth, assert his own energy. And again, like Satan, whose hellish kingdom is a shadowy copy of God's luminous one, or like those suavely unregenerate animal grooms Mr. Fox and Bluebeard, he manages to achieve a great deal because he realizes that in order to subvert legitimacy he must first impersonate it; that is, to kill patriarchy, he must first pretend to be a patriarch.

Put another way, this simply means that Heathcliff's charismatic maleness is at least in part a result of his understanding that he must defeat on its own terms the society that has defeated him. Thus, though he began his original gynandrous life at Wuthering Heights as Catherine's whip, he begins his transformed, soulless or Satanic life there as Isabella's bridal hook. Similarly, throughout the extended maneuvers against Edgar and his daughter which occupy him for the twenty years between Isabella's departure and his own death, he impersonates a "devil daddy," stealing children like Catherine II and Linton from their rightful homes, trying to separate Milton's cook from both her story and her morality, and perverting the innocent Hareton into an artificially blackened copy of himself. His understanding of the inauthenticity of his behavior is consistently shown by his irony. Heathcliff knows perfectly well that he is not really a father in the true (patriarchal) sense of the word, if only because he has himself no surname; he is simply acting like a father, and his bland, amused "I want my children about me to be sure" (chap. 29) comments upon the world he despises by sardonically mimicking it, just as Satan mimics God's logic and Edmund mimics Gloucester's astrologic.

On the one hand, therefore, as Linton's deathly father, Heathcliff, like Satan, is truly the father of death (begotten, however, not upon Sin but upon silliness), but on the other hand he is very consciously a mock father, a male version of the terrible devouring mother, whose blackly comic admonitions to Catherine II ("No more runnings away! ... I'm come to fetch you home, and I hope you'll be a dutiful daughter, and not encourage my son to further disobedience" [chap. 29]) evoke the bleak hilarity of hell with their satire of Miltonic righteousness. Given the complexity of all this, it is no wonder Nelly considers his abode at the Heights "an oppression past explaining."

Since Heathcliff's dark energies seem so limitless, why does his vengeful project fail? Ultimately, no doubt, it fails because in stories of the war between nature and culture nature always fails. But that point is of course a tautology. Culture tells the story (that is, the story is a cultural construct) and the story is etiological: how culture triumphed over nature, where parsonages and tea-parties came from, how the lady got her skirts—and her deserts. Thus Edmund, Satan, Frankenstein's monster, Mr. Fox, Bluebeard, Eve, and Heathcliff all must fail in one way or another, if only to explain the status quo. Significantly, however, where Heathcliff's analogs are universally destroyed by forces outside themselves, Heathcliff seems to be killed, as Catherine was, by something within himself. His death from self-starvation makes his function as Catherine's almost identical double definitively clear. Interestingly, though, when we look closely at the events leading up to his death it becomes equally clear that Heathcliff is not just killed by his own despairing desire for his vanished "soul" but at least in part by another one of Catherine's parallels, the new and cultivated Catherine who has been reborn through the intervention of patriarchy in the form of Edgar Linton. It is no accident, certainly, that Catherine II's imprisonment at the Heights and her rapprochement with Hareton coincide with Heathcliff's perception that "there is a strange change approaching," with his vision of the lost Catherine, and with his development of an eating disorder very much akin to Catherine's anorexia nervosa.

* * *

If Heathcliff is Catherine's almost identical double, Catherine II really is her mother's "non-identical double." Though he has his doubles confused, Bersani does note that Nelly's "mild moralizing" seems "suited to the younger

Catherine's playful independence."[65] For where her headstrong mother genuinely struggled for autonomy, the more docile Catherine II merely plays at disobedience, taking make-believe journeys within the walls of her father's estate and dutifully surrendering her illicit (though equally make-believe) love letters at a word from Nelly. Indeed, in almost every way Catherine II differs from her fierce dead mother in being culture's child, a born lady. "It's as if Emily Brontë were telling the same story twice," Bersani observes, "and eliminating its originality the second time."[66] But though he is right that Brontë is telling the same story over again (really for the third or fourth time), she is not repudiating her own originality. Rather, through her analysis of Catherine II's successes, she is showing how society repudiated Catherine's originality.

Where, for instance, Catherine Earnshaw rebelled against her father, Catherine II is profoundly dutiful. One of her most notable adventures occurs when she runs away from Wuthering Heights to get *back* to her father, a striking contrast to the escapes of Catherine and Isabella, both of whom ran purposefully away from the world of fathers and older brothers. Because she is a dutiful daughter, moreover, Catherine II is a cook, nurse, teacher, and housekeeper. In other words, where her mother was a heedless wild child, Catherine II promises to become an ideal Victorian woman, all of whose virtues are in some sense associated with daughterhood, wifehood, motherhood. Since Nelly Dean was her foster mother, literally replacing the original Catherine, her development of these talents is not surprising. To be mothered by Milton's cook and fathered by one of his angels is to become, inevitably, culture's child. Thus Catherine II nurses Linton (even though she dislikes him), brews tea for Heathcliff, helps Nelly prepare vegetables, teaches Hareton to read, and replaces the wild blackberries at Wuthering Heights with flowers from Thrushcross Grange. Literary as her father and her aunt Isabella, she has learned the lessons of patriarchal Christianity so well that she even piously promises Heathcliff that she will forgive both him and Linton for their sins against her: "I know [Linton] has a bad nature ... he's your son. But I'm glad I've a better to forgive it" (chap. 29). At the same time, she has a genteel (or Urizenic) feeling for rank which comes out in her early treatment of Hareton, Zillah, and others at the Heights.

Even when she stops biblically forgiving, moreover, literary modes dominate Catherine II's character. The "black arts" she tries to practice are essentially bookish—and plainly inauthentic. Indeed, if Heathcliff is merely impersonating a father at this point in the story, Catherine II is merely impersonating a witch. A real witch would threaten culture; but Catherine II's vocation is to serve it, for as her personality suggests, she is perfectly suited to (has been raised for) what Sherry Ortner defines as the crucial female function of mediating between nature and cultures.[67] Thus it is she who finally restores order to both the Heights and the Grange by marrying Hareton Earnshaw, whom she has, significantly, prepared for his new mastery by teaching him to read. Through her intervention, therefore, he can at last recognize the name over the lintel at Wuthering Heights—the name Hareton Earnshaw—which is both his own name and the name of the founder of the house, the primordial patriarch.

With his almost preternatural sensitivity to threats, Heathcliff himself recognizes the danger Catherine II represents. When, offering to "forgive him," she tries to embrace him he shudders and remarks "I'd rather hug a snake!" Later, when she and Hareton have cemented their friendship, Heathcliff constantly addresses her as "witch" and "slut." In the world's terms, she is the opposite of these: she is virtually an angel in the house. But for just those reasons she is Urizenically dangerous to Heathcliff's Pandemonium at the Heights. Besides threatening his present position, however, Catherine II's union with Hareton reminds Heathcliff specifically of the heaven he has lost. Looking up from their books, the young couple reveal that "their eyes are precisely similar, and they are those of Catherine Earnshaw" (chap. 33). Ironically, however, the fact that Catherine's descendants "have" her eyes tells Heathcliff not so much that Catherine endures as that she is both dead and fragmented. Catherine II has only her mother's eyes, and though Hareton has more of her features, he too is conspicuously not Catherine. Thus when Edgar dies and Heathcliff opens Catherine's casket as if to free her ghost, or when Lockwood opens the window as if to admit the witch child of his nightmare, the original Catherine arises in her ghostly wholeness from the only places where she can still exist in wholeness: the cemetery, the moor, the storm, the irrational realm of those that fly by night, the realm of Satan, Eve, Sin, and Death. Outside of this realm, the ordinary world inhabited by Catherine II and Hareton is, Heathcliff now notes, merely "a dreadful collection of memoranda that [Catherine] did exist, and that I have lost her!" (chap. 33).

Finally, Catherine II's alliance with Hareton awakens Heathcliff to truths about the younger man that he had not earlier understood, and in a sense his consequent disillusionment is the last blow that sends him toward death. Throughout the second half of the novel Heathcliff has taken comfort not only in Hareton's "startling" physical likeness to Catherine, but also in the likeness of the dispossessed boy's situation to his own early exclusion from society. "Hareton seem[s] a personification of my youth, not a human being," Heathcliff tells Nelly (chap. 33). This evidently causes him to see the illiterate outcast as metaphorically the true son of his own true union with Catherine. Indeed, where he had originally dispossessed Hareton as a way of revenging himself upon Hindley, Heathcliff seems later to want to keep the boy rough and uncultivated so that he, Heathcliff, will have at least one strong natural descendant (as opposed to Linton, his false and deathly descendant). As Hareton moves into Catherine II's orbit, however, away from nature and toward culture, Heathcliff realizes the mistake he has made. Where he had supposed that Hareton's reenactment of his own youth might even somehow restore the lost Catherine, and thus the lost Catherine-Heathcliff, he now sees that Hareton's reenactment of his youth is essentially corrective, a retelling of the story the "right" way. Thus if we can call Catherine II C^2 and define Hareton as H^2, we might arrive at the following formulation of Heathcliff's problem: where C plus H equals fullness of being for both C and H, C^2 plus H^2 specifically equals a negation of both C and H. Finally, the ambiguities of Hareton's name summarize in another way Heathcliff's problem with this most puzzling Earnshaw. On the one hand, Hare/ton is a nature name, like Heathcliff. But on the other hand, Hare/ton, suggesting Heir/ton (Heir/town?) is a punning indicator of the young man's legitimacy.

It is in his triumphant legitimacy that Hareton, together with Catherine II, acts to exorcise Heathcliff from the traditionally legitimate world of the Grange and the newly legitimized world of Wuthering Heights. Fading into nature, where Catherine persists "in every cloud, in every tree," Heathcliff can no longer eat the carefully cooked human food that Nelly *offers* him. While Catherine II decorates Hareton's porridge with cut flowers, the older man has irreligious fantasies of dying and being unceremoniously "carried to the churchyard in the evening." "I have nearly attained *my* heaven," he tells Nelly as he fasts and fades, "and that of others is ... uncoveted by me" (chap. 34). Then, when he dies, the boundaries between nature and culture crack for a moment, as if to let him pass through: his window swings open, the rain drives in. "Th' divil's harried off his soul," exclaims old Joseph, *Wuthering Heights*' mock Milton, falling to his knees and giving thanks "that the lawful master and the ancient stock [are] restored to their rights" (chap. 34). The illegitimate Heathcliff/Catherine have finally been replaced in nature/hell, and replaced by Hareton and Catherine II—a proper couple just as Nelly replaced Catherine as a proper mother for Catherine II. Quite reasonably, Nelly now observes that "The crown of all my wishes will be the union of" this new, civilized couple, and Lockwood notes of the new pair that "together, they would brave Satan and all his legions." Indeed, in both Milton's and Brontë's terms (it is the only point on which the two absolutely agree) they have already braved Satan, and they have triumphed. It is now 1802; the Heights—hell—has been converted into the Grange—heaven; and with patriarchal history redefined, renovated, restored, the nineteenth century can truly begin, complete with tea-parties, ministering angels, governesses, and parsonages.

* * *

Joseph's important remark about the restoration of the lawful master and the ancient stock, together with the dates—1801/1802—which surround Nelly's tale of a pseudo-mythic past, confirm the idea that *Wuthering Heights* is somehow etiological. More, the famous care with which Brontë worked out the details surrounding both the novel's dates and the Earnshaw–Linton lineage suggests she herself was quite conscious that she was constructing a story of origins and renewals. Having arrived at the novel's conclusion, we can now go back to its beginning, and try to summarize the basic story *Wuthering Heights* tells. Though this may not be the book's only story, it is surely a crucial one. As the names on the windowsill indicate, *Wuthering Heights* begins and ends with Catherine and her various avatars. More specifically, it studies the evolution of Catherine Earnshaw into Catherine Heathcliff and Catherine Linton, and then her return through Catherine Linton II and Catherine Heathcliff II to her "proper" role as Catherine Earnshaw II. More generally, what this evolution and de-evolution conveys is the following parodic, anti-Miltonic myth:

There was an Original Mother (Catherine), a daughter of nature whose motto might be "Thou, Nature, art my goddess; to thy law / My services are bound." But this girl fell into a decline, at least in part through eating the poisonous cooked food of culture. She fragmented herself into mad or dead selves on the one hand (Catherine, Heathcliff) and into lesser, gentler/genteeler selves on the other (Catherine II, Hareton). The fierce primordial selves disappeared into nature, the perversely hellish heaven which was their home. The more teachable and docile selves learned to read and write, and moved into the fallen cultured world of parlors and parsonages, the Miltonic heaven which, from the Original Mother's point of view, is really hell. Their passage from nature to culture was facilitated by a series of teachers, preachers, nurses, cooks, and model ladies or patriarchs (Nelly, Joseph, Frances, the Lintons), most of whom gradually disappear by the end of the story, since these lesser creations have been so well instructed that they are themselves able to become teachers or models for other generations. Indeed, so model are they that they can be identified with the founders of ancestral houses (Hareton Earnshaw, 1500) and with the original mother redefined as the patriarch's wife (Catherine Linton Heathcliff Earnshaw).

The nature/culture polarities in this Brontë myth have caused a number of critics to see it as a version of the so-called Animal Groom story, like Beauty and the Beast, or the Frog Prince. But, as Bruno Bettelheim has most recently argued, such tales usually function to help listeners and readers assimilate sexuality into consciousness and thus nature into culture (e.g., the beast is really lovable, the frog really handsome, etc.).[68] In *Wuthering Heights*, however, while culture does require nature's energy as raw material—the Grange needs the Heights, Edgar wants Catherine—society's most pressing need is to exorcise the rebelliously Satanic, irrational, and "female" representatives of nature. In this respect, Brontë's novel appears to be closer to a number of American Indian myths Lévi-Strauss recounts than it is to any of the fairy tales with which it is usually compared. In particular, it is reminiscent of an Opaye Indian tale called "The Jaguar's Wife."

In this story, a girl marries a jaguar so that she can get all the meat she wants for herself and her family. After a while, as a result of her marriage, the jaguar comes to live with the Indians, and for a time the girl's family becomes friendly with the new couple. Soon, however, a grandmother feels mistrust. "The young woman [is] gradually turning into a beast of prey.... Only her face remain[s] human ... the old woman therefore resort[s] to witchcraft and kill[s] her granddaughter." After this, the family is very frightened of the jaguar, expecting him to take revenge. And although he does not do so, he promises enigmatically that "Perhaps you will remember me in years to come," and goes off "incensed by the murder and spreading fear by his roaring; but the sound [comes] from farther and farther away."[69]

Obviously this myth is analogous to *Wuthering Heights* in a number of ways, with alien and animal-like Heathcliff paralleling the jaguar, Catherine paralleling the jaguar's wife, Nelly Dean functioning as the defensive grandmother, and Catherine II and Hareton acting like the family which inherits meat and a jaguar-free world from the departed wife. Lévi-Strauss's analysis of the story makes these likenesses even clearer, however, and in doing so it clarifies what Brontë must have seen as the grim necessities of *Wuthering Heights*.

> In order that all, man's present possessions (which the jaguar has now lost) may come to him from the jaguar (who enjoyed them formerly when man was without them), there must be some agent capable of establishing a relation between them: this is where the jaguar's (human) wife fits in.
>
> But once the transfer has been accomplished (through the agency of the wife):
>
> a) The woman becomes useless, because she has served her purpose as a preliminary condition, which was the only purpose she had.

b) Her survival would contradict the fundamental situation, which is characterized by a total absence of reciprocity. The jaguar's wife must therefore be eliminated.[70]

Though Lévi-Strauss does not discuss this point, we should note too that the jaguar's distant roaring hints he may return some day: obviously culture must be vigilant against nature, the superego must be ready at all times to battle the id. Similarly, the random weakening of Wuthering Heights' walls with which Brontë's novel began—symbolized by old Earnshaw's discovery of Heathcliff in Liverpool—suggests that patriarchal culture is always only precariously holding off the rebellious forces of nature. Who, after all, can say with certainty that the restored line of Hareton Earnshaw 1802 will not someday be just as vulnerable to the onslaughts of the goddess's illegitimate children as the line of Hareton Earnshaw 1500 was to Heathcliff's intrusion? And who is to say that the carving of Hareton Earnshaw 1500 was not similarly preceded by still another war between nature and culture? The fact that everyone has the same name leads inevitably to speculations like this, as though the drama itself, like its actors, simply represented a single episode in a sort of mythic infinite regress. In addition, the fact that the little shepherd boy still sees "Heathcliff and a woman" wandering the moor hints that the powerfully disruptive possibilities they represent may some day be reincarnated at Wuthering Heights.

Emily Brontë would consider such reincarnation a consummation devoutly to be wished. Though the surface Nelly Dean imposes upon Brontë's story is as dispassionately factual as the tone of "The Jaguar's Wife," the author's intention is passionately elegiac, as shown by the referential structure of *Wuthering Heights*, Catherine-Heathcliff's charisma, and the book's anti-Miltonic messages. This is yet another point Charlotte Brontë understood quite well, as we can see not only from the feminist mysticism of *Shirley* but also from the diplomatic irony of parts of her preface to *Wuthering Heights*. In *Shirley*, after all, the first woman, the true Eve, *is* nature—and she is noble and she is lost to all but a few privileged supplicants like Shirley-Emily herself, who tells Caroline (in response to an invitation to go to church) that "I will stay out here with my mother Eve, in these days called Nature. I love her—undying, mighty being! Heaven may have faded from her brow when she fell in paradise; but all that is glorious on earth shines there still."[71] And several years later Charlotte concluded her preface to *Wuthering Heights* with a discreetly qualified description of a literal heath/cliff that might also apply to *Shirley's* titanic Eve:

> ... the crag took human shape; and there it stands, colossal, dark, and frowning, half statue, half rock: in the former sense, terrible and goblin-like; in the latter, almost beautiful, for its coloring is of mellow grey, and moorland moss clothes it; and heath, with its blooming bells and balmy fragrance, grows faithfully close to the giant's foot.[72]

This grandeur, Charlotte Brontë says, is what "Ellis Bell" was writing about; this is what she (rightly) thought we have lost. For like the fierce though forgotten seventeenth-century Behmenist mystic Jane Lead, Emily Brontë seems to have believed that Eve had become tragically separated from her fiery original self, and that therefore she had "lost her Virgin Eagle Body ... and so been sown into a slumbering Death, in Folly, Weakness, and Dishonor."[73]

Her slumbering death, however, was one from which Eve might still arise. Elegiac as it is, mournfully definitive as its myth of origin seems, *Wuthering Heights* is nevertheless haunted by the ghost of a lost gynandry, a primordial possibility of power now only visible to children like the ones who see Heathcliff and Catherine.

> No promised Heaven, these wild Desires
> Could all or half fulfil,
> No threatened Hell, with quenchless fire
> Subdue this quenchless will!

Emily Brontë declares in one of her poems.[74] The words may or may not be intended for a Gondalian speech, but it hardly matters, since in any case they characterize the quenchless and sardonically impious will that stalks through *Wuthering Heights*, rattling the windowpanes of ancient houses and blotting the pages of family bibles. Exorcised from the hereditary estate of the ancient stock, driven to the sinister androgyny of their *Liebestod*, Catherine and Heathcliff nevertheless linger still at the edge of the estate, as witch and goblin, Eve and Satan. Lockwood's two dreams, presented as prologues to Nelly's story, are also, then, necessary epilogues to that tale. In the first, "Jabes Branderham," Joseph's nightmare fellow, tediously thunders Miltonic curses at Lockwood, enumerating the four hundred and ninety sins of which erring nature and the quenchless will are guilty. In the second, nature, personified as the wailing witch child "Catherine Linton," rises willfully in protest, and gentlemanly Lockwood's unexpectedly violent attack upon her indicates his terrified perception of the danger she represents.

Though she reiterated Milton's misogyny where Brontë struggled to subvert it, Mary Shelley also understood the dangerous possibilities of the outcast will. Her lost Eve became a monster, but "he" was equally destructive to the fabric of society. Later in the nineteenth century other women writers, battling Milton's bogey, would also examine the annihilation with which patriarchy threatens Eve's quenchless will, and the witchlike rage with which the female responds. George Eliot, for instance, would picture in *The Mill on the Floss* a deadly androgyny that seems like a grotesque parody of the *Liebestod* Heathcliff and Catherine achieve. "In their death" Maggie and Tom Tulliver "are not divided"—but the union they achieve is the only authentic one Eliot can imagine for them, since in life the one became an angel of renunciation, the other a captain of industry. Significantly, however, their death is caused by a flood that obliterates half the landscape of culture: female nature does and will continue to protest.

If Eliot specifically reinvents Brontë's *Liebestod*, Mary Elizabeth Coleride reimagines her witchlike nature spirit. In a poem that also reflects her anxious ambivalence about the influence of her great uncle Samuel, the author of "Christabel," Coleridge *becomes* Geraldine, Catherine Earnshaw, Lucy Gray, even Frankenstein's monster—all the wailing outcast females who haunt the graveyards of patriarchy. Speaking in "the voice that women have, who plead for their heart's desire," she cries

> I have walked a great while over the snow
> And I am not tall nor strong.
> My clothes are wet, and my teeth are set,
> And the way was hard and long.
> I have wandered over the fruitful earth,
> But I never came here before.
> Oh, lift me over the threshhold, and let me in at the door ...

And then she reveals that "She came—and the quivering flame / Sank and died in the fire."[75]

Emily Brontë's outcast witch-child is fiercer, less dissembling than Coleridge's, but she longs equally for the extinction of parlor fires and the rekindling of unimaginably different energies. Her creator, too, is finally the fiercest, most quenchless of Milton's daughters. Looking oppositely for the queendom of heaven, she insists, like Blake, that "I have also the Bible of Hell, which the world shall have whether they will or no."[76] And in the voice of the wind that sweeps through the newly cultivated garden at Wuthering Heights, we can hear the jaguar, like Blake's enraged Rintrah, roaring in the distance.

NOTES

Epigraphs: King Lear, 4.6.126–30; The Marriage of Heaven and Hell, plates 5–6; Poems, J. 959.

1. Mark Schorer, "Fiction and the Analogical Matrix," in William M. Sale, Jr., ed., Norton Critical Edition of *Wuthering Heights* (New York: Norton, 1972, revised), p. 376.

2. Winifred Gérin notes, for instance, that Mrs. Brontë wrote a "sprightly essay," entitled "The Advantages of Poverty in Religious Concerns," which her husband noted that he had "sent for insertion in one of the periodical publications" (Gérin, *Emily Brontë* [Oxford: The Clarendon Press, 1971], p. 3). See also Annette Hopkin, *The Father of the Brontës* (Baltimore: Johns Hopkins Press for Goucher College, 1958), passim.

3. Published instances of the Brontë juvenilia include Charlotte Brontë, *The Twelve Adventurers and Other Stories*, ed. C. W. Hatfield (London: Hodder, 1925); Charlotte Brontë, *The Spell*, ed. G. E. MacLean (London: Oxford University Press, 1931); Charlotte Brontë, *Tales from Angria*, ed. Phyllis Bentley (London: Collins, 1954); Charlotte Brontë, *Five Novelettes*, ed. Winifred Gérin (London: The Folio Press, 1971); Charlotte Brontë, *Legends of Angria*, compiled by Fannie E. Ratchford and William Clyde De Vane (New Haven: Yale University Press, 1933); and Emily Jane Brontë, *Gondal's Queen: A Novel in Verse*, arranged by Fannie E. Ratchford (Austin: University of Texas Press, 1955). Charlotte Brontë's most notable criticism of her sisters' work appeared in *Wuthering Heights, Agnes Grey, together with a selection of Poems by Ellis and Acton Bell*, Prefixed with a Biographical Memoir of the authors by Currer Bell (London: Smith, Elder, 1850).

4. Leo Bersani, *A Future for Astyanax*, p. 203.

5. Ibid., pp. 203, 208–09.

6. Gérin, *Emily Brontë*, p. 47.

7. Norton Critical Edition of *Wuthering Heights*, p. 72. All references will be to this edition.

8. Catherine Smith, "Jane Lead: The Feminist Mind and Art of a Seventeenth-Century Protestant Mystic," forthcoming in Rosemary Ruether, ed., *Women and Religion*.

9. See Thomas Moser, "What is the matter with Emily Jane? Conflicting Impulses in *Wuthering Heights*," *Nineteenth–Century Fiction* 17 (1962): 1–19.

10. Fannie E. Ratchford, *Gondal's Queen*, p. 22. As Ratchford shows, many of Brontë's best poems were written as dramatic monologues for A.G.A. In addition, a number of critics have seen A.G.A. as a model for the first Catherine.

11. Terence Eagleton, *Myths of Power* (London and New York: Macmillan, 1975), p. 58.

12. See Claude Lévi-Strauss, *Tristes Tropiques* (New York: Atheneum, 1965), pp. 214–16: "There is something almost scandalous, to a European observer, in the ease with which the (as it seems to us) almost incompatible activities of the men's house are harmonized. Few people are as deeply religious as the Bororo.... But their spiritual beliefs and their habits of every day are so intimately mingled that they seem not to have any sensation of passing from one to the other."

13. Ratchford, *Gondal's Queen*, p. 186.

14. Ibid., pp. 192–93.

15. See Q. D. Leavis, "A Fresh Approach to *"Wuthering Heights*," Norton Critical Edition, p. 313; Mark Schorer, "Fiction and the Analogical Matrix," p. 371; Leo Bersani, *A Future for Astyanax*, p. 203; Elliot Gose, *Imagination Indulg'd* (Montreal: McGill, Queen's University Press, 1972), p. 59.

16. Robert Kiely, *The Romantic Novel in England* (Cambridge, Mass.: Harvard University Press, 1972), p. 233.

17. Emily Jane Brontë, "Often rebuked, yet always back returning," in C. W. Hatfield, ed., *The Complete Poems of Emily Jane Brontë* (New York: Columbia University Press, 1941), pp. 255–56. Hatfield questions Emily's authorship of this poem, suggesting that Charlotte may really have written the piece to express her own "thoughts about her sister" (*loc. cit.*), but Gérin discusses it unequivocally as a piece by Emily (Gérin, *Emily Brontë*, pp. 264–65).

18. Byron, *Manfred*, 2.4.134–48; see also Gérin, *Emily Brontë*, p. 46.

19. As we noted in discussing Austen, in a letter to G. H. Lewes (12 January 1848) Charlotte remarked that she had never read *Pride and Prejudice* until he advised her to, so it is unlikely that Emily had read any Austen, especially not the comparatively obscure *Northanger Abbey*.

20. Mircea Eliade, *The Myth of the Eternal Return* (New York: Pantheon, 1954).

21. The Complete Poems of Emily Jane Brontë, pp. 255–56.

22. To distinguish the second Catherine from the first without obliterating their similarities, we will call Catherine Earnshaw Linton's daughter Catherine II throughout this discussion.

23. The realistically iconoclastic nature of Catherine's interest in riding, however, is illuminated by this comment from a nineteenth-century conduct book: "[Horseback riding] produces in ladies a coarseness of voice, a weathered complexion, and unnatural consolidation of the bones of the lower part of the body, ensuring a frightful impediment to future functions which need not here be dwelt upon; by overdevelopment of the muscles equitation produces an immense increase in the waist and is, in short, altogether masculine and unwomanly" (Donald Walker, *Exercises for Ladies*, 1837, quoted in Cunnington, *Feminine Attitudes in the Nineteenth Century*, p. 86).

24. See Bersani, *A Future for Astyanax*, and J. Hillis Miller, *The Disappearance of God* (Cambridge, Mass.: Belknap Press of Harvard University Press, 1963), pp. 155–211.

25. Q. D. Leavis, "A Fresh Approach to *Wuthering Heights*," p. 321.

26. For a brief discussion of androgyny in *Wuthering Heights*, see Carolyn Heilbrun, *Toward a Recognition of Androgyny* (New York: Knopf, 1973), pp. 80–82.

27. There are thus several levels of irony implicit in Nelly's remark that "no parson in the world ever pictured heaven so beautifully as [Catherine and Heathcliff] did, in their innocent talk" (p. 48).

28. C. P. Sanger, "The Structures of *Wuthering Heights*," Norton Critical Edition, pp. 296–98.

29. Bersani, *A Future for Astyanax*, p. 201.

30. Even in his way of speaking-laconic, old-fashioned, oracular—old Mr. Earnshaw seems like a fairy-tale character, whereas Hindley and Frances talk more like characters in a "realistic" novel.

31. Eagleton does discuss the Lintons' dogs from a Marxist perspective; see *Myths of Power*, pp. 106–07.

32. Elizabeth Janeway, "On 'Female Sexuality,'" in Jean Strouse, ed., *Women and Analysis* (New York: Grossman, 1974), p. 58.

33. See Claude Lévi-Straus, *The Raw and the Cooked: Introduction to a Science of Mythology*, vol. 1 (New York: Harper & Row, 1969).

34. Dickinson, *Letters*, 2:408.

35. Charlotte Brontë elaborated upon the terrors of "ladylike" education in *The Professor, Jane Eyre*, and *Villette*. For a factual account of the Cowan Bridge experience, see also Gérin, *Charlotte Brontë*, pp. 1–16.

36. Blake, The Marriage of Heaven and Hell, plate 5.

37. Mark Kinkead-Weekes, "The Place of Love in *Jane Eyre* and *Wuthering Heights,*" in *The Brontës: A Collection of Critical Essays*, ed. Ian Gregor (Englewood Cliffs: Prentice-Hall, 1970), p. 86.

38. See Dorothy van Ghent, *The English Novel: Form and Function* (New York: Harper & Row, 1961), pp. 153–70.

39. As we noted in discussing the metaphor of literary paternity, Jean-Paul Sartre thought of books as embodiments of power, and it seems relevant here that he once called his grandfather's library "the world caught in a mirror" (Marjorie Grene, *Sartre*, p. 11).

40. Sylvia Plath, "The Stones," in *The Colossus* (New York: Vintage, 1968), p. 82. 41. Sanger, "The Structures of *Wuthering Heights,*" p. 288.

42. Plath, "Tulips," *Ariel*, p. 11.

43. Leavis, "A Fresh Approach to *Wuthering Heights,*" p. 309; Bersani, *A Future for Astyanax*, pp. 208–09.

44. Plath, "Lady Lazarus," *Ariel*, p. 6. 45. Plath, "Contusion," *Ariel*, p. 83.

46. See A. Alvarez, *The Savage God* (London: Weidenfeld & Nicolson, 1971). 47. Marlene Boskind-Lodahl, "Cinderella's Stepsisters," p. 352.

48. Ibid., pp. 343–44.

49. For a comment on this phenomenon as it may really have occurred in the life of Emily's sister Charlotte, see Helene Moglen, *Charlotte Brontë: The Self Conceived*, pp. 241–42.

50. See Maxine Hong Kingston, *The Woman Warrior* (New York: Knopf, 1976), p. 48: "Even now China wraps double binds around my feet."

51. Dickinson, *Poems*, J. 1072 ("Title divine—is mine! / The Wife—without the Sign!").

52. Charlotte Brontë, "Editor's Preface to the New Edition of *Wuthering Heights* (1850)," Norton Critical Edition, p. 11.

53. Q. D. Leavis, "A Fresh Approach to *Wuthering Heights,*" p. 310.

54. Interestingly, even in this speech the characteristic obsession of "Milton's daughters" with Greek and Latin recurs. The only books in the library she *hasn't* read, Nelly notes, are in "that range of Greek and Latin, and that of French," and even about those she can say that "those I know one from another" (p. 59).

55. Bersani, *A Future for Astyanax*, pp. 221–22.

56. Q. D. Leavis, "A Fresh Approach to *Wuthering Heights,*" p. 321.

57. Bersani, *A Future for Astyanax*, pp. 208–09.

58. Showalter, *A Literature of Their Own*, pp. 133–52.

59. Ortner, "Is Female to Male as Nature is to Culture?" in *Women, Culture, and Society*, p. 80.

60. The concept of "androgyny," as some feminist critics have recently noted, usually "submerges" the female within the male, but Emily Brontë's vision is notably gynandrous, submerging the male, as it were, within the female.

61. *The Rainbow*, "Wedding at the Marsh," chap. 5.

62. John Donne, "Problemes," VI, "Why Hath the Common Opinion Afforded Women Soules?"

63. *Lear*, 1.2.15–16.

64. Ibid, 2.4.57.

65. Bersani, *A Future for Astyanax*, pp. 221–22.

66. Ibid.

67. Ortner, "Is Female to Male as Nature Is to Culture?"

68. Bettelheim, *The Uses of Enchantment*, pp. 277–310.

69. Lévi–Straus, *The Raw and the Cooked*, pp. 82–83.

70. Ibid.

71. Charlotte Brontë, *Shirley*, chap. 18.

72. Charlotte Brontë, "Editor's Preface," p. 12.

73. Jane Lead, *A Fountain of Gardens*, 2:105–07.

74. "Enough of thought, Philosopher," in *The Complete Poems of Emily Jane Brontë*, p. 220.

75. "The Witch," *Poem by Mary E. Coleridge*, pp. 44–45.

76. Blake, The Marriage of Heaven and Hell, plate 24.

NANCY ARMSTRONG

Emily Brontë In and Out of Her Time

Although she wrote but one novel, Emily Brontë continues to carry on a precarious relationship with a nineteenth-century intellectual tradition that consistently endorsed humanistic values, either by advancing the claims of the individual, or by maintaining those of the community. The temptation for readers is to stabilize this relationship either by seeing Brontë as a Romantic reactionary who rejected the kind of fiction coming into vogue during the 1840's or by aligning her work with the utilitarian tradition that gave rise to literary realism. In attempting to pin down the genre of *Wuthering Heights*, however, the problem has not been resolved. It has only become more apparent: if, as Terry Eagleton claims, a drably spiritless form of realism displaces the "'pre-industrial' imaginative creativity" in Brontë's fiction, it is also true that "the real world" is eclipsed by an earlier Romantic form of the imagination, as J. Hillis Miller maintains.[1] How such politically and philosophically hostile positions can coexist in her sister's novel is the very question Charlotte Brontë tried—and with no little success—to defer in her preface to the 1850 edition of *Wuthering Heights*. By describing the author as one who combined the skills of a budding regional novelist with the powers of a full-blown visionary artist, Charlotte made Emily's novel, in effect, *sui generis*, the interaction of a remote social milieu with a unique personal

From *Genre* 15, 3 (fall 1982), pp. 243–264. © 1982 by The University of Oklahoma.

vision.[2] From the earliest to some of the more recent of Brontë's readers, then, the effort has been to resolve the problem and not to clarify it.

Any attempt to classify the novel, even if this entails making it a kind unto itself, rests upon Heathcliff and how one describes his character. Most often such attempts proceed on the ground that he is full of meaning and that by finding the key to decode him one will also discover what familiar set of nineteenth-century categories makes the novel a coherent whole. To see Heathcliff in this way is to see him as a conventional mediator, however, and, if nothing else, the history of failed attempts at resolving the debate over the genre of *Wuthering Heights* testifies to the fact that this is precisely what Heathcliff is *not*. True, he calls forth and appears to validate both modes of Enlightenment thinking, those which continue to make themselves felt on into the nineteenth century in the conflict between utilitarianism and Romanticism, to name but one such manifestation. But in doing so, Heathcliff actually problematizes the literary categories that depend upon these oppositions, namely, the distinction between romance and realism. Thus it is due to the breakdown of such primary cultural differences in Brontë's fiction that the whole question of its genre arises.

Rather than understand Heathcliff as a "both/and" device for symbolically closing the gap between cultural codes, it is more accurate to consider him as an impossible third term, an empty category by which Brontë rejected the conventional alternatives for resolving a work of domestic fiction even while she could not imagine anything beyond these alternatives. Such a dilemma is not unique to Brontë, nor is it even a strictly literary one. This order of relationship between text and context can occur whenever history fails to provide the adequate materials for imaginative representation. In *The Political Unconscious* Fredric Jameson has described Hegel's historical situation in similar terms, as being one in which his thinking could go no further. Like any author of his age, Hegel could use only what linguistic materials were available in his cultural moment. He was, in this sense, a product of his time. To be dependent on these materials for his thinking was for Hegel to be caught "in an impossible historical contradiction," caught, as Jameson explains, "between the alternatives of Romantic reaction and bourgeois utilitarianism."[3] Rather than remain within the ideology of the moment, however, he projected an "impossible third term" beyond these historical alternatives, the notion of Absolute Spirit. But this, according to Jameson, does not make Hegel an idealist in any conventional sense. He is rather someone who felt the limits placed on the imagination by the concrete materials his culture gave him to work with even while he sought to make those limited materials represent the totality of cultural history.[4] He could represent what was beyond his power to imagine only by an act of negation and so created an empty category that awaits manifestation at some future moment.

While the limitations of imagination felt by a young female novelist writing during the 1840's from a remote corner of Yorkshire could hardly be those of a Hegel, still, there are obvious parallels to be drawn between them. Through at least half of Brontë's novel, Heathcliff's rise into power dramatizes the apotheosis of the Romantic hero, his intrusion into and transformation of a convention-bound world. But at some point it becomes clear that Romantic conventions will no longer do as a way of negotiating the text and of understanding the world to which it refers. By making them manifest in an energetic new form, Heathcliff actually cancels out Romantic possibilities and reduces that system of belief to mere superstition. From this point on, not surprisingly, the novel proceeds according to norms and expectations that are much more characteristic of Victorian realism. The meaning of Heathcliff's desire for Catherine Earnshaw changes so as to place such desire beyond the bounds of middle-class thinking and therefore outside the discourse of domestic fiction. But just as certain as her awareness of change is Brontë's unwillingness to see this change as an improvement or gain rather than as a kind of trade-off, an exchange of psychosexual power for economic power in which each calls the value of the other into question.[5]

By taking the conventions of an earlier literature as the subject matter of a new kind of fiction, she demonstrates that fiction could no longer be written from the Romantic viewpoint and still be considered a novel. At the same time, the alternative offered to her as a novelist could not represent the totality of personal experience as she saw it. Out of this dilemma, we might imagine, came Heathcliff, who, in participating in both literary traditions, actually reveals the limitations of each. This is why he remains an enigma to readers, then, not because he is both noble savage and entrepreneur, but because he is ultimately neither. He only prefigures a time and discourse in which the boundary between self and society is no longer so necessary to the making of fiction.

i

Upon his first introduction as a "dark-skinned gypsy in aspect, in dress and manners a gentleman" (p. 15), Heathcliff calls warring systems of meaning into play. As in this paradigmatic instance, it is never entirely certain whether gypsy features should be read as positive or negative, as befitting or contradicting an aristocratic appearance, for the potential is there for meaning to go one of two ways. In the social discourse of the age, the gypsy was naturally viewed with all the disdain and apprehension attending his utter lack of social position. But literary tradition, on the other hand, had portrayed the gypsy in a sentimental light, associating the character type with the virtues and pleasures of uncivilized life and infusing it with an egalitarian ethos.[6] Heathcliff's dualism is not due, then, to a quirk of the author's personality, but rather to a conflict within middle-class thinking which condemned sensuality in the lower classes while placing enormous stock in the natural feelings and instincts of the common individual. It was out of precisely this conflict in the thinking of the time that the novel emerged as an elaboration of middle-class experience. Out of this conflict, too, came the virulent criticism, launched from the very beginning against the novel on the grounds that it falsified life. To the sensibility that located nobility in the most humble of men, Lawrence Stone, among others, has attributed the phenomenal appetite for biography and novels of sensibility that accompanied industrialization in England, but manifestations of this kind of sentimentality also proved one of the more irresistible targets for detractors of the fledgling literary form.[7] Particularly revealing in the angle of its attack, one review heaps scorn on the fiction of its day for portraying "in coarse colours the workings of more genuine passions in the bosom of Dolly, the Dairy-maid or Hannah, the housemaid."[8]

What can be said of the gypsy is also true of the aristocrat, the other half of the equation comprising Heathcliff's character. The proliferation of courtesy books and schools for instructing *nouveaux riches* in the taste and behavior of their social superiors, as well as the migration of businessmen from the city to country manors, indicates that the aristocracy was also viewed with a great deal of ambivalence.[9] It represented not only the chief obstacle to be overcome by the upward aspiring, but also the ideal to which one aspired in order to rise. In this respect, too, Heathcliff provides an unstable field of meaning, sometimes implying a natural superiority on his part over the degenerate Earnshaws, sometimes a natural degeneracy that merits his exclusion from their line. In associating aristocratic power with sadism and violence, neither this novel nor others before it—those of Richardson and Radcliffe come immediately to mind—were mirroring the actual relationship between the two classes. Even supposing there once were such clearly drawn battlelines between them, the conflict between the bourgeoisie and old aristocracy, as it was thematized in fiction, quickly became a way of talking about something else.[10] Above all it was a convenient means of projecting onto an earlier and largely imaginary social landscape the conflicts among middle-class factions sharply divided on issues of social and economic reform. The device pitted all those disparate groups comprising the readership against a monolithic Other, a representation of the aristocracy that could only exist as a belated form of feudalism. In the very act of airing differences, then, a novelist could also create a sense of homogeneity among the various interest groups who saw themselves in what Defoe called "the middle estate." Because novels ultimately reconciled the contradictions within a single historical perspective and set of class interests, it seems only natural for groups of characters who appear to be hotly contending for power to unite in a single harmonious community at the end of a novel.

Perhaps the most telling evidence of the ideological homogeneity underlying eighteenth and early nineteenth-century fiction is the frequency with which the acquisition of power through competition entails an act of submission to some form of patriarchal power, aggressive individualism thus coming to serve and not threaten the more traditional idea of power. One feature novels so diverse as those of Defoe, Richarson, Fielding, Austen, or Scott have in common is the homage they pay to the notions of aristocratic taste and *noblesse oblige*. They simply relocate these values in the aspiring classes with which the protagonists are usually affiliated. The aim of such narratives seems only obvious, to resolve the conflict between hostile conceptions of power, one based on the *laissez-faire* principle and the other, on primogeniture, and their protagonists accordingly incorporate some of the positive features adhering to each. In many of the key respects, Heathcliff recalls these earlier protagonists who pit their virtue, instinct, or wit against conventionalized behavior and inherited power only to erase these differences once they have gained entry into the institutions oppressing them. When he is thrust upon the Earnshaws "as a gift of God, though its dark almost as if it came from the devil" (p. 38), when Nelly tells Heathcliff "he's fit for a prince in disguise" (p. 54), or when Catherine Earnshaw declares him to be "more myself that I am" (p. 72), the possibility is created for Heathcliff to become one of the Earnshaws in the manner of his heroic prototypes. But this is only because the Romantic assumptions are kept in play that he is—figuratively speaking—an aristocrat concealed beneath a barbarous exterior, that his desire has all the force of nature behind it, and that such a noble savage can eventually redeem the community by making manifest his desires within it.

But Heathcliff's character includes features besides those of a Romantic hero. These have an economic and political logic all of their own and acquire their rhetorical force from the association between gypsies and the laboring classes, a conception of man that stubbornly resists idealization.[11] We should recall that *Wuthering Heights* was written against the background of swelling industrial centers and Chartist uprisings that had reached alarming proportions by the forties, as had the hoards of migrant workers who were newly arrived on the English social scene.[12] Against such a background Heathcliff's Napoleonic features set him in direct opposition to the vested interests of the readership who would hardly be well served by any unleashing of popular energy or further democratizing of social authority.

Simply by giving his character a particular point of origin in the slums of a major industrial city rather than leaving the matter open to more romantic possibilities, Brontë made her protagonist capable of acquiring whatever negative meaning adhered to such a potentially hostile social element. In a realistic schema it follows, therefore, that father Earnshaw is not humane but demented for picking up a child, "starving, and houseless, and as good as dumb in the streets of Liverpool" and taking it into his family (p. 39). Heathcliff proves true to the worst implications of the type, furthermore, by enchanting the master's daughter, supplanting the legitimate son in the father's affections, and so breeding dissension in the family for a generation to come.

Brontë defers these obvious and timely possibilities for meaning, however, and allows her reader to sympathize with this character in defiance of middle-class norms. The novel begins by designating the year of its telling as 1801, which is to move the events of the story backwards by several decades into the previous century. Moreover, the story of the family's dissolution and restoration unfolds, as Charlotte reminds us in her preface, on the "wild moors of the north of England" (p. 9). Much like Scott's settings, this remote landscape endows a contemporary crisis with all the trappings of an archaic one and summons up a context in which Heathcliff's insurgency seems to justify the emergence of middle-class power. One finds, for example, the Earnshaws exercising power over the hapless orphan in a manner reminiscent of the villainous aristocrats in earlier fiction. If old man Earnshaw's policies seem rather capricious ("A Nothing vexed him, and suspected slights of his authority nearly threw him into fits," p. 41), the next generation is clearly perverse. Hindley Earnshaw exercises power out of class anger, fraternal rivalry, and thwarted sexual desire. His aim is to obstruct legitimate desires, those to which one is entitled by nature rather than rank, and he succeeds in twisting Heathcliff's spontaneous desire for Catherine into a lust for vengeance. At Thrushcross Grange, on the other hand, one finds the other half of Brontë's fictional world governed by a conspicuously genteel breed, the man of sensibility. But the very refinement that makes both Lockwood and the Lintons before him so much at home in the parlor and library proves utterly useless, even debilitating, and just as destructive as open tyranny in dealing with the crises generated by Heathcliff's desire. Heathcliff may be relatively powerless without the cultural accoutrements of a gentleman, but it is also true that men with little more than their education and good manners to fall back on founder stupidly amidst the social and emotional turbulence at Wuthering Heights. That such characters are virtually out of their element in the novel itself is demonstrated on more than one occasion, by Lockwood's pratfall in the Earnshaw's threshold, for instance, or by his failure to acknowledge his own desire for the young Catherine Earnshaw as well as the truth in his dream of her mother. The Lintons demonstrate this same order of false consciousness whenever events require them to restrain their emotions humanely or to respond with genuine compassion.[13]

It is important to note that between them the heads of these families possess all the features necessary for a benevolent patriarchy that could reward natural merit while preserving established traditions. The problem lies in combining the features of the Lintons and Earnshaws to make such a harmonious whole. When broken down into the components of a brutal tyrant and ineffectual gentleman, the socioeconomic data of the novel create the double-bind situation that tears Catherine Earnshaw asunder. "Did it never occur to you," she explains to Nelly, "that if Heathcliff and I were married, we should be beggars? whereas, if I marry Linton, I can aid Heathcliff to rise, and place him out of my brother's power" (p. 73). Should she dare to enjoy immediate gratification, then Catherine would cut herself off from economic power. To acquire that power, however, she must forgo her desire for Heathcliff. An extraordinary act of sublimation or displacement of desire is therefore the precondition for entering into relationships at the Grange. Such a conspicuous lack of a narrative means for harnessing desire and exhausting it productively within a domestic framework is all we are given to sustain the belief that Heathcliff alone can reconstitute the family along more tolerable lines. By the end of the century, to be sure, Freud would have formulated the narrative model for substitution and sublimation that could resolve this dilemma. But in the absence of the narrative logic for bridging this gap between intolerable cultural alternatives we are left with the Romantic doctrine which says that a poor and uneducated individual may "conceal depths of benevolence beneath a stern exterior" (p. 89).

But the Romantic critique of rigidly hierarchical thinking can itself become subject to a critique, especially when its logic unfolds within the structure of a novel. There is the irony that Heathcliff can retain his role as the hero of the tale so long as he remains virtually powerless, the unwitting object of pathos. This in itself constitutes a departure from Romantic prototypes whose rebellion appears to advance the general good and bring about social reform. There is the further irony as well that even as an object of pathos Heathcliff is ruthlessly cur-like and therefore incapable of submitting to paternal authority. (The more primitive fear of separation from the maternal figure is what ultimately regulates his desire.) Nelly cautions him that this antisocial nature of his must be concealed if he hopes to succeed in bettering his position. "Don't get the expression of a vicious cur that appears to know that the kicks it gets are its deserts, and yet hates all the world, as well as the kicker, for what it suffers," she tells him (p. 82). That he can possess these bestial qualities while still serving as the protagonist through at least half of the novel—through all of the novel, according to some—is also what differentiates this character from historically later counterparts, the entrepreneurs of Dickens's and Thackerary's fiction, for instance.

Heathcliff can no longer serve as the mediator if the novel has redefined the problem that needs mediation. Originally, this problem is clearly a matter of how to satisfy the claims of the individual within the categories of the existing social order. Heathcliff's acquisition of power can indicate neither the triumph of the individual nor the affirmation of the community, however, much less some reconciliation of the conflict between the two, for these become historically discontinuous viewpoints as the history of his rise into power unfolds. The impedance of the individual's claims for the sake of preserving class boundaries only seems to be the central conflict which the narrative needs to resolve. Once competition has been injected into the system and power has emerged from below, value shifts immediately to those institutions that have been dismantled in the process, as well as to the fictions swept away by the harsh facts of the economic struggle his rise entails. What once served as the novelist's answer to problems posed by her cultural milieu has evidently become the problem itself, and having been redefined, the problem must now be resolved by some other means. It is no longer a matter of how to gratify the individual in the face of social constraints; it has become a matter of how to maintain the values of the community in a competitive world.

In the second half of the novel, nature remains the repository of the authentic self and the constituent element in Heathcliff's character, but nature no longer serves as a source of benign possibilities. It resembles nothing quite so much as the inhumane battleground mapped out in Darwin's biology, the source of one's most perverse impulses as well as his will to power. As nature bares its teeth and claws at this point in the novel, the social order undergoes a corresponding change. A competitive principle rooted in the accumulation of capital provides the transforming agency that moves Heathcliff from the margins of society to its very center. Once there, he displays all the vices that have accompanied political power, the Lintons' sophistication, their veneer of civility, as well as the Earnshaws' brutality. It is money alone that empowers him to infiltrate the timeless institutions of marriage, inheritance, and property ownership and to shape these institutions to serve his own interests. Upon gaining possession of both the Heights and the Grange, Heathcliff initiates a new form of tyranny that undoes all former systems of kinship and erases the boundaries between class as well as between family lines.

Out of this dissolution of boundaries, however, a new division emerges. Catherine regards the change in Heathcliff as a splitting away of his socioeconomic features from his emotions, a division that has drained away all his sensuality and lent a spiritual quality to their passion. "That is not Heathcliff," she insists, "I shall love mine yet; and take him with me— he's in my soul" (p. 134). Whenever it is that one finally makes the equation between Heathcliff's sexual desires and his worldly ambition, between his ambition and gross bestiality, it is then that the romance of individualism is punctured, the essentially competitive nature of Brontë's protagonist demystified, and the politics underlying sexual desire in the novel exposed. Accordingly, Heathcliff becomes the opponent and not the proponent of middle-class values, What residue still clings to him of earlier prototypes— noble savages, fiery rebels, and plucky rogues alike—is abruptly placed in the past or relegated to the realm of memory and fiction. This is none other than the bewildering situation into which Lockwood stumbles at the beginning of the novel, one where character cannot be understood unless one has the history of relationships that Nelly's gossip provides.

The kind of world that will come into being under Heathcliff's domination is what Catherine Earnshaw tries to make the bedazzled Isabel Linton recognize:

> "Tell her what Heathcliff is—an unreclaimed creature, without cultivation; an arid wilderness of furze and whinstone. I'd as soon put that little canary into the park on a winter's day as recommend you to bestow your heart on him! It is deplorable ignorance of his character, child, and nothing else, which makes that dream enter your head. Pray don't imagine that he conceals depths of benevolence and affection beneath a stern exterior. He's not a rough diamond—a pearl-containing oyster of a rustic—he's a fierce, pitiless, wolfish man.... I know he couldn't love a Linton; and yet he'd be quite capable of marrying your fortune and expectations. Avarice is growing with him a besetting sin." (pp. 89–90)

In no uncertain terms does Brontë equate the Romantic doctrine of presence with "ignorance," a view of character which says that surface features point to meaning beyond the material manifestations of the self. The kind of fiction arising from this older notion of language, the self, and the world seems to fall into oblivion at this point in the novel, leaving the reader with a tangible sense of what the world is like with no spirituality in it. Resembling on a small scale Hegel's dismally spiritless "world of prose," this world, too, is one where "the individual human being must repeatedly, in order to preserve his own individuality, make himself a means for other people, serve their limited ends, and transform them into means in order to satisfy his own narrow interests."[14] This failure of Romantic conventions to represent adequately the relationships comprising her narrative is Brontë's way of acknowledging the fact that fiction could no longer be written from a Romantic viewpoint and still be considered a novel.

So it is that in the second half of the novel, the conventions of earlier literature, thus dismantled, become the subject matter of a new kind of fiction. The structure of social relationships erected from the ruins of the old calls forth a cast of characters much more in line with Victorian norms and expectations. Not unlike those of Dickens and Thackeray, for that matter, Brontë's fictional world fast becomes a veritable bestiary of predators and victims wherein only the latter retain some vestige of their humanity. Conventionalized behavior rather than impulse or desire seems to be the true mark of one's character. Capitalism replaces a belated feudalism as the chief source of villainy, and competition is treated as a fact of life that converts sentient beings into objects in the marketplace. At the same time, an idealized notion of the long-banished aristocracy, still conveniently remote from a society operating according to the *laissez-faire* principle, comes to serve as the repository of ethical value. But Dickens and Thackeray do not change from one historical frame of reference to another. For all the inconsistencies swarming about in their cultural milieu, they operate consistently from within Victorian categories and paradigms. Brontë's novel, on the other hand, appears to fall into their world from another of necessity, as the idealist categories of Romantic discourse break down. Out of the pieces of earlier fiction then comes a new kind of narrative art where value no longer resides in the claims of the individual but rather in the reconstitution of the family. The result is that problems are posed and questions asked in one set of literary conventions that cannot be answered by the other, which is to say what most critical readings strive to deny, that this is an essentially disjunctive novel.

It is worthwhile, first, to consider how the original patriarchs acquire the force of nostalgia as they pass into obsolescence. Hindley Earnshaw's grand finale is an uncharacteristically selfless attempt to rescue the heirs of both houses from the villain usurping their authority. "I'll do you a kindness in spite of yourself," is his promise to Isabel, "and Hareton, justice!" (p. 145). In its utter futility, Hindley's wrath takes on some of the heroic aura that Heathcliff's has lost in its potency. Edgar Linton's deathbed scene similarly idealizes the past by recasting his rather lame gentility in the light of Christian beatitude. "All was composed," as Nelly describes the scene, "Catherine's despair was as silent as her father's joy. She supported him calmly in appearance; and he fixed on her his raised eyes that seemed dilated with ecstasy. He died blissfully...." (p. 225). So these figures of authority shed their social garb and merge with the sacred traditions of the past to create a romance of culture. This is to represent culture as necessarily detached from social practices and relegated not only to the past but also to the tale whose business it is to preserve and transmit these traditions.

The second generation of characters comprises a social world devoid of culture in this limited sense. Though frail and victimized, for example, Linton Heathcliff is the least idealized of all Brontë's characters, unworthy even to serve as the object of pathos. The predacious tendencies of the father and the affectations of the mother—all that is "harsh" and "peevish" in these two extremes—combine to form a character that both parodies and fulfills his heritage. Lacking the bourgeois energy of the father, Linton is described as the "worst bit of sickly slip that ever struggled into its teens" (p. 195). Just as his weakness does not make him kind, neither does it imply any of the education and gentility that, in Edgar Linton's case, brought the constraints of a humanistic tradition along with them. "Linton can play the little tyrant well," Heathcliff points out, "He'll undertake to torture any number of cats if their teeth be drawn, and their nails pared" (p. 219). Given that the family history in this novel is also a genealogy of political myths, this grotesque combination of features can only represent what results from the interpenetration of capitalism and the process of dynastic succession. It is not true that one manner of distributing wealth amends or complements the other in this novel. Quite the contrary, when brought together in Linton Heathcliff, these forms of social authority prove mutually undercutting, contradictions surface, and the literary machinery that once reconciled them is thoroughly dismantled. We find, for example, that all the Gothic devices of abduction, rape, incest, and necrophilia enabling Linton to marry his cousin against her will are engineered by common law and empowered by acquired wealth. This is to foreclose any possibility of sweeping away the injustices of a degenerate aristocracy by the coming in of a new social order. A version of the middle-class hegemony itself is what perverts established traditions in the second half of Brontë's novel and brings Gothic devices to the service of realism instead of romance.

To turn the contemporary world into such a nightmare is to invert the procedures of earlier Gothic Fiction and anticipate the sensation novels that came into fashion during the 1860's.[15] By developing the character of Hareton Earnshaw, however, Brontë hit upon what may be considered a typically Victorian way out of the dilemma of a world thrown open to competition. Heathcliff's aggressive individualism plays itself out in a psychotic nightmare and historical cul-de-sac, but, as this becomes apparent, the story of an upward aspiring hero begins anew in an epicycle of the plot that originally brought Heathcliff into power. The second time around the emergence of power from below, so to speak, bears with it no traces of rebellion against paternal authority. Rather than unleashing popular energy, this protagonist's rise entails the harnessing and exhaustion of subversive forms of desire. Hareton Earnshaw is quite literally a noble savage, for one thing, and although he, like Heathcliff, originally occupies a servile position, his rudeness cannot be construed as the gross sensuality of the laboring classes. It is the natural vigor of "the ancient stock." Much like the boy heroes spawned by Thomas Hughes's *Tom Brown*, Hareton's rough and readiness lends itself readily to acculturation through the persuasive power of a pretty girl and the influence of the written word.[16] His mastery of the two houses and not Heathcliff s, significantly, signals an amalgamation of the ruling classes where there had been grave division (all their intermarriages having proved fatal). Nor does this unification entail any dissolution of social boundaries, but rather a situation, as Joseph calls it, where "the lawful master and the ancient stock had been restored to their rights" (p. 264). While Hareton's rise into power does represent the reform of an intolerably authoritarian society along more humanitarian lines, this reform is accomplished by means of a return to the past which restores the lines of inheritance and reconstitutes the family as it was prior to Heathcliff's intervention.

This kind of narrative resolution obviously won the immense popularity it did during the 1850's because it revised the fictional struggle between the bourgeoisie and the old aristocracy to accommodate later Victorian norms. The same middle-class interests could no longer be served by a fable in which the ruling class was defeated in the course of an industrial revolution. Quite the contrary, the struggle must now be represented as that of an entrenched middle class allied with the old aristocracy and beleaguered by the barbarians who were clambering to get in. The benevolent patriarchy towards which Brontë's narrative moves by reshuffling the features of character, reversing the relationships among individuals, and playing their story backwards and forwards ultimately denies the optimistic individualism that first set it in motion.

In contrast with the other characters in the novel, it is Heathcliff who embodies the contradiction produced as the novel shifts its frame of reference from one side of some historical faultline to the other. Once we dissolve the text back into this large context, it becomes clear why he seems to be several characters even though his name and competitive nature never vary. Against the background of a too rigid class structure where the individual appears to be radically undervalued, even such negative terms for the gypsy as "imp," "fiend," or "devil" can only recall his Romantic prototypes and lend him a positive value. By the 1840's, however, middle-class intellectuals were giving up on the individual as the guarantee of a reality superior to that designated by material facts. As Heathcliff's triumph over the institutions which had been oppressing him turns into something on the order of a reign of terror, it seems clear that the individual's desire has been overvalued to the detriment of the community. Desire loses its salutary power, value is reinvested in traditions that bind family and class, and Heathcliff's demonic features, as the factor disrupting these traditions, take on an ominously literal meaning. A resolution for the novel is grounded on revisionary principles where love is no longer to be equated with natural desire, nor the community with nature itself:

> The intimacy between Hareton and young Cathy, thus commenced, grew rapidly, though it encountered temporary interruptions. Earnshaw was not to be civilized with a wish; and my young lady was no philosopher and no paragon of patience; but both their minds tending to the same point—one loving and desiring to esteem, and the other loving and desiring to be esteemed—they contrived in the end to reach it. (p. 249)

If this were truly the mediation and final note it seems to be, however, it is difficult to imagine readers having all that much trouble placing *Wuthering Heights* squarely within the mainstream of Victorian literature.[17] After all it is not that unusual for the protagonist of a novel to violate social boundaries as Heathcliff does. What is more, the social climbers of the fiction of the thirties and forties tend to differ from their earlier counterparts in this significant respect: lacking a pedigree, they cannot penetrate the old squirarchy without destroying it. Thus Heathcliff joins ranks with such characters as Dickens's Oliver Twist, Charlotte Brontë's Jane Eyre, Mrs. Gaskell's Mary Barton, and Thackeray's Becky Sharp in this respect. For they also threaten to become usurpers, criminals, or tyrants in their own rights by pursuing individualistic goals, and their demonic features must also be neutralized before the social tensions in these novels can convincingly give way to social cohesion.

It appears that *Wuthering Heights* was caught in the same shifting winds of history as were other major novels of the period. It is easy to see how, on the one hand, novels that played out a fantasy of upward mobility provided the middle-class readership with a fable of its own emergence into power as Ian Watt has suggested.[18] During the thirties and forties, however, when the obvious evils of industrialism made that power seem less the stuff of utopian fantasy and more of a fact to be defended, we should not be surprised to find that aggressive individualism changes its meaning to play a villainous role in history. Directly counter to the readership's interests at Brontë's point in time, not only would such a protagonist provide a critique of middle class policies but, in doing so, he would expose the roots of middle-class power as grounded in an amoral and competitive nature.

And this is not simply the wisdom of hindsight. Such a backside to Romantic ideology is evident in poems of despair like Wordsworth's "Elegaic Stanzas Suggested by a Picture of Peele Castle," for instance, or Keats's "To J.H. Reynolds Esq.," and it is seen still more clearly in novels whose narrative strategies undergo a similar reversal. Competitive mettle is devalued and power recentered in established bloodlines, just as it is in *Wuthering Heights*, when the orphaned Jane Eyre receives an inheritance prior to marriage with Rochester, an almost gratuitous gesture, or so it seems to many readers, at the point when her struggle for a social position is won. The same principle obtains in the long and perilous quest undertaken in the effort to document Oliver Twist's genteel lineage when his history is otherwise complete, the orphan's adoption into polite society secured, and all former threats to his well-being have been soundly eliminated. But nowhere, to my mind, is the origin of social authority more conspicuously transformed than it is in *Wuthering Heights*.

ii

How *Wuthering Heights* ultimately evades the kind of literary determinism I have been proposing becomes evident when the text has been mapped out against this background. Only then can we see how Brontë took issue with a public opinion that suppressed certain kinds of fantasy in order to sanction others as realistic. Even while playing to the expectations of her contemporaries, this novel, we find, maintains the relative independence of artistic play from the fluctuations of social history. This is not to say that *Wuthering Heights* transcends the limits of her materials or the whole set of suppositions that made it possible for one to think and write novelistically at her moment in history, yet Brontë does make it clear that in insisting on her freedom to imagine, she felt those very constraints. All the images of breaking out and of renewed confinement that characterize not only her work but Charlotte's as well may serve as metaphors for the self in a tradition-bound world, but they also function on a quite different level, as a way of acknowledging the problem in writing that arises when the conventions for representing the self in opposition to society will no longer do. The division of the semantic universe into parlor and heath, male and female, past and present, real and fictive obstructs the narrative process which depends upon making something new of all these deadlocks, and continuing the story therefore requires periodic acts of violence.

More telling, paradoxically, than what can be said are the seams and joints, chinks in the armor of realistic narration, that the author refuses to seal even by some violent conjunction. The omission of the one event on which hinge all changes of fortune in the novel gives us a clear indication of her departure from literary norms. We are told that during a three-year's absence Heathcliff miraculously changed and then reappeared, still savage at heart, bearing all the outward and visible signs of a gentleman. Yet this change itself must take place outside the province of literature. "Like a planet revolving around an absent sun," the novel reminds us, "an ideology is made of what it does not mention; it exists because there are things which must not be spoken of."[19] And what may not be brought into the open, in this case, is the very transformation that makes other novels so gratifying, the Napoleonic moment where the ruthless acquisitor and pretender to power becomes the redeemer and rightful claimant, a benevolent patriarch. Even though Brontë excludes the moment where this radical inversion of meaning takes place, the absence itself points to the discontinuity within the materials of her chosen genre as manifest in the character of the protagonist whose "development" usually smooths them away. It also points to the consistently competitive element in Heathcliff that is the more disturbing for the lack of a rational cause.

We are likely to become aware of this problem first as a rupture in the narrative flow. Nelly breaks off her story at the point where Heathcliff disappears, in response to which Lockwood implores, "With all my heart! Don't interrupt me. Come and take your seat here ... now continue the history of Mr. Heathcliff from where you left off, to the present day" (p. 80). This hunger for intelligibility is only whetted by the interruption in the story. It is never entirely satisfied. Even after the telling of the tale resumes, there remains a disturbing break in the chain of events comprising what Lockwood calls "the history of Mr. Heathcliff. "Significantly, Lockwood endeavors to mend the break by drawing upon a repertoire of novelistic devices meant just for this purpose but which must now be couched in the interrogative: "Did he finish his education on the continent? or escape to America, and earn honors by drawing blood from his foster country? or make a fortune more promptly, on the English highways?" (pp. 80–81). By cataloguing the permissible explanations for a rise in social position such as Heathcliff enjoys, Brontë makes her reader only too aware that the truth is neither in the novel nor among the conventions novelists use for diverting power into the hands of ordinary individuals. Implying a kind of ironic self-consciousness on the order of that permeating a work like *Tristram Shandy* or even *Bouvard et Pécuchet*, the very arbitrariness of the novelist's catalogue drains away its explanatory power, leaving behind the mere husks of words for us to play with. By giving voice to the novel reader's expectations through Lockwood's relatively naive commentary, Brontë raises the questions such conventions were supposed to answer but in answering actually suppressed.

There is not only Heathcliff's strange disappearance from the text to deal with, but also his strange refusal to do so. The persistence of forms of Romantic supernaturalism in the novel disturbs the otherwise conventional ending and further separates the author's viewpoint from the beliefs and values she ascribes to the reader. In death Heathcliff becomes part of nature and, as such, continues to compete with Edgar Linton for possession of Catherine Earnshaw, only now for the privilege of mingling with her corpse through the process of their physical decomposition. Such demonstrated perversity notwithstanding, Brontë maintains nature's superiority to culture in certain respects, and she has Heathcliff pursue his desires through to their own sort of resolution. Counter to the beliefs of what Lockwood calls "the busy world," Heathcliff demonstrates the primacy of man's essential nature over and against a more modern notion of character that trusts to familiar roles and places material limits on the self. He has a "conviction" that spirits "can, and do exist, among us" and feels Catherine's ghostly presence as "certainly as you perceive a substantial body in the dark" (p. 229). That this is something more than a delusion on his part is indicated by Lockwood's similar encounter with her ghost, by Heathcliff's "frightful, life-like gaze of exultation" on his deathbed (p. 264), and by Nelly's testimony that "country folk, if you asked them, would swear on their Bible that he walks" (p. 265). Heathcliff's apotheosis as the demon lover of folklore and superstition exactly inverts the assumption of scientific thinking that nature remains securely locked within its rational categories. Contrary to Heathcliff's magical thinking, Lockwood's empiricism merely flattens characters into stereotypes and suppresses the desires that alone can revitalize a rigidly endogamous society. Essentially hostile to social categories of any kind, these aspects of character remain in the novel as the signs of absent desire. As such, they comprise a separate world of romance, a fantasy of power that is both obsolete and imminently threatening.

Viewed from this perspective, the process of domestication allowing the characters to fall more in line with familiar social roles in the manner of domestic realism does not constitute a mediation of the conflict between self and society so much as a contraction and fragmentation of the novel's original fantasy materials, a process of displacement that is the more sophisticated for baring its own devices. Like the Romantic poet, Brontë seems to locate value in the natural aspects of the self and conceive social roles as confining, but she also accepts a materialistic view of nature as the ultimate reality, never retreating as Keats did, for example, from a world "where every maw / The greater on the lesser feeds evermore."[20] In confronting the Victorian dilemma of man's identification with this depraved nature, she refuses to soften the harsh facts of competition underlying human history or to countenance the possibility of amelioration by such means. Nature's utter hostility to humanistic values locates her fiction within a later Victorian context, that is clear. In maintaining sympathy for what is more primal in the self than rules whose business it is to constrain the individual, the author casts in her lot with artists of an earlier age.

In this way her writing carries on a precarious relationship with a nineteenth-century intellectual tradition that continuously endorsed humanistic values either by advancing the claims of the individual or by maintaining those of the community. The first metamorphosis of Heathcliff from a "gipsy brat" into someone who is "in dress and manners a gentleman" tells us that the Romantic tradition fails to answer adequately the questions posed by an industrialized world. But the second metamorphosis of Heathcliff from the social interloper, a *nouveau riche*, into the bogeyman of popular lore and superstition reveals that this is precisely what the novel must hide if it is to remain a novel: the subversive desire at the origins of middle-class power, hence the history of the discourse in which the novel itself participates. The second change in the rules governing the formation of character in the novel reroots economic power within a domestic world whose function is to harness competitive energy and convert desire into the means for some ulterior end. The presence of the supernatural is dangerous, in turn, because it antedates science and undermines the rational categories that domestic realism affirms. If Heathcliff's first metamorphosis tells us something cannot be spoken if the novel is to remain a novel, then the second uncovers the act of repression that has enabled Victorian fiction to emerge. With the division of the protagonist in two, the ascension of Hareton, and the return of Heathcliff as a ghost, the boundaries between romance and realism are reestablished in the novel, but the philosophically hostile positions of Enlightenment thinking achieve a disturbing kind of equivalence there as well.

Under circumstances such as these it becomes rather evident that the author of the novel, as Foucault would say, "is not simply an element of speech ... Its presence is functional in that it serves as a means of classification. A name," he explains, "can group together a number of texts and thus differentiate them from others. A name also establishes different forms of relationships among texts."[21] By situating her sister's name in circumstances that might explain away the peculiar discontinuities shaping *Wuthering Heights*, Charlotte's biographical sketch and preface to the second edition perform this classificatory function where neither the novel itself nor Emily's pseudonym apparently could. It was Charlotte Brontë who separated *Wuthering Heights* from her own fiction and Anne's, with which it was initially confused. It was Charlotte who cautioned the readership that "an interpreter ought always to have stood between her [sister] and the world" (p. 8) and thereby implied that Emily's was an essentially private language. Most criticism has followed in the path cut by this first attempt to detach *Wuthering Heights* from the literary categories of the 1840's by placing the author backwards or even forwards in history but rarely within her own moment in time. Nevertheless, these biographical constructions themselves must incorporate the paradox of male and female features of discourse, those of budding novelist, full-blown visionary and even the weary skeptic inscribed within her technique, as well as the biographical material for both a classic instance of hysteria and a case of aesthetic martyrdom on the order of Keats's. We should not be too surprised consequently to discover that despite the biographical mythology still clinging to the text its boundaries remain unstable and shifting, the viewpoints within it comprising the sort of discontinuities that emerge only from a series of texts, reversible and capable of speaking from several perspectives at once. In resisting our categories, however, *Wuthering Heights* allows one to see not only the transformations giving rise to a distinctively Victorian fiction, but also the radical act of forgetting that enables such discourse to exist.[22]

NOTES

1. Terry Eagleton, *Myths of Power, A Marxist Study of the Brontës* (New York: Harper & Row, 1975), p. 12, and J. Hillis Miller, *The Disappearance of God* (New York: Schocken, 1965), p. 160. Also see Marilyn Butler's *Romantics, Rebels and Reactionaries* (Oxford: Oxford Univ. Press, 1981), pp. 178–88, for an informative description of the Romantic counter-revolution to Enlightenment individualism during the 1820's.

2. As if the Haworth environment were not a consummately literate one, Charlotte claims Emily wrote about "the inhabitants, the customs, the natural characteristics of the outlying hills and hamlets in the West-Riding of Yorkshire" without realizing they "are things alien and unfamiliar" to the reader (p. 9). At the same time, Charlotte insists that her sister's novel is not to be regarded as naive representationalism at all, at least where Heathcliff is concerned. He is the pure product of Emily's "creative gift," she explains, something of which the writer was "not always the master—something that at times strangely wills and works for itself." *Wuthering Heights*, ed. William M. Sale, Jr. (New York: Norton, 1972), p. 12. (All subsequent citations to *Wuthering Heights* and its prefatory materials are to this edition and have been included in the text.)

3. Fredric Jameson, *The Political Unconscious* (Ithaca: Corneal Univ. Press, 1981), p. 51.

4. Jameson, The Political Unconscious, p. 53.

5. In his discussion of *Wuthering Heights*, Jameson, like Eagleton and Miller, assumes that Heathcliff embodies all the contradictory themes in the novel because he is "in reality a mechanism for mediating these themes," *The Political Unconscious*, p. 127. But any approach that proceeds according to this assumption, I maintain, will necessarily tip the scales toward romance or realism without clarifying the problem that has made any such resolution inherently limited and dissatisfying.

6. For an extended discussion of the gypsy's usage in nineteenth-century discourse, see John Reed's informative chapter on the subject in his *Victorian Conventions* (Athens, Ohio: Ohio Univ. Press, 1975), pp. 362–400.

7. Lawrence Scone, *The Family, Sex and Marriage in England, 1550–1800* (New York: Harper & Row, 1977), pp. 221–68, 325–405.

8. George Canning in *The Microcosm*, 26 (May 14, 1787), reprinted in *Novel and Romance, 1700–1800, A Documentary Record*, ed. Joan Williams (New York: Barnes & Noble, 1970), p. 344.

9. See, for example, John E. Mason's *Gentlefolk in the Making* (Philadelphia: Univ. of Pennsylvania Press, 1935), pp. 220–91, and Mark Girouard's *Life in the English Country House* (New Haven: Yale Univ. Press, 1978), pp. 213–99.

10. Pertinent here is Lévi-Strauss's comparison between myth and "what appears to have largely replaced it in modern societies, namely, politics. When the historian refers to the French Revolution," he maintains, "it is always as a sequence of past happenings, a non-reversible series of events the remote consequences of which may still be felt at present. But to the French politician, as well as to his followers, the French Revolution is both a sequence belonging to the past—as to the historian—and a timeless pattern which can be detected in the contemporary French social structure and which provides a clue for its interpretation, a lead from which to infer future developments" ("The Structural Study of Myths," *Structural Anthropology*, trans. Claire Jacobson and Brooke Grundfest Schoepf (New York: Basic Books, 1963), p. 209). That the battle between the aristocracy and bourgeoisie won by the latter during the course of an industrial revolution constitutes such a myth for the English is particularly clear in Alan MacFarlane's study, *The Origins of English Individualism*, which he concludes with these words: "What is absolutely clear is that one of the major theories of economic anthropology is incorrect, namely the idea that we witness in England between the sixteenth and nineteenth centuries the 'Great Transformation' from a non-market, peasant, society where economics is 'embedded' in social relations, to a modern market, capitalist, system where economy and society have been split apart." Instead, MacFarlane's findings lead him to take Adam Smith at his word when Smith claimed he founded "classical economics on the premise of the 'rational' economic man, believing that he was describing a universal and long-evident type," *The Origins of English Individualism* (New York: Cambridge Univ. Press, 1979), p. 199.

11. According to Harry Payne's "Elite *versus* Popular Mentality in the Eighteenth Century," the qualities of "blood, magic, belief, and tradition," once ascribed to the ruling class, came to be associated with the laboring classes and taken as signs of their gross sensuality. This semiotic shift in the categories of class occurred at precisely the time when the ruling classes took it upon themselves to police, reform, and educate those socially less privileged. This new kind of contact with the masses is what, Payne surmises, bred awareness of their differences from an educated elite who prided themselves on "gentility, science, innovation, ... taste, and economic realism," *Studies in Eighteenth Century Culture*, 8 (1979), 21.

12. For an important connection between gypsies and early emerging labor force, see Ralph Samuel's "Comers and Goers," *The Victorian City*, ed. H. J. Dyos and Michael Wolff (London: Routledge & Kegan Paul, 1976), p. 110.

13. See Charlotte Brontë's dispute with the novel of manners in a letter written to W. A. Williams, in 1859. Here she berates Jane Austen rather unmercifully, contending that while her distinguished predecessor describes "the surface of the lives of genteel English people curiously well, ... the passions are perfectly unknown to her," *The Brontë's: Their*

Friendships, Lives, Correspondence, ed. T. J. Wise and J. A. Symington (London: Oxford, 1932), III, p. 99.

14. Quoted in Fredric Jameson's *Marxism and Form* (Princeton: Princeton Univ. Press. 1971), pp. 352–53.

15. In her informative study of the little known "sensation novel," Winifred Hughes offers a description of it that could easily apply to much of the Brontës' fiction as well: "Although remarkably few examples of modern prose fiction can be characterized as 'pure' romance or 'pure' realism, one vision or the other normally dominates. The sensation novel, however, deliberately strains both modes to the limit, disrupting the accepted balance between them," *The Maniac in the Cellar, Sensation Novels of the 1860s* (Princeton: Princeton Univ. Press, 1980), p. 16.

16. See, for example, Bruce Haley, *The Healthy Body and Victorian Culture* (Cambridge: Harvard Univ. Press, 1978), pp. 141–60.

17. "The conclusion," says Terry Eagleton in reference to this relationship, "while in a sense symbolically resolving the tragic disjunctions which precede it, moves at a level distanced from those disjunctions to preserve their significance intact," *Myths of Power*, pp. 118–19. Having far more difficulty with the idea of mediation, Leo Bersani sees this gesture at closure as something of a betrayal or act of bad faith on the part of the author, "the expulsion of difference," as he puts it, that makes her novel resemble "other novels," *A Future for Astyanax, Character and Desire in Literature* (Boston: Little, Brown and Company, 1969), p. 222. If we may take these two responses as indicative, it seems that in offering readers this form of traditional closure, what Brontë did was to create a transparently false sense of continuity among its materials and, at the same time, stir up yet one more discontinuity among those materials.

18. In *The Rise of the Novel*, Ian Watt argues that the popularity enjoyed by fiction and journalism was "not so much that Defoe and Richardson responded to the new needs of their audience, but that [being 'middle-class London tradesmen'] they were able to express those needs from the inside much more freely than would previously have been possible" (Berkeley: Univ. of California Press, 1957, p. 59).

19. Pierre Macherey, "Lenin, A Critic of Tolstoy," A *Theory of Literary Production*, trans. Geoffrey Wall (London: Routledge and Kegan Paul, 1978), p. 132.

20. *The Poetical Works of John Keats*, 2nd ed., ed. H. W. Garrod (Oxford: Clarendon Press, 1958), 11. 94–95.

21. Michel Foucault, "What is an Author?," *Language, Counter-Memory, Practice*, ed. Donald F. Bouchard, trans. Donald F. Bouchard and Sherry Simon (Ithaca: Cornell Univ. Press, 1977), p. 123.

22. An earlier version of this paper was presented at the Sixth Annual Brontë Conference, University of Leeds, 1981.

STEVIE DAVIES

Baby-Work:
The Myth of Rebirth in Wuthering Heights

Catherine Linton, as her mind turns toward its last agony, the departure from the "little frame" in which the warring gods of her spirit contend, moves from violence to a disconcerting lull in which she starts to pull feathers out of her pillow and arrange them methodically on the sheet according to their different species. Her calm absorption in this work of sorting is more frightening than the hysterical fits that preceded it. It is almost as if she had broken through into another world or dimension, abstracted from the chronology of ordinary time, the limits of accepted space, into a quiet place which is inaccessible to anyone else, a sealed solitude. Nelly Dean, who watches and listens, is clearly alarmed and dismayed: she covers her sense of threat by labelling Catherine's occupation "childish," a "childish diversion." She feels that if only Catherine—who is a nuisance—could be got to pull herself together and behave like a normal person, everything could be solved. Nelly's response is the sort that is appropriate and efficient in dealing with a small child's tantrum: you turn your back, avert your eyes and apply an abrasive scepticism. She is right in one sense that Catherine is being "childish," for she has diverted herself entirely. She has gone straight through that invisible wall that separates our adult selves from our childhood selves, as if entering the looking-glass. In the looking-glass world (and Catherine is about to see herself reflected in the mirror which she

From *Emily Brontë: The Artist as a Free Woman*, pp. 95–113. © 1983 by Stevie Davies takes for the old wooden press where she slept in her childhood) perception of time is altered. Childhood is now, immediate.

But old age is simultaneous too: Catherine sees Nelly all grey and bent, as she will be, fifty years from this date. Catherine can speak back into the "real" world from the dreamworld, but she communicates as if from far away. All Nelly is definitely aware of is the chaos Catherine is creating in the room as she starts tearing feathers out of the pillow by the handful and scattering them wholesale, blithely unconcerned that Nelly is going to have to pick up the mess and put things to rights. (Nelly as narrator of *Wuthering Heights* is constantly concerned with tidying and putting to rights for Lockwood's and the reader's sake the chaotic material of her story.) She feels cross and surly. "'Give over that baby-work!' I interrupted." Getting hold of the annoying pillow, she drags it by force out of the plucking hands that are destroying it. All that she—and we—have to compare such an irruption with is the destructive wantonness of childhood in its "baby-work," which is wanton because it does not conceive of consequences. "Baby-work" is an experiment on the wrong side of the boundary between anarchy and survival. Yet the minute we have heard Nelly reduce Catherine's strange activities to this level, we know that she is wrong. We sympathize with Nelly in her task of coping with the feather-spreading, uncontrollable girl on the bed in her delirium: by making us wryly amused at her predicament in the earthy Yorkshire idiom of her reaction to it, Nelly also helps us to cope with it. But we have seen Catherine expressing herself in an activity which cannot accurately be construed as meaninglessly destructive. Beneath the elemental tantrum is taking place a kind of "work" which is mysterious and purposeful. This "baby-work" involves an urge toward a fundamental and radical order, which underlies the common "civilized" order and deeply criticizes it. Beside the work of sorting and grading the feathers in the pillow, social order appears as a kind of primitive chaos.

There is a very ancient story with its roots in Egyptian and Greek mystery religions, of Psyche and a sort of "baby-work" in which she was engaged. Psyche, having lost her lover, Cupid, by exposing him to light, was forced out of her cave into the terrible light of the upper world. The vindictive goddess Venus gave Psyche an impossible task to perform. She was given a huge heap of mixed seeds to sort; a time-limit; and a threat of death in the event of failure. Nobody could do what was required of Psyche: it is not in human nature to fulfil this pointless and immensely detailed task. Psyche was aided by the powers of nature. The end of her story was initiation into full possession of her husband. Psyche is the human spirit—our souls in their first rising to consciousness, losing hold of our primal source and our first intuitive affinities; forcibly separated from our twinned "other self" (Cupid);

released into a light which we cannot love, for it exposes us, abandoned and rejected, to a riddling life burdened with tasks whose meaning is lost on us. Life is imagined as a quest, a seeking, shot through with yearning. Yet some potent forces work for us, mysteriously buried in the dark underworld of our nature, where darkness is creative; seeds are growing. The pointless "baby-work" leads, as in all great structuring myths, to rediscovery, reunion and return in a changed form to an earliest truth with which we are finally able to deal.

The legend of Psyche is an allegory of the soul's expulsion, quest, and reunion with the beloved. *Wuthering Heights*, with its story of Catherine's wilful separation from her "twin," Heathcliff, her exile at Thrushcross Grange, the riddle of her delirium and the "baby-work" of her pregnancy and delivery of the new Catherine, is an original myth of loss, exile, rebirth, and return. It has the self-contained and opaque quality of all myth. It imagines the human soul as being female, seeking a lost male counterpart. The "secret" of *Wuthering Heights* is not a displaced incest motif, nor is it asexual, as critics claim. Catherine, having betrayed the union with her own truest likeness, is involved in a sexual search, but sexual union is not the subject of the story, rather it is the metaphor for a search which is metaphysical and "human" in the largest sense. Both Psyche's and Catherine's stories concern a metamorphosis. As the pupa opens to reveal the caterpillar, the caterpillar is bound into the chrysalis, and the chrysalis at its right season is unbound to reveal the new and sticky-winged butterfly which was there at every stage—an eternal and traditional image of rebirth—so Psyche must emerge; her world must darken and bind her; she must toil, despair, change, open, in order to rediscover. But she finds the beloved in her own person. Emily Brontë too stresses the suffering of those metamorphoses, the cramping pain of constriction, the terrible aspects of those rites of passage which initiate one into a new state. Catherine's is not a personal success-story like Psyche's. Emily charts two stages of metamorphosis: dead Catherine gives rite of passage to living Cathy. Like Psyche's the path is full of the most impossible riddles. She cannot trust her eyesight. The agony of death is the same as the agony of birth. It is dreadful to be born; hard to grow up; incomprehensible to die—and Emily Brontë will not say where exactly the new self in her myth of rebirth is located—whether in Heathcliff, in the second Cathy, in the heath where Catherine is buried. Emily preserves the mystery.

All along the way we are presented with images of the most astonishing beauty which, rooted in pain, loss, and dissolution bear suggestions of new life, and the release of the soul from the mortal carcass in which it is borne, as if waiting to hatch and fly. This is most deeply connected with the "baby work" of which Nelly complains so bitterly. Catherine reacts with ire to the thought of Edgar self-enclosed and adult, composedly reading in his book-lined study, for it is unbearable to her ego to think of him absorbed in the cocoon of his adult preoccupations: "'What in the name of all that feels, has he to do with *books*, when I am dying?'" She reacts with childish pique to his apparent safety from her tantrums. But at the same time, she responds with a deeper childlikeness of spirit which relates her both to her own orphaned childhood and to the child who is yet to be derived from her, Cathy. The challenge to her power is the catalyst that starts off the "childish diversion" with the pillow, accompanied by a speech that echoes Ophelia's in her madness in Shakespeare's *Hamlet*, but which turns the reader's imagination progressively out of doors—away from books, rooms, the confined space of the present moment, into the immensity of the external world of the heath and of Heathcliff:

> "That's a turkey's," she murmured to herself; "and this is a wild-duck's; and this is a pigeon's. Ah, they put pigeon's feathers in the pillows—no wonder I couldn't die! Let me take care to throw it on the floor when I lie down. And here is a moorcock's; and this—I should know it among a thousand—it's a lapwing's. Bonny bird; wheeling over our heads in the middle of the moor. It wanted to get to its nest, for the clouds touched the swells, and it felt rain coming. This feather was picked up from the heath, the bird was not shot—we saw its nest in the winter, full of little skeletons. Heathcliff set a trap over it, and the old ones dare not come. I made him promise he'd never shoot a lapwing, after that, and he didn't. Yes, here are more! Did he shoot my lapwings, Nelly? Are they red, any of them? Let me look."

All this while, Catherine is removing feathers from her pillow and sorting them. As she sorts them, she names them. As she names them, she relates them to her own destiny. There is a language of flowers, trees, birds, and animals which has still not died out. It is related to that folklore legend for which, given its tough, enduring roots in her inheritance, Emily Brontë had a tenacious memory. Each bird Catherine names springs into life in our imaginations from the bits of feather which are its sole mortal remains, taken by human hands from the carcass of a bird known to us both for its own beauty as a natural creature and for its traditional meaning and suggestions. The domesticated turkey gives way to the wild duck which is an emblem of freedom but hunted by man. Then the Yorkshire superstition that pigeon's feathers restrain the human spirit from passing out of the body is supplied by Catherine as an explanation of why she cannot "burst the fetters" of her condition by willing death so intensely. The pigeon is gregarious, tame, obedient, associated with domesticity and the "homing" instinct that binds her to Thrushcross Grange: she is bound to a continuing and unwanted life in a social order in which she is expected to act the wife's part, that tame, unspirited profession. The moorcock leads out beyond the range of the domestic world in which she is suffocating. Outside all this is the lapwing nesting upon the upland heath, in some shallow exposed basin of the earth, rearing its young at the mercy of every intruder. The lapwing and its baby birds are an exact emblem of Catherine's nature and her plight.

Catherine speaks as if in a waking dream, of a place in which she will never again be a presence; nor is the lapwing at that moment a presence. It is midwinter, and the lapwings have probably migrated. Male lapwings return to choose the site of a breeding-ground in mid-February or March: by that time, when Linton brings her the wild golden crocuses Catherine will be dying. She is within this "shattered prison," her body, enclosed within that other prison of Edgar's house, in extremity, and engaged in the "baby-work" of undoing the stuffing of a pillow, the symbol of all the warmth and comfort that pads and dulls her existence at Thrushcross Grange. Someone has made this pillow, the paranoid's "they"; some enemy to the person she is. She takes what "they" have fabricated to pieces and restructures it; traces the finished (dead) product back to its living sources. Birds have died to make the pillow on which she is meant to lay her head. In the pillow many species' feathers are anarchically mingled: muddle, chaos, is revealed as the basis of the pillow—that, and cruelty too, for much killing of beautiful natural creatures had to be done in order to make up the pillow. Catherine reveals in this most poignant moment that the civilized world, priding itself on its rationality, mildness, and gentle behaviour (Edgar reading in his library) depends on exploitation. She pulls out the inside and analyses it down into its unthinkable reality. Her will is to undo it all: unweave the mess that poses as order and remake the lives on which it preyed. The urge is to return to source. The task, like Psyche's, is not in any way viable unless the riddle can be solved, the code broken, which explains the system in which we all grow. There is a strong sense that this passage is making some emotional and philosophical assault on us with which we are called upon to come to terms. The likelihood is that we respond to the unanswerable by turning with Nelly to the safe haven of a request to "Give over with that baby-work."

But as we move out in imagination on to the heath where the single lapwing swerves and rides the air currents, turning for its nest, we also move back in time, to a single occasion before that great loss of Heathcliff which cut through Catherine's life like a physical bereavement. The piteous image of the nest in the "middle of the moor," seen in winter by the two children "full of little skeletons" is a central symbol within *Wuthering Heights*. We later gather that Catherine, speaking this memory to Nelly, who has decided not to comprehend it, is pregnant. She speaks, in a tradition known in Yorkshire, of the moorland bird as a symbol of the soul liberated from the body, or wandering the earth yearning for heaven. One of Emily Brontë's profoundest affinities is with the wild birds who are almost the sole living inhabitants of the moors. She had observed their habits and behaviour, and studied the natural science of Bewick's History of British Birds, painstakingly copying out in minute detail the engravings there. *Wuthering Heights* bears the fruit of this knowledge. Like humankind, the bird-life of the novel speaks of a search for liberty, soaring between the mountains; like our race, their fertility is burdened with seasonal change, the cruelty that is within nature, the high mortality-rate which took such a toll in Emily's own life and which in her art she both expressed realistically and tried to heal in the course of a mythic, cyclical structure. *Wuthering Heights*, in the person of Catherine, tells of a world which is a mighty orphanage, in which at best we are fostered for a limited period, on sufferance. But equally through the person of Catherine, it suggests the process through which we may guess at the existence of kin, seek them out, bond and mate with them, whether on this side of the grave or on the other. And so the birds of Catherine's reverie symbolize her predicament, and suggest its universal nature. The lapwing is near relation of the golden plover whose overhead whistling has, in a northern legend, been associated with the doomed Jews, wandering eternally after the crucifixion; the plaintive curlew's low-pitched fluting was associated in the north with the "Seven Whistlers," portending death. Emily Brontë is able to harness the power of these ancient legends of birds whose inhuman music calls like an agent of destiny into the human world. Yet the creatures Catherine lists are also felt as real, living and warm presences, linked to people not just as messengers but because they are so like us. The lapwing especially is known by its behaviour-patterns as a parent-bird. Its "pee-weet" note extends when its young are in danger to an acutely distressful call, uttered in tumbling flight. The parent-birds feign to be crippled or to drag a wing in order to draw off danger from the exposed nest. The woman who looks back on the outing to the moors where she and Heathcliff were most at home sees an image of beauty—"Bonny bird"; freedom "wheeling over our heads," shot through with menace, inexhaustible longing for home which belongs equally to human and to animal nature, as an instinct rather than a decision. Catherine imagines the bird as having freely moulted the feather she has picked out of her pillow, but the bird was as subject to vicissitude as she now is, pathetic in its longing as she will be in a few minutes, lying back on the much-criticized pillows, "her face bathed in tears ... our fiery Catherine was no better than a wailing child!" The lapwing is like her in being a parent, with the elements gathering against her: rain is coming. In the midst of its soaring flight it is a prisoner, like Catherine, dashing for home before calamity can strike. Catherine is five months pregnant: she is herself a nest from which the future will derive. Yet her image is of that time after the breeding-season in which (winter then as now) she and Heathcliff were out again and saw the nest "full of little skeletons." This desolating vision of a small family of forms bereaved at their very inception, yet held cocooned in the circle of the nest, their home become a tomb open to the winter skies, is an image for what Catherine feels she holds within her, fertility that is blighted because it comes of Linton. Equally it is an emblem of her own childhood, orphaned like this, exposed in a family of two with Heathcliff after the death of her father and protector, to the enmity and indifference of an uncaring sky.

We always are, in Emily's mythology, the child we were. At the very centre of the novel, in the protracted death of Catherine, the birth of Cathy, this truth is affirmed and reaffirmed. In looking at that nest, barred with a trap, with its starved, exposed little skeletons, we remember that terrible first grief of Catherine as a child:

> The poor thing discovered her loss directly—she screamed out—
>
> "Oh, he's dead, Heathcliff! he's dead!"
>
> And they both set up a heart-breaking cry. I joined my wail to theirs, loud and bitter.

The only adult present, Joseph, somewhat less than true to the vigorous spirit of the departed, and utterly, satirically unmoved by the grief of the orphans that remain, lets forth a blast of chilling moral air by wanting to know "what we could be thinking of to roar in that way over a saint in Heaven." In their mutual shock and grief, Catherine and Heathcliff become one with the narrator, Nelly: their loss is hers, and the infuriating Catherine with her naughty ways, her petulance and her need, becomes for Nelly "the poor thing." Catherine, after so many times teasing her father till he was moved to say the unthinkable "'Nay, Cathy ... I cannot love thee,'" had come on the last evening of his life to lay her head quietly against him; Heathcliff's young head pillowed on her lap; moved to kiss him goodnight, put her arms round his neck and found him dead. Nelly cannot get to the children in their grief. She looks in through their bedroom door late that night and sees that:

The little souls were comforting each other with better thoughts than I could have hit on; no parson in the world ever pictured Heaven so beautifully as they did, in their innocent talk.

We have been allowed to see a nest of little orphans, cut off for ever from the parent who was their only guarantee of shelter. They are exposed to the rancorous humours of Joseph; the jealousies of Hindley; the intermittent mothering that Nelly can or will give. Our minds touch upon that memory when we read of the dead lapwing chicks in their nest on the moors, cradled in their grave. What Catherine remembers of that vision of the dead young birds carries for us another painful acknowledgment. It was Heathcliff who in his young, unmitigated cruelty, set the trap that introduced the fledglings so early to their mortality. Catherine starts looking for evidence of blood upon the feathers she has pulled from the pillow. Heathcliff, whom she has said she does not love but rather *is*—like a part of her own identity, a force of her own nature—is implicated in the cruelties of the human and the natural world. Later in the novel he will "lay the trap" over the nest of the child Hareton and his own son, Linton Heathcliff, degrading the one and tormenting the other without any hint of remorse. The "little soul" whom Nelly watched with awe in his bereavement communing with Catherine suffers only to cause more suffering. In her poetry, Emily Brontë had constantly reverted to the theme of a rejected child handicapped throughout life because of rough early conditions,

> bred the mate of care,
> The foster-child of sore distress.

Pain begets cruelty; rejection unkindness, reciprocally, so that we act as transmitters down the generations of the wrongs that are done us. It is less a case of original sin than of original pain. That is why Emily Brontë everywhere insists on universal forgiveness for all offences whatever. Seeing through the walls of the adult self to the defenceless child each person contains, it is not thinkable to cast the first stone. Catherine recognizes Heathcliff's "fierce, pitiless, wolfish" nature: "'he'd crush you, like a sparrow's egg, Isabella.'" He is the barbarous cruelty of the heath itself, with its lowering weather; the wild part of Catherine's own nature which she had thought to have tamed, but also the victim of that pattern with which Emily was so personally familiar, whereby the world is a system for orphaning the young; bringing to destitution; killing mothers; undoing twins; betraying affinities. Heathcliff, who is the agent of so much destruction in *Wuthering Heights*, is as automatically an innocent as any being born into such a system.

At the very centre of the whole novel, Catherine suffers, dies, and gives birth. If we take a radius from that point, we encompass the whole novel, so that the structure is a perfect circle. Like the great myths of antiquity, *Wuthering Heights* presents us not only with a story of rebirth but also with a myth of return. The narrative at once presses forward and doubles back to its source. From the first Hareton Earnshaw who built the Heights in 1500, we are brought to the last Hareton Earnshaw, who restores the ancient line. Though the novel is precisely timed and documented to the year, the day, the hour, almost to a fault, and the very first word is a date (1801), the forward push of heredity and causality, with its vigilant eye on the clock, is retarded by a process of recapitulation. From Catherine's speech about the lapwings, we can move to almost any other point in this great prose poem and find some echo or resonance. Devices such as repetition and recapitulation of places, persons, events, names, and even of the letters which begin those names— the mysterious H's of Hindley, Hareton, Heathcliff, suggestive of a family cluster of improbable likenesses, and even a provocative code which tempts us to try and break it—reinforce this sense of a circling reality. Lockwood's narrative encircles Nelly's, which in turn encircles other stories told in their own persons by Zillah, Catherine, Isabella, Heathcliff, in letters, or retold dreams, or simply verbally. The beginning echoes in the end; the end in the beginning. Fractionally before the mathematical centre (so perfectly is the whole novel balanced), the elder Catherine dies and the younger is born; yet the dead Catherine is felt by a reader as just as strong and living a presence in the second half as her daughter and namesake. In the cross-breedings of the two families, the mild Lintons and the harsher Earnshaws, washed through and renewed by fresh blood, there is a sense of something fated and inevitable. The personalities of the characters, though so odd and eccentric, come to seem, in this inexplicable pattern of return to source, as impersonal as their setting, the wind that is busy on the moors and the abeyance of self that is under the moors.

The novel is not so much about individuals as about humanity. It is less about humanity than humanity in a setting. It is far less about humanity in the person of the male of our species ("man," "forefathers," "God the father," "masterpiece") as about humanity in the person of the female. The author of Genesis, looking back to our origins, had felt called upon to attribute to Adam a sort of womb where his ribcage was, by biological sleight and to the confounding of common sense, deriving woman from man. For a person as radical as Emily Brontë, and innocent of the offence her perceptions might cause the vulnerable minds of the orthodox, writing of the theme of genesis, this would simply not seem sensible, credible, or even efficient according to the laws of practical economy. She expresses instead a female vision of genesis, expulsion, and rebirth in terms of the metaphor of fertility and childbirth. Wordsworth and the Romantic poets, whom she deeply admired, had taken the imagination back to childhood, to muse over the idea of the child as "father of the man," a metaphor for our beginnings. Emily Brontë, in a way that is radical and difficult because no language has existed in patriarchal England to express it (foremothers, mistress piece, God the mother?), relived the idea according to the more natural metaphor of the child as mother of the woman. Catherine's mothering of Cathy at the centre of the book relates past to present; projects present into future, so that past and future meet at source. The ethic of this feminine way of encountering reality is that of universal forgiveness; the metaphysic is one of final but mysterious redemption; the means of expression is that of a coded, secret utterance which, though we feel we understand fully while we read, has the knack akin to that of dream-language of slipping just out of comprehension when we awaken.

Toward the centre of *Wuthering Heights* occurs the transition where past meets future, youth meets age, death meets life. It is very like the structure of Shakespeare's tragicomedies: "thou mettest with things dying, I with things new born," where, through the channel of labour from which a living girl-baby is drawn from the birth-canal of her dying mother we are led to brood upon the deepest mysteries of human existence: a living cycle which includes and transcends individual deaths and mortal-seeming bereavements. Emily Brontë starts chapter 2 of part 2 with a characteristic telling of the time: "About twelve o'clock, that night, was born the Catherine you saw at Wuthering Heights." She directs us to the moment of transition, the crucial turning point at which the threshold between two worlds is doubly crossed. The baby Catherine has come in; the mother Catherine's soul crosses with that of her child, on its way out. Twelve o'clock is the midpoint, at which the old day has given place to the new. All is grief and loss in this new day: the baby who has come in seems not, yet, to count. Nelly describes the aspect of Catherine lying dead as a scene of peace, but we do not always trust Nelly's evaluations, suspecting her of sentimentality at some times, as of vinegar sourness at others. Yet when she describes the moment of Catherine's departure to Heathcliff outside, there is a sense of perfect truthfulness:

> "How did she die?" ...
> "Quietly as a lamb ... she drew a sigh, and stretched herself, like a child reviving, and sinking again to sleep; and five minutes after I felt one little pulse at her heart, and nothing more."

Nelly is filling in information for Heathcliff, her head turned from Lockwood. She opens a window for us, into the immediate past, through which we have a chance of apprehending Catherine's last moments in this world. Emily Brontë constantly reveals just as tender and naturalistic an observation of the gestures and behaviour of babies and children as of the moorland creatures whose nature she knew by heart. If you have seen a little girl in a deep sleep, coming gently to the surface, perhaps roused by some dream, and then relapsing downward into the inner world without breaking the surface of consciousness, then you have seen Catherine's death as Emily Brontë meant you to imagine it. A child observed in sleep is poignant, existing in a remote world: to us who watch her, helpless, to herself unaware of being vulnerable, beyond the need for help. Nelly transmits an image of the soundest peace, in which the hearer may draw comfort as if from a well. In her telling, death has lost its sting; the grave its victory. She speaks of Catherine "sighing." A sigh which normally speaks to us of pain, is presented as the breath of life, prelude to "revival." We feel that Catherine does revive in some other world. The child goes home. Nelly touches Catherine's breast; records the final sign of life, "one little pulse." Her tenderness for this woman whom she has not much liked is shown quickened as Catherine, who has just borne a child, herself becomes one. As her daughter wakes into this world, we are given to believe that the mother wakens into another, as she had predicted and as Nelly feels constrained to echo: "Incomparably beyond and above you all." Nelly reinforces the idea of regression to childhood as the way out of the imprisoning mortal condition by going on to say that "'her latest ideas wandered back to pleasant early days.'" The mighty circle of *Wuthering Heights*, in which the Hareton Earnshaw who built the Heights in 1500 returns to the Hareton Earnshaw who will marry this new young Cathy on January 1, 1803, is informed by smaller circles, leading us to muse on the final and original identity of "late" and "early"; first and last; mother and daughter. There is no linear path from present into the future, as if the world were laid out flat as a map; the map, Emily Brontë everywhere tells us, is a useful fiction which must not be mistaken for the shape of reality. In moving forward over the round world we recapitulate our mutual and personal history. Thus Nelly speaks of Catherine's "latest" thoughts (the last things) as "wandering back" to "early days" (her source and birth). To "wander" suggests those rambles on the moors which offered prospects of Paradise to Catherine and Heathcliff, together with freedom from adult authority; to "wander" in mind means to go mad; to "wander back" means the joy of retracing steps without deliberate purpose but with the sure instinct of homing birds—like the pigeons Catherine has been seen feeding; of whose feathers in the stuffing of her pillows she had bitterly complained as keeping her soul hampered in the flesh. We are reminded too of Catherine's hallucination, when, going out of her mind at the onset of her illness, she had lost seven years of her life:

I did not recall that they had been at all. I was a child; my father was just buried, and my misery arose from the separation that Hindley had ordered between me and Heathcliff—I was laid alone, for the first time.

In her delirium, Catherine had not managed to "wander back" far enough into childhood, but fell back only to the moment of exile which is a source of her present pain, confirmed by her own voluntary betrayal of Heathcliff for Linton at the age of seventeen. That return landed her in a sudden, inexplicable liaison with a "stranger; an exile, and outcast." Her wandering mind could do no more than settle her at the crucial moment of loss.

For Emily Brontë, the adult self is felt as a stray fragment of a greater whole, of which we may intensely dream or hallucinate, but not recover until we meet as children at our starting-point. For the elder Catherine, Heathcliff is this whole; for the younger, it will be Hareton to whom she goes home by some true instinct bred perhaps of the Linton tempering of her constitution, of her mother's mortal suffering, and of some maternal-seeming destiny suggested but never explained by the novel. In a last, deep relaxation of her fretful being, Catherine is shown by Nelly as being able to shed the years and be the child she was. In her poetry, Emily had many times implied this possibility. Near the eve of her coming-of-age, she speaks of the damp evening landscape "breathing of other years":

> Oh, I'm gone back to the days of youth,
> I am a child once more.

In an undated but probably late poem, she expressed the myth of going back which Catherine enacts in her dying moments, in a metaphor of going out on the moors which also includes the idea of wandering in mind:

> Often rebuked, yet always back returning
>   To those first feelings that were born with me,
> And leaving busy chase of wealth and learning
>   For idle dreams of things which cannot be:
>
> I'll walk where my own nature would be leading:
>   It vexes me to choose another guide:
> Where the gray flocks in ferny glens are feeding;
>   Where the wild wind blows on the mountain side.

What have these lonely mountains worth revealing?
More glory and more grief than I can tell:
The earth which wakes *one* human heart to feeling
Can centre both the worlds of Heaven and Hell.

Here the poet dramatizes the regressive process which she sees as the key to the sources of creativity and value by inverting the grammar: "turning back" becomes "back returning." "Often" is resisted by "always"; "rebuked" superseded by "return." In *Wuthering Heights*, Nelly enacts the adult world's "rebuke" of the child consciousness in man, which constantly performs an abrupt about-turn and goes sprinting back for home in accordance with the laws of its "own nature": "'Give over with that baby-work! ... Lie down and shut your eyes, you're wandering. There's a mess!'" Nelly spends most of her time expostulating as the lawless child-heroes give her the slip; wander off on the moors; push each other around; play serious games. To her infuriated demand that they grow up, they reply by silently eluding her grasp (as the second Cathy will do, by a stealth foreign to her guileless nature, to reach the Heights), and circling back to their starting-places. Heathcliff finally resists the onward pressure of time to move into the future by starving himself to death, until, "washed by rain," with his hand grazed upon the open window, and his unclosable dead eyes staring into the mortal world as his living eyes had gazed into the immortal one, he is placed with Catherine in the one grave. They sleep together. Over his grave, Hareton "with a streaming face" weeps like a child, not in proportion to the usage he received from the "sarcastic, savage" corpse he is burying, but according to the laws of his own strong and loving nature, and because he finds himself in some way kin to the foster-father who abuses him. Hareton is true to his childhood roots; Heathcliff returns to his, as the author holds we do return, not in a "second childhood" of senility, but first childhood, where we began.

Heathcliff himself, the destroyer, vengeful, avaricious, lying, and sadistic as he is, remains (especially at the moment of his most abject loss, in the centre of the book) profoundly and organically in touch with this process of recreation. He was the cuckoo in the nest who disturbed the world of the Heights, and outraged its symmetry of brother and sister balancing brother and sister at Thrushcross, whose intermarriage might in the course of things have taken place. He was the bane of Hindley and will be the potential undoing of Hareton. The only creation we can attribute to him is his sickly, spineless, and degenerate son, Linton Heathcliff, sired on Isabella in a fit of hate. Yet Heathcliff is associated by Emily Brontë with a kind of harmony and fertility which underlie all the other levels of order and disorder that superimpose in complex strata in the novel. Beneath the immaculate and fastidious social order symbolized by Thrushcross Grange and the Lintons' way of life, Catherine has discerned a predatory disorder, through her "baby-work" of undoing the pillow. At a yet deeper level, beneath the disharmony of Catherine's early death and Heathcliff's huge, inexplicable loss, is revealed a buried principle of a benign though pagan shaping-out of a destiny that is ultimately fruitful and kind. Emily Brontë allows us to glimpse this mysterious reparation which lies at the core of loss, through the most delicate allusions to the relationship between man and his natural setting, especially birds and trees. Nelly describes his appearance as she approaches him with the news of Catherine's death:

> He was there—at least a few yards further in the park; leant against an old ash tree, his hat off, and his hair soaked with the dew that had gathered on the budded branches, and fell pattering round him. He had been standing a long time in that position, for I saw a pair of ousels passing and repassing scarcely three feet from him, busy in building their nest, and regarding his proximity no more than that of a piece of timber. They flew off at my approach, and he raised his eyes and spoke:
> "She's dead!" he said.

It is spring. The buds in the ash in March are large and sticky; here they are covered in early-morning dew which overflows them on the bare head of the oblivious watcher beneath, keeping vigil. The ash is old, having seen many seasons. Heathcliff is felt to be deeply related to the surge of new life in the old stock, inevitably, subconsciously so. In Nelly's description, he seems to belong to the landscape as an intrinsic part of it—as if he were planted there, rooted not as a human and active entity but as a different species, quiet as the trees with which he is surrounded. He is recognized as a harmless part of nature by the inhabitants of the natural world going about their business— the ring ousels building their nest, who are not afraid to come within three feet of his stock-still body because they are ignorant that he is human and their natural enemy. They recognize Nelly sure enough, and depart. The ring ousels are emblems of fertility; in their pairing and nest-building they speak to us of the future. Emily Brontë will have known that this is a species in which both sexes build the nest, incubate and tend the brood; that they are related to the thrush (appropriate, then, to Thrushcross), and are reckless in protecting their young from predators. We remember the nest of little skeleton chicks over which Catherine mourned, and perhaps look forward to the later image of her daughter Cathy as a "bird flying back to a plundered nest which it had left brim-ful of chirping young ones." Heathcliff is a force causing such destruction to the young, yet here at the centre of the novel he seems to be imitating an opposite role. The ousels have returned early to their familiar nesting-site to build from the coarse grasses which they are conveying across Heathcliff's line of vision. We are directed to the moment at the very turn of the year. Indoors the baby is new in its crib; the breeding birds are in a pair outside, building for the future. In this scene, the mateless Heathcliff—outside the human community, alongside these emblems of fidelity, the homing instinct, protectiveness, warmth—stands spiritless as "a piece of timber." Contrary to his own intentions, and against his will to destroy and uproot, he is in deep harmony with the scene, even a contributor to it.

   In the second half of the novel, Heathcliff tries to thwart and mutilate the products of this fertility. Yet toward the end, it becomes clear that he cannot destroy anything; that he is in a strange way the agent of a harmony for which he cannot wish. Far from thieving the property of the Heights and the Grange from their rightful owners, his efforts marry the two inheritances by bringing the two heirs into proximity. The "little dark thing, harboured by a good man to his bane" as Nelly muses, is not ultimately a "bane" at all, but an instrument of regeneration and of harmonious balance between eternal oppositions. *Wuthering Heights* hinges on a fruitful but—in rational terms—baffling paradox: order and disorder, creation and destruction, being born and dying, looking in and seeing out, enclose and define each other, as if in a series of multiple parentheses. Within this pattern Heathcliff, for all his efficient manipulations, is caught static. He is, at the centre, a "piece of timber," rooted in the seasonal cycle, at whose foot the breeding birds are free to fulfil their instinctual nature. At the end of his career he is again static, ceasing to act because his cycle is fully lived out:

> I have to remind myself to breathe—almost to remind my heart to beat! And it is like bending back a stiff spring ... it is by com-pulsion that I do the slightest act not prompted by one thought, and by compulsion that I notice anything alive or dead, which is not associated with one universal idea.

Under his very eyes, Hareton ("'the ghost of my immortal love'") and Cathy, who are in some respects so like himself and Catherine in their earlier lives, but tempered, reshaped and reshaping, are moving toward each other, to mate and build. Heathcliff is in process of turning back into the bedrock earth from whose rough nature he seems made: heath and cliff. Emily Brontë suggests a mode of existence intermediate between "human" and "nature," in which the subconscious continuum of our living—to breathe with our lungs, to pump the blood round with the heart—is coming to a deliberate standstill. Heathcliff, to stay alive at all, has to make a mental labour of the unthinking processes of survival. It is all said in the brilliant image of "bending back a stiff spring": incarnate existence has become to him a matter of mechanics predetermined to tend in an undesired direction. Nelly stresses in these latter moments of Heathcliff's life that he really does not seem quite human. But all she can suggest to explain him is that he might be a "goblin" or a "ghoul, or a vampire." She knows this to be very feeble and embarrassing when she reflects that she "had tended him in infancy," the vampire species having no known childhood. Joseph is much happier with his explanation when he shuffles in to view the corpse, announcing with malevolent joy that "'Th' divil's harried off his soul.'" There is a beautifully wry note in Nelly's description of Joseph as "the old sinner," as he grins back at his master's face set in rigor mortis, and, labelling him a fiend, looks ready to dance for joy all round the deathbed. When Heathcliff is buried, Nelly feels anxious that he bears no surname, simply the one (surely not a "Christian") name, which is inscribed simply and singly upon his gravestone. Heathcliff has moved from a death-in-life to a life-in-death with Catherine. He has passed through the window; reverted, as Gimmerton Kirk will do, to the moor. Personality is annulled, but a new, impersonal, more absolutely vital existence is felt to begin as the heath which is his original claims its namesake.

At the centre, Nelly, having seen Catherine on her passage out of the world and Cathy on her way in, enters the park expecting that Heathcliff had been out "among the larches" all night. It is characteristic of the author to name the species of tree rather than to refer to generalized trees. The larch is a fir but not ever-green, shedding needles annually from delicate, slender boughs and with the spring reclothing itself in soft pale-green. Midway between the evergreen and deciduous worlds, it looks like the one, behaves like the other. Heathcliff is absorbed in his waiting into the wood. He beats his head against the trunk of the ash in his agony: "I observed several splashes of blood about the bark of the tree, and his hand and forehead were both stained; probably the scene I witnessed was a repetition of others enacted during the night." This extreme behaviour has often been seen as a bizarre intrusion of Gothic in which the obligatory maniac behaves like a howling beast rather than a man. But there is a deeper, mythic meaning to these actions. Heathcliff now has a double nature: he both lives and does not live. Catherine, who is conceived of as his own being will be buried and he left above ground, "with his soul in the grave." In this absolute loss he meets the boundaries of human nature but cannot get across. Nelly sees him as an animal. It is easier for her to formulate the idea of the nonhuman in these terms. The breeding birds see him as a tree. We see his blood shed upon the bark of the ash and staining it; his forehead too is stained with blood as if baptismally. In the image of the blood-stained tree Emily Brontë suggests an analogy to the sacrificial slaughter either of animal or man, by which the ancient mystery religions sought to appease the deities and ensure a fruitful new year. Heathcliff's pain is absolutely acute. The year, the hour, the day turn; the baby is born, the birds mate. The old mother passes, while the man's blood, like that of the sacrificial king of ancient pagan religions, seeps into mother earth.

The happiness of the future, Emily Brontë asserts, is built on the destruction of the past, and is seen by the reader to depend on it. In one of the most poignantly beautiful images of *Wuthering Heights*, stated matter-of-factly two chapters later, Nelly says of the second Catherine, whose birth had killed her mother: "For the rest, after the first six months, she grew like a larch; and could walk and talk too, in her own way, before the heath blossomed a second time over Mrs. Linton's dust." "Six months" takes us to September, the year's turning into winter: Cathy has it in her to resist and overcome winter. Since the moorland heather blooms in August to September, the same sentence takes us through yet another full cycle, placing an image of hope and renewal (the purple bells of heather) directly upon an image of loss and mortality (Mrs. Linton reduced to "dust"). The child has in her the best of the Lintons and the best of the Earnshaws, in fruitful mixture. If she is "like" her mother she is also "like" Heathcliff, since we must believe Catherine's conviction that "I am Heathcliff." As he stood in the terrible night of Cathy's birth amongst the larches, and shed his blood upon the bark of a tree, so Cathy "grew like a larch." In some mysterious way, Heathcliff is intrinsically linked to the second Cathy, and has given up some of his life to her.

JOSEPH ALLEN BOONE

Wuthering Heights:
Uneasy Wedlock and Unquiet Slumbers

Although now recognized as a nineteenth-century classic, *Wuthering Heights* (1847) has always impressed its critics as something of an anomaly in the English tradition of the novel, and its difference is nowhere so marked as in its unconventional attitudes toward love and marriage. Indeed, the "disjointed" and "strangely original" qualities of the text's form that its initial reviewers found unsettling have everything to do with its equally strange and original representation of love.[15] In pitting its vision of life-affirming relationship against the destructive course of identity frustrated, violated, and sundered by societal norms of wedlock, Emily Brontë's unconventional tale of passion unfolds onto multiple planes of plot, reality, and perspective that defy the boundaries of traditional fictional order. The result is a textual openness, an explosiveness of possibility, that flouts the proper "end of fictitious writings"[16] prescribed by the novel's Victorian critics and readers alike. Its final denial of the easy moral, in turn, becomes Brontë's strategy for affirming a radical paradigm of self-in-relationship that runs counter to the sexual polarity, self-limitation, and inequality endemic to most English marriage fiction.

That Brontë's unorthodox critique establishes itself, in some degree, in opposition to her society's dominant sexual ideology is a fact established in the best of recent criticism of *Wuthering Heights*. One might look, for

From *Tradition Counter Tradition: Love and the Form of Fiction*, pp. 151–172. © 1987 by the University of Chicago.

example, at the novel's recurrent figure of the oppressive male "master" for a clue to this dimension of Brontë's vision. The correlation between male control of the family and excessive and often arbitrary displays of power first surfaces in old Earnshaw, who despite his kindness is thrown "into fits" by "slights of his authority,"[17] and continues in his son and heir Hindley, who, from the safety of his domestic "paradise on the hearth" (27), mercilessly persecutes the young Heathcliff and Catherine; it will resurface in the very different personalities of Edgar Linton, Heathcliff, and Heathcliff Linton. In turn, Brontë measures the negative consequences of male tyranny in the novel's accumulating pattern of forcibly sundered relationships, as well as in the internal divisions of identity that mirror such losses. And, crucially, this thematic pattern of division is registered in the structural schisms or ruptures that make up so much of the fabric of *Wuthering Heights*, beginning with its dual narrators and continuing in its divisions between the worlds of "reality" and ghosts, between recollected and anticipated levels of time, between modes of ending. Coexisting with this multiplication of parts is another, more radical kind of narrative doubleness engendered by the constant duplication of characters, events, gestures, settings: everything seems uneasily to replicate itself in similar but different forms, progressively upsetting readerly assumptions of stable reality and narrative coherence alike. Standing against this structural pattern of division and doubling, moreover, is a single thematic constant, the image of oneness and difference embodied in the passionate bond of Catherine and Heathcliff Moving from an overview of this pivotal relationship to the multiplication of developmental and perspectival strategies that envelop it, we may begin to see how both these patterns participate in a subversion of the traditional marriage plot and the tenets underlying its construction.

I

Brontë's reworking of received notions of romantic affiliation is given its fullest expression in the affinity uniting Catherine and Heathcliff as untraditional soul mates: "He's more myself than I am," Catherine will say of this uniquely nonpolar attraction in her famous speech of chapter 9, "Whatever our souls are made of, his and mine are *the same*.... Nelly, I *am* Heathcliff" (68, 70; emphasis added). The mystical intensity of this assertion of "like" selves, it is essential to realize, originates in a childhood inseparability so powerfully conveyed that, despite its fleeting nature and representation in only a very few pages, it colors the reader's impression of their adult passion and of the rest of the novel. The singularity of being that ensues from the youths' absolute identification comes alive in a series of vivid figures of oneness, union, and merger; these range from the diary entry in which Catherine tells of pinning her and Heathcliff's pinafores together in the arc of the dresser to create a shelter from their oppressors, to recollections of their moorland escapes joined "under [the] shelter" of a single cloak (27, 50). No image, however; is as evocative of their oneness as the enclosed oak-paneled bed that the two share at the Heights until Heathcliff is fourteen and Catherine twelve. This womblike structure, to which the narrative keeps returning at pivotal moments, at once suggests their umbilical closeness, serves as a private "space" within which each can nurture the other's nascent identity, and hints at the highly charged eroticism that will seem to unfold naturally, almost imperceptibly, from these moments of early physical intimacy.

As such an image also suggests, the children seem to share a sibling-like affinity; even their adult passion will retain this sense of a brother–sister relationship. The intimation of kinship, however, is less suggestive of literal incest than of Brontë's attempt to redefine romantic attraction in terms of erotic identification rather than sexual antagonism. One mark of such an intention may lie in a plaintive comment the younger Cathy later makes: "People hate their wives, sometimes; but not their sisters and brothers" (192).[18] Cathy, of course, oversentimentalizes the reality of the typical sibling bond—a wishful fallacy shared by a variety of Victorian novelists including Austen, Dickens, Eliot, and Gaskell, and exposed in Brontë's text by the negative relations of actual brothers and sisters. But Cathy's articulation nonetheless holds an intensely real meaning as a *metaphoric* expression of an alternative to reigning preconceptions of marriage as the union of opposingly gendered, and hence inevitably antagonistic, factions. For, unlike the hatred visible between many husbands and wives, brother and sister ideally participate in a noncombative mode of male–female relationship, one that is unthreatening because gender difference is rendered secondary to the bond of blood-likeness, familiarity, and friendship. By characterizing the future lovers Catherine and Heathcliff as foster siblings, then, Brontë begins to undermine the ideology of sexual attraction embedded in traditional conjugal arrangements.

At the same time, to the degree that the blood tie of kinship points to a common source greater than the difference of gender, sibling "oneness" becomes a symbol for a potential state of psychological integration. Hence, Catherine's youthful representation as Heathcliff's "rough-headed counterpart" (51) has suggested to readers since the novel's publication a working out of the Platonic myth of androgyny: "He and she are, so to speak, but a single person," wrote a French essayist in 1857, "he is the male soul of the monster, she the female."[19] One needs to be careful, however, in applying the slippery term "androgyny" to these two characters. For readings that designate Heathcliff the sundered "masculine" component and Catherine the "female" half of a Platonic (or even "monstrous") whole mistakenly transform the nearly identical personalities of Catherine and Heathcliff into sexually defined opposites. This is precisely the conventional notion of love against which Brontë pits her vision. Rather, what one finds in the young Catherine and Heathcliff are states remarkably free of the constraints typically imposed by social constructions of "masculinity" or "femininity"; theirs is the place of difference vis-à-vis the exacting geography of gender mapped out by their world. Nelly's narration, for example, calls attention time and again to the defiant, unsubmissive side of Catherine's unrestrained childhood personality that has led Patricia Spacks to label her "an anti-heroine, in every respect opposed to her century's ideal prototype of the adolescent woman." Conversely, Gilbert and Gubar have suggestively demonstrated some of the ways in which Heathcliff's youthful status at the Heights—as victim of oppression, as unnamed "it" (39) without rights or birthright, as mediator marking the boundary between natural and cultural realms—replicates the anthropological status of women in patriarchal social organizations. The psychological continuum connecting Catherine and Heathcliff as symbiotic and symbolic twins tantalizingly subverts traditional demarcations of sexual identity.[20]

The affinity that Catherine and Heathcliff discover in the wild Eden of their preadolescent years also has specifically external origins, ones which reinforce Brontë's critique of conventional romantic norms. To the extent that Catherine's real brother, Hindley, mercilessly persecutes them, they are drawn together in empathy and rebellion as equals whose cause lies in human rather than sexual values;[21] to the extent that Hindley totally neglects their upbringing, the two are granted a temporary respite from the socializing pressures of nuclear family life that would more readily fix them in restrictively gendered modes of behavior. The social and psychological freedom that they gain as "unfriended" orphan "creatures" (46) is epitomized in the unconstrained, savage life they lead on the moors, their haven from the values of the dominant order. As such, they inhabit that "free territory" or "wild zone" that recent feminist criticism has made a compelling metaphor for those overlooked gaps in patriarchal logic where invisibility becomes the avenue to autonomy and power.[22] Privy to this "space" as youths, Catherine and Heathcliff, classic outsider figures, become the insiders, free to exist on their beloved moors as self-sufficient allies and unconscious equals who define as their antagonists the world's representatives, not each other.

In opposition to this bond of "like" selves, Brontë uses the social marriage of Catherine and Edgar to depict the consequences of a relationship based on conventional polarity: Catherine's soul is lightning, Linton's moonbeam; her blood feverous, his ice-water (72, 101). Since "opposites" are supposed to attract according to popular love ideology, to surface appearance the newly-wed Lintons have achieved the golden mean requisite to the conventional wedlock ideal. But as the disharmony that erupts upon Heathcliff's return betrays, Catherine and Edgar's conjugal happiness exists only as long as their precarious balancing of disparate wills manages to exclude all conflict or personal desire. Furthermore, this uneasy balance of opposites is doomed because it is rooted in basic inequality. "There were no mutual concessions," Nelly says of Catherine's domineering and Edgar's mild personalities, "one stood erect and the other yielded" (81). Once roles reverse, and Edgar decides to wield his legal right as "master," it will be his preemptory command that Catherine choose between himself and Heathcliff that explodes once and for all Nelly's wishful assertion that they are "in possession of a deep and growing happiness" (81). The sentimental ideal of love, touted as the source of peaceful concord, is thus exposed to be the opposite, a breeding ground of violence and hatred, because its basic premise, the union of contraries, is rooted in a sense of initial and unequal antagonism.

Hindley's marriage to Frances, Isabella's elopement with Heathcliff, and Lockwood's sterile romantic fantasies all reveal a similar lesson: the dominant social order promotes conceptions of love that, whether insipid, erotic, or voyeuristic, allow men access to power through their control of women. It is with the petulant Frances perched on his knee that Hindley feels the strength to begin his retaliatory persecution of Heathcliff. Isabella's illusory conception of Heathcliff as a Byronic "hero of romance" (126), which results in her becoming the sexual instrument of his scheme of revenge, issues in a hatred as destructive as her mistaken love. Lockwood's coolly teasing game of glances with the "fascinating creature" (15) at the seaside prefigures his equally sterile fantasies of becoming the younger Cathy's "favoured possessor" (21). "Something more romantic than a fairy tale it would have been ... had she and I struck up an attachment" (240–41), Lockwood can *safely* fantasize at the very moment he is taking leave of the region. In exposing the politics of sexual power hidden within such "fairy tale[s]" of sentimental romantic "attachment," the novel highlights, by contrast, the radical difference of a love based on likeness and equality.

II

As I have already intimated, the web of interrelationships giving substance to Brontë's critique of love relationship is complemented by an extremely complex narrative structure, one in which the doubling and division of developmental lines of plotting become a powerful agent adding to the novel's uneasy and explosive tensions. On the most apparent level, the division of the text into two halves after its midpoint—the moment of Catherine's death and of the second Cathy's birth in chapter 16—suggests a "classic" double plot structure governed by the sequentially ordered trajectories of mother and daughter. But if one chooses to evaluate the novel's organization in terms of a singular focus on Heathcliff's development, *Wuthering Heights* may appear as *one* continuous plot which overlaps and encloses the generational stories of the two Catherines. Because of this overlapping of developmental structures, a truly synchronous rather than sequential double plot may also be seen operating after chapter 16: the unresolved story of Heathcliff's frustrated love, becoming that of his revenge and agony, develops beside the history of the second Cathy. All these modes of "doubling," moreover, occur within a narrative format in which the disruption of temporal sequence through the use of dual narrators makes the two "halves" of the text seem almost to unfold simultaneously (the latter stages of the second Cathy's history, observed and narrated by Lockwood at the beginning of the novel, are happening while Nelly narrates the history of the first Catherine). The fact that no one has ever been able to argue successfully that only one "plot," or for that matter one character, dominates *Wuthering Heights* should alert us, indeed, to the multivocal principles underlying its structure.[23]

Within this doubling framework, the clash between the desiring self and marital identity is most graphically represented in the bildungsroman variations that structure the mother–daughter history. In contrast to the traditional female bildungsroman, in which the heroine's acquisition of mature identity is confirmed by marriage, the trajectories of courtship and wedlock forming the narrative of the two Catherines become the means of raising profoundly disturbing questions about the social institution of marriage. For by methodically undermining the threshold moments, rites of passage, significant scenes, and climactic actions of conventional romantic fiction, Brontë's text italicizes its damning portrait of the harrowing effects of wedlock on female identity by presenting it in repeating plots that mirror each other in an uneasy blend of parallel and chiasmic structures as disorienting as they are gripping.

The original Catherine first "enters" the text in Lockwood's opening narration not as a living character but as a disembodied name, tracings of which Lockwood finds etched on the windowsill of her former bedchamber: "*Catherine Earnshaw*, here and there varied to *Catherine Heathcliff*, and then again to *Catherine Linton*" (25). These markings not only suggest Catherine's fundamental uncertainty about who she is or will become, but also forecast, in exact order, the successive crises of identity shaping the plot of her life and, in inverse order, her daughter's development from Linton to Earnshaw status. As Lockwood's overnight experience at the Heights opens into

Nelly's retrospective narrative in the immediately following chapter, the text presents the "real" Catherine—as opposed to the tracings that remain on the windowsill—in a fairytale-like tableau equally prophetic of her destiny. Asking her father to bring her a riding whip from Liverpool, a present critics have associated with the "ungirlish" power she delights in wielding, Catherine instead gets HeathCliff.[24] Not insignificantly, then, Nelly's narrative originates in the very event that triggers the most formative stage of Cathy's youthful development—the brief but idyllic blossoming of a rebellious self-sufficiency that unfolds on the moors with Heathcliff as her comrade.

The loss of freedom that brings this narrative stage to a halt at Thrushcross Grange in chapter 6 forms the decisive turning point in Catherine's story and in the novel as a whole. This loss, indeed, is underscored in that the event precipitating it is literally absent from the present-time of Nelly's narration, reported to her only after the fact by Heathcliff.[25] One moment he and Catherine are joined together—another image of their oneness—in the act of spying into the alien, civilized world of the Linton family; the next, forcibly separated as Catherine, wounded by the watchdog Skulker, is detained within. As a significant threshold in the bildungsroman of Catherine's youth, this event ironically reverses the rising pattern of most fictions of female growth: twelve years of age and on the verge of sexual maturation, incapacitated by her wound and forced to undergo a six weeks' confinement, the pubescent Catherine is initiated by the Lintons into superficially appealing modes of "feminine" social privilege—a rite of passage into female sexuality that, significantly, is recorded as a "fall" from the sufficiency of her prior existence.[26] Emerging from her symbolic captivity at the Grange as "quite a beauty ... a lady now" (50–51), Catherine manifests an internal division of self and sexual role that results, as even Nelly notes, in her "adopt[ing] a double character without exactly intending to deceive anyone" (62). For although she and Heathcliff attempt to remain "constant companions still" (63), her feminized self increasingly inclines toward Edgar Linton in what becomes a compressed courtship narrative. The tightly interwoven sequence of action in chapters 7, 8, and 9, charting the gradual evolution of their attraction in face of Heathcliff's prior claim, culminates in Catherine's decision to marry Edgar, her complementary opposite and hence conventionally appropriate suitor. The specific event of Catherine and Edgar's engagement, moreover, is structured to expose their sentimental romance for what it is—a relationship rooted in an antagonism that portends its own violent end. Ironically, it is Catherine's slapping of Edgar in a moment of anger that elicits her suitor's immediate, offstage proposal: "I saw the quarrel had merely effected a closer intimacy," Nelly reports, "... and enabled them ... to confess themselves lovers" (66). One could hardly ask for a more perfect example of the *discordia concors* principle discussed above in chapter 2 as a historical model for traditionally conceived romantic attraction.

Yet strategically juxtaposed with this rapprochement, and antithetical to conventional courtship plotting in several ways, is Catherine's "confessional" speech to Nelly in chapter 9. For what she has to say of her two "suitors" brings to a head the conflict between social role and personal identity that she is undergoing. The dream she reports to Nelly of being cast out of heaven (which she associates with the Grange, Linton's home) and of waking "sobbing for joy" on the "heath" that is her true "home" (and, by synecdoche, Heathcliff) reveals an intuitive recognition of the self-deprivation involved in accepting Edgar (72), as do the contrasting types of language she uses to describe her feelings for both youths. Furthermore, in contrast to the temporary obstructions blocking union in traditional courtship formulas, Catherine's answer to Nelly's question, "All seems smooth and easy—where is the obstacle?", reveals that barrier to be something more than temporary: "*Here!* and *here!* ... in my soul, and in my heart" (71). The obstacle, that is, is her authentic self, which by analogy is also the self of Heathcliff ("Nelly, I am Heathcliff," Catherine continues). It is inevitable, then, that marriage to Edgar spells a permanent alienation from "heath" and "home" for Catherine, canceling the personal sense of wholeness that her bond of identification with Heathcliff has represented.

Given this fact, it is ironically appropriate that the narrative climax of the plot of Catherine's presumed "courtship" should ignore the situation of the betrothed suitors, focusing rather on the psychological impasse created by the sundering of Catherine and Heathcliff's relationship. For when she learns that Heathcliff has run away, Catherine undergoes an immediate *internal* breakdown (mirroring their *external* severance) that leaves her a literally debilitated, more capriciously "feminine" ghost of her former fierce self, "broken" for her place in the marital order. The displacement of the subsequent espousals of Catherine and Edgar to an ambiguously worded, one-sentence paragraph near chapter's end cooperates in upending the rhythm of climax and smooth succession that propels the traditional erotic narrative; the gap of three years that intervenes before the marriage is finalized, moreover, further renders its occurrence anticlimactic by intimating, among other things, that Catherine has been silently, desperately, holding out for Heathcliff's return.

In the wedlock plot that unfolds in the following chapter, the dialectic between marital destiny and selfhood almost instantly resurfaces in acts of psychic and narrative violence. For in Brontë's careful arrangement of Nelly's narrative, the return of Heathcliff is made to seem nearly simultaneous with Catherine's marriage; thus, his mysterious reappearance becomes, like the welling up of the forbidden, an external manifestation of Catherine's hitherto suppressed acknowledgment of her forfeited identity. The geometric configuration that results as Catherine finds herself torn between the demands of her husband and Heathcliff nightmarishly repeats the premarital struggle leading to her emotional collapse in chapter 9. The consequence, again, is internal fragmentation. Locking herself into her bedroom at the end of chapter 11 in a despairing assertion of autonomy, Catherine actually reenacts her self-imprisonment in wed/lock, in the process precipitating a descent into schizophrenia, the ultimate loss of identity. Hence, in the psychodramatic "mad" scene of chapter 12, Catherine is unable to recognize her reflection in the mirror as "Mrs. Linton" (106) because, in becoming Edgar's wife and complement, she has lost her true mirroring self, Heathcliff. It is entirely appropriate, then, that in her mad reveries the "whole last seven years" have grown a "blank"; she returns, in a striking instance of narrative analepsis, to the memory of being "enclosed in the oak-panelled bed" at the Heights and "*laid alone* for the first time.... wrenched from ... my all in all, Heathcliff" (107; emphasis added). This traumatically repressed (and hitherto narratively suppressed) event, it dawns on the reader, was the *immediate* consequence of Catherine's initiation, exactly seven years ago, into the Grange and womanhood. The desire to erase these intervening years and return in memory to an undivided state is less a regressive turning away *from* reality, therefore, than an affirmation of the reality of a lost identity, "savage, and hardy, and free," preexisting the fiction of self she has assumed in marriage; as Catherine says in a statement where madness speaks the words of truth, "I should *be myself* were I once among the heather on those hills" (107; emphasis added). Instead, as "Mrs. Linton, the lady of Thrushcross Grange," the maddened Catherine finds herself inhabiting an alien role in an alien plot as "the wife of a stranger" and as an "exile, and outcast" (107) from her previous life with Heathcliff. Ironically, it is at this point that Edgar finally enters Catherine's sickroom, and her reaction—"I'm past wanting you" (109)—marks a sobering conclusion to the ill-fated narrative of their marriage.

In terms of the bildungsroman structure of the narrative of Catherine's life, the issue of her illness is a "permanent alienation of intellect" (112) and loss of the will to live: like Clarissa Harlowe, Catherine discovers that death, the elimination of self, becomes the only liberation from a fragmented existence. The end of Catherine's devolving trajectory, then, is quite the opposite of the glorified and idealized *Liebestod*, or death-longing, of Continental love literature; her death neither fulfills nor resolves anything, and it simultaneously frustrates the conventional assumption that mature female identity lies in marriage, marking, to the contrary, an ultimate fragmentation of identity.[27] And as a narrative "exit," Catherine's demise not only imposes an unbridgeable chasm between herself and the living Heathcliff but violently ruptures the text at its midpoint, the consequences of which are manifest in the uneasily multiplying levels of narration and nightmare that follow.

Out of this splintering of lives, of text, the novel seems to begin again with the birth of the second Cathy—in a sense, Brontë's third opening, following Lockwood's beginning in chapter 1 and Nelly's in chapter 4. The uncanny doubling of "Catherines" that ensues, creating an atemporal as well as genealogical relation between the two plots, serves to bring into perspectival alignment the unchanging system of oppression against which the violated self must struggle. For within the brackets of Nelly's retelling, the stages of Cathy's growth to adulthood, like Catherine's before her, chart an education into female powerlessness—an education whose inevitable end, as glimpsed in the narrative time occupied by Lockwood, seems to be the embittered self-division of one who "feel[s] like death" (233).

Drawing upon a complex pattern of repetitions and reversals, the second phase of Brontë's demystification of the cultural ideal of sheltered womanhood begins by reversing the literal direction of the first Catherine's trajectory. Thus, the plot of young Cathy's unconscious quest for identity begins where her mother's ended, in the Victorian world of the Grange, and moves toward the Heights. Raised to believe herself everyone's "'love,' and 'darling,' and 'queen,' and 'angel'" (162), Cathy's growing adolescent longing to explore the moors beyond the Grange's walled-in gardens signals a strong unconscious desire to differentiate, to break out of the constraints of a limiting storybook identity (as "'love' and 'darling,'" etc.), and a return of the rebellious spirit that was once her mother's. Cathy's rebellious desires, however, are circumscribed by her Edenic confinement in "innocence," a fact directly linked to the next stage of developmental plotting. It is precisely her inability to recognize "evil," to perceive the network of power controlling the world of the Heights as well as her home, that transforms her eventual escape from the park into an entrance into an even worse prison. Blind to Heathcliff's design in abetting her moorland rambles, Cathy finds herself embroiled in an exploitative affair with her cousin Linton Heathcliff, a "fiction" of romance based on sentimental norms in which the differences that existed between her parents have become totally antithetical extremes. From the first moment of their reacquaintance at the Heights—Cathy's "whole aspect sparkling" and Linton's "languid" (175)—their opposing natures portend mutual disaster. Worse, Cathy's dutiful upbringing, repressing her sparks of self-assertion, traps her in a destructive mode of erotic masochism as she selflessly submits to the misery—and mastery—of Linton's peevish moods.

This courtship variation reaches a climax in a rite of passage as pivotal as the older Catherine's adolescent detainment by the Lintons at the Grange. Mirroring that event in reverse direction, Cathy leaves the Grange world of her youth irrevocably behind as Heathcliff dupes Nelly and herself into crossing the forbidden threshold of the Heights, where they become his literal prisoners. What follows is an unending nightmare as Cathy's most vital relationship (to her dying father) is severed and any sense of autonomy crushed as Heathcliff forces her to agree to marry his son Linton. The plot thus replicates the situation of the first Catherine—confinement in an alien environment, marriage as a tool of self-diminishment—but with a difference that makes clear the social ethos underlying the trials of both: for the older Catherine's more subtle seduction by the trappings of privilege becomes, in the younger Cathy's experience, a blatant rape of her individual will by male-sanctioned powers of authority. And as Cathy's new husband fulfills his father's prophecy that he "can play the little tyrant well" (219) despite his physical weakness, his litanic repetition of the phrase, "It's mine" (223), in a terrifyingly solipsistic speech claiming all of his wife's belongings as his own, confirms the degree to which Cathy's victimization is coterminous with her sex. Through the strategic placement of such unnerving "domestic" scenarios, the patriarchal ideal of wedlock is shown to mask a state of absolute female captivity; the sentimental notion of a complementary union of opposites, exposed as an instrument of sexual domination and a perversion, of human love.

The plot of Cathy's "education" into female adulthood reaches its nadir when after her father's funeral Heathcliff assumes control of the Grange as its new master: "He made no ceremony of knocking or announcing his name; he was master, and availed himself of the master's privilege to walk straight in, without saying a word" (227). Just as the women's crucial threshold entrances have entailed losses of authority, Heathcliff's signifies successful mastery: structure again becomes a comment on gender. By sundering young Cathy from her last familiar associations with this action, Heathcliff willfully perpetuates the pattern of expanding disaster that began with his own separation from Catherine. First held captive against her will, Cathy now becomes, again like her mother, a victim of negative self-enclosure; withdrawal from others becomes at once her only protection and a formidable obstacle to any recovery of her violated self-esteem. In bringing this "story" to a close, Nelly perceives that the only solution (or, textually speaking, resolution) for Cathy lies in the very institution that has debilitated her: "and I can see no remedy at present, unless she could marry again; and that scheme, it does not come within my province to arrange" (236). The irony implicit in this reversal of the expectations associated with marital "schemes" in fictional plotting

could not be greater, for it will take an "arranger" far more innovative than
Nelly—or the writer of conventional romances—to extract Cathy from the
impasse of her deadlocked and deathly situation.

But Cathy's history is only one consequence of her mother's unsettling
death; structurally juxtaposed and intersecting with her linear development
is the adjacent developmental plot of Heathcliff's life following Catherine's
death. Heathcliff's trajectory echoes Catherine's in that external separation—
now made final by death—completes a process of internal division, a "fall"
into what Carolyn Heilbrun has called an "anti-androgynous world."[28] From
an initially marginal and noncategorizable position of difference, Heathcliff
transforms himself after Catherine's death into what Isabella calls "half a
man" (149)—that is, a prototypically "masculine" oppressor who unfeelingly
appropriates people's lives and possessions as a way of avenging himself on
the social caste system responsible for his initial separation from Catherine.[29]
But the final irony is that for all his acquired "power" as master and tyrant,
he also ends up leading an imprisoned inner existence, one epitomized in the
plot of his unceasing unrest in the last half of the novel.

While the dual foci of the novel's second half pit Heathcliff's actions
against those of his primary victim, the younger Cathy, another structural
effect—the splintering of perspective that emerges between the violent
present-time of his revenge and the timeless eternity of his agony—forestalls
a totally negative condemnation of his increasingly diabolic role. For the
more he lives in the past (mourning his lost unity with Catherine) and the
more he anticipates the future (envisioning that opening in time that will
allow their unworldly reunion), Heathcliff is propelled out of a temporal
framework altogether; this technique works to suspend our judgment of his
present actions and to point us instead toward their cause. A vivid example
occurs in chapter 29, where the developmental plots involving Heathcliff and
Cathy jarringly intersect with Heathcliff's crossing the threshold of Cathy's
home as its new master. For the eventfulness of the moment—representing
the ostensible apex of Heathcliff's drive toward revenge in one plot and the
nadir of Cathy's loss of self-possession in the other—is very nearly nonexistent
from Heathcliff's perspective. His mind, rather, is fixed on the unbearable
frustration of his eighteen-year separation from the *other* Catherine, which
has led him the night before, as he confides to Nelly, to reopen her grave in
an impossible attempt to erase the division between the living and the dead
(one recalls Catherine's analogous attempt to erase seven years of time in
chapter 12). Coming to epitomize all the years of unrest that Heathcliff has
suffered without his "life" and "soul" (139), his action is itself a repetition of a
hitherto suppressed narrative event, his parallel attempt to unearth Catherine's

corpse the evening of her burial.[30] The latter structural displacement gains all the more power from the present circumstance of its telling: for, at the greatest moment of his revenge upon the Lintons, Heathcliff is ironically for all purposes *absent*, living entirely in the past moment of Catherine's death. The separation between temporal realms could not be greater, a structurally juxtaposed effect that is reiterated in the following chapter as Nelly's story unexpectedly enters "present" narrative time; the past has caught up with the present that involves Lockwood, yet the Heathcliff whom Lockwood visits in the current novel-time of chapter 31 is by now almost entirely an inhabitant of the past.

These jarring narrative shifts are, of course, part of the novel's larger perspectival structure, in which the temporal and spatial dislocations caused by the presence of multiple narrators ultimately strengthen the reader's awareness of an uneasy past whose effects continue to disrupt the present. For Brontë's complex manipulation of multiple frames of narration not only mediates between reader and text but also works, significantly, to disturb any semblance of the univocal recuperation characteristic of conventional fictional closure. The effect is a tension similar to that created by the division and doubling within the novel's developmental structures.

Such disorientations in perspective predominantly occur as a result of the continual "flashes" of present narrative time that punctuate Nelly's history, forcing the reader to assimilate great leaps in time and space. One such significant dislocating moment occurs when the crisis of chapter 9— Catherine and Heathcliff's separation—is cut short by a return to Lockwood's first-person narration. However brief and seemingly incidental, his account of his illness brings the two narrative levels into sudden, disturbing proximity: the same doctor who treats Catherine the page before is now taking care of Lockwood; Heathcliff, who has just disappeared from the text of Nelly's tale, reappears at Lockwood's bedside. And even more unsettling is Lockwood's failure to connect the living reality of his visitor with the "hero" (80) of the story he immediately asks Nelly to continue, treating the past as an impersonal fiction that does not touch his safe reality. The intrusion of living representatives of the past—Dr. Kenneth, Heathcliff—into current time, of course, underlines the *radically altered* circumstances of the present that have resulted from the cataclysmic rupture of the lovers just narrated.

With the exception of the novel's final chapters, the greatest number of such interruptions in continuity occur in the sequence (chapters 12–15) detailing the stages of Catherine's decline from madness to death. Her internal fragmentation, therefore, is heightened by these jumps back and forth in the spatial and temporal frames. A further dislocation occurs when at the beginning of chapter 15 the reader suddenly learns that Lockwood is no longer listening to, but retelling, what has been told him; Nelly has finished her tale, which, "only a little condensed" (130), Lockwood now claims to pass faithfully on to his audience, a decentering device whereby the once-removed past becomes twice-removed, qualifying still further the judgments of its various narrators.[31] In contrast to the spatial fragmentation of the Catherine plot, the trajectory of young Cathy's experience forms an almost unbroken narrative line of descent into nightmare—the horror of which is brought home to the reader, with a shock, with Nelly's interjected comment, "These things happened last winter, sir" (204). Upon Heathcliff's removal of Cathy from Nelly's field of observation, her narration (temporarily kept in motion by the insertion of Zillah's account of Cathy's miserable life at the Heights) necessarily draws to an inconclusive close. "Thus ended Mrs. Dean's story," Lockwood recounts, then promptly decides to bring his sojourn in the region to an "end" as well, an act simultaneously terminating his own narrative.

Yet it is Lockwood's "re-entrance" into the text in chapter 32—the novel's fourth "beginning"—that reopens the spatial structure of the novel as well as the temporal possibility of more story. The opening of the chapter, marked by the date "1802," circles the reader back to the novel's first sentence, also designated by a date, "1801." The events enclosed within this year-long cycle are thus shut away, so to speak, into the past, while the chapters that follow form a separate unit that in fact becomes an eerie repetition, in miniature, of the *whole* novel: Lockwood comes to the region; Nelly tells him another two-part story (this time, of the young lovers Cathy and Hareton and of the strange death of Heathcliff); Lockwood passes judgment and leaves. Once again, a kind of sequential double plotting is achieved as the novel seems to repeat itself, with the significant difference that this doubling-back simultaneously functions as coda and conclusion to all that has gone before—a conclusion, as we shall now see, that maintains a doubleness worthy of Brontë's radical rewriting of the traditional love-plot.

III

It is commonly said that *Wuthering Heights* consists of two endings, not necessarily reconcilable, in its dual movement toward earthly and unearthly union.[32] In chapter 32, Nelly recounts for the returned Lockwood (who has already stumbled into Cathy and Hareton reading together) the story of the young couple's courtship, which she ends with a prototypically Victorian affirmation of wedlock ("The crown of all my wishes will be the union of these two" [250]). Nelly's conventional hopes, however, should not necessarily pass as Bronze's own, as they have for generations of critics. The critical gesture of summarily dismissing the Cathy–Hareton romance as "a rather sugary frill" unconsciously repeats the sexism underlying Thomas Moser's judgment that its love interest is "simply a superficial stereotyped tale of feminine longings" belonging "with countless pieces of sub-literary fiction in women's magazines."[33] In contrast to such views, I would like to suggest that this final love story is essential to the revisionary cast of Bronze's structural and thematic designs. Not only does the anticipation of this union, happy as it is, strategically share narrative time with the very different plot of Heathcliff's end; its paradigm of romantic bonding equally serves, as we shall see, to propel the narrative forward into an unknown and unwritten future.

In crucial ways Cathy and Hareton's relationship hauntingly evokes yet revises that of the first generation of lovers. Like their forebears, they also come to share an attraction grounded in affinities of situation and inherited similarities of temperament—"opposition" between them is a mistaken, not an elementally gendered, condition. Foremost, as Heathcliff's victims, both discover an essential sameness in their experiences of degradation: the widowed Cathy's stultifying captivity at the Heights, echoing her mother's adult deprivations at the Grange, parallels Hareton's keenly suffered entrapment in brutish ignorance, a condition that Heathcliff perversely enforces in order to repeat his own debasement at Hindley's hands. Hence, since both youths have been stripped of their rightful identities by Heathcliff, the first stage of their growth toward mutual love details, appropriately, how each becomes the other's avenue to regained autonomy. Hareton serves as Cathy's lifeline to the world of the living as she finally breaks out of her self-imprisoning despair to acknowledge his presence for the first time, simultaneously admitting her sense of loss and static self-enclosure: "Oh, I'm tired—I'm *stalled*, Hareton!" (237). In a parallel movement, Hareton's yearning to escape his own "stalled" condition ("Will you ask her to read to us, Zillah? I'm stalled of doing naught" [235]) reaches a poignant climax when Cathy teaches him to read, an act of mental liberation (not of feminization, as too many critics have claimed)[34] that symbolically gives Hareton back his robbed identity as he learns to spell his name, Earnshaw, inscribed above the Heights' entrance. Likewise, it should be noted—to counter critics leaping to "obvious" interpretations of "Freudian" symbols—that Brontë does not rob Hareton of his phallic potency when he chooses to forego his gun and pipe for Cathy's company; rather, he is stripped of his *learned* masculine defenses, of the tactics of withdrawal into a privileged male realm, that have stood in the way of his achievement of adult humanity.

Second, the sameness binding the second generation of lovers is also registered in their kinship as cousins, a literal "return" of the sibling ideal once uniting Heathcliff and Catherine. The structure of the sequence in chapter 32 leading to the convergence of the two—both tellingly identified by Nelly as "my children" (254)—makes clear the link between blood-like affinity and romantic love in the novel's revisionary erotics. Breaking from feminine norms of passivity by actively campaigning for Hareton's attentions, Cathy first presses upon him the claim of actual kinship ("I should like you to be my cousin now"), then follows it with the claim of friendship ("And you'll be my friend?"). A paragraph later the two have become "sworn allies" and thence, in Nelly's proleptic summation, declared lovers whose minds, "tending to the same point, contrived ... to reach it" (247–49). If the ensuing childlike playfulness of the lovers is worlds removed from the tumultuous and troubled passion of the first generation, hence more "conventional," its calm register should not negate for the reader the radical difference that their love, tempered by the context of their preceding oppression, has made: in Brontë's vision, identification with rather than against each other has created a common ground, transcending normative boundaries of class and gender, that allows for the rebirth of childlike joy, the foundation of a new Eden of possibility located in the world rather than on the moors, that is aptly signified by the lovers' playful (but never again naive) innocence.

Therefore, as friends who share a natural and erotic affinity that does not deny their differences, as adults and equals not defined solely in terms of gender roles, and, finally, as comrades in a common cause against Heathcliff's tyranny, Cathy and Hareton create a relationship that goes far in repudiating the Victorian stereotype of ethereal love. In its place their hard-earned alliance gives birth to a dynamic ideal, one that like Brontë's narrative is neither "stalled" nor rigidly defined but poised on the brink of realization. Hence the end is also a beginning for these two lovers. Planning to marry on New Year's Day, they will leave the Heights behind to begin the future in a new year and a new world in which nothing is certain but the united strength of their alliance. "*They* are afraid of nothing," Lockwood grudgingly admits, as Cathy and Hareton ramble into the Heights and out of his narration: "Together they would brave Satan and all his legions" (265–66). In a final movement worthy of the text's manifold entrances and openings, Cathy and Hareton prepare to cross the threshold of an open future.

This sense of visionary possibility, however, is posited against a very different kind of fulfillment simultaneously occurring in Nelly's tale of Heathcliff's "'queer' end" (245), one that presupposes a mode of irresolution in which ambiguity and unrest predominate. Again, the message lies in the structural sequence, for the organization of chapters 33 and 34 demonstrates that Heathcliff cannot achieve his desired reunion in death with Catherine as long as he lives to avenge himself on his enemies and thus tacitly accepts a definition of manhood antithetical to the united difference he once shared with Catherine. Appropriately, then, it is the doubled visual image of his lost love, reflected in the newly allied Cathy and Hareton, that leads to Heathcliff's abjuration of revenge and makes possible his unearthly reunion: "[T]hey lifted their eyes together to encounter Mr. Heathcliff," Nelly tells Lockwood, "Perhaps you have never remarked that their eyes are precisely similar, and they are those of Catherine Earnshaw.... I supposed this resemblance disarmed Mr. Heathcliff (254).[35] Within minutes, Heathcliff confesses that "I don't care for striking, I can't take the trouble to raise my hand ... where is the use?" (255). In proportion to the lessening grip of his constricting obsession with mastery, the "disarmed" and metaphorically unmanned Heathcliff conversely expands in a newly receptive passivity that, in rewriting the erotic dynamic of traditional novelistic terms of masculine "fulfillment," will *make possible* his and Catherine's reunion. "*I am swallowed* in anticipation of its fulfillment" (256; emphasis added), he thus says as he acquiesces to the promise of death and reunion.

The two final days of Heathcliff's life, recounted in chapter 34, record the surreal process by which the "other" world, where Catherine waits, moves into and begins to coexist with commonplace reality for a few moments before reversing direction and leading Heathcliff outward in its wake. For, as the window "swinging open" (264) by his deathbed—Catherine's enclosed bed—suggests, death has become that opening in the wall, a final entrance into another and uncertain realm where their twin phantoms ceaselessly roam the moors. Resting neither in heaven nor in hell, they occupy, once again, the purgatorial "wild zone" that once made possible their most essential selves. While the Heathcliff plot thus attains an aesthetically satisfying close, the fact that such satisfaction comes at the expense of life underlines, in a way no reader can ignore, the severity of the actual conditions that have made fulfillment impossible in his and Catherine's lives: if the tenor of their doomed desire ultimately seems metaphysical, it has been raised to such a pitch by the specifically cultural and psychological origins of their tragedy. This sense of thwarted love haunts the text in the concluding hints of unease—do their ghosts *really* roam the moors?—that can never be answered.

Not only do these conclusions in earthly union and unearthly reunion play off each other, but the several self-contradicting denouements offered by each narrator also prevent *Wuthering Heights* from resolving into a univocal pattern. Both Nelly and Lockwood attempt—for their own peace of minds— to impose closed patterns on the sequence of final events. Nelly, for example, first offers Lockwood the closed, conventionally worded assurance of the young lovers' bliss at the end of chapter 32; then she moves on to narrate Heathcliff's "poor conclusion" (254) in the final chapter, at first expressing the hope that Heathcliff rests "soundly" in his grave but qualifying and unsettling her own interpretation as she relates the rumors that his and Catherine's ghosts walk the moors (265). Lockwood's narrative voice resumes, and he too first turns to the lovers, as if confirming one type of plot, yet he also moves on to the concurrent plot involving the first generation as he visits their graves. Here, like Nelly, he also attempts to paint a reconciliatory picture of repose. But, again like Nelly, he qualifies his own attempt in the penultimate moment of closure; for his dismissal of "unquiet slumbers" for "the sleepers in that quiet earth" (266) is belied by the supernatural imagery inundating the novel's final paragraph—moths, harebells, and soft wind all signify the presence of restless ghosts in folklore.[36] This repeating pattern of assertion followed by qualification in Nelly and Lockwood's final statements, in itself meticulously crafted and aesthetically perfect, holds Brontë's text in open suspension to its very end.

Thus, Heathcliff's entrance into an undefined and indefinable perpetuity in death, like Cathy and Hareton's movement across the threshold of a visionary future in life, ultimately turns outward to the reader, who is left to grapple with the thematic reverberations emanating from the repeating, multiple levels of structure in the novel; the final diffusion of both sets of protagonists into worlds beyond the text suggests at once the deathly hazards of identity razed by societal and sexual expectations and left forever uneasy, and the possibility of a mode of love that by guaranteeing autonomy and mutuality may create a new world. Suspending the promise of the one union against the ghostly reverberations of the other, Brontë instills in her text a difference, and in its ending an endless double movement, that reaffirms her unorthodox vision of a love that is passionate—and yet more.

NOTES

15. See, respectively, the reviews in the *Examiner*, January 1848, and in the *Britannia*, January 1848, rpt. in Allott, pp, 220, 223.

16. Review, *Britannia*, rpt. in Allott, p. 225.

17. Emily Brontë, *Wuthering Heights*, Norton Critical Edition (New York: W.W. Norton, 1972), p. 41. All further references to this work appear in the text.

18. Young Cathy's statement, significantly, is made in response to her cousin Linton Heathcliff's possessive desire to make her his wife in order to ensure himself of her total loving devotion. Hypotheses of Heathcliff and Catherine's passion as incestuous hinge on interpretations of Heathcliff as Mr. Earnshaw's bastard (and hence given the name of an Earnshaw son who died in infancy).

19. Émile Montégut, Review, *Revue des deux mondes*, 1 July 1857, rpt. in Allott, pp. 377–78. For contemporary echoes, see Adrienne Rich, "Jane Eyre: The Temptations of a Motherless Woman," *Ms.*, October 1973, p. 68, and Heilbrun, *Toward a Recognition of Androgyny* (New York: Harper Colophon, 1973), p. 80.

20. Patricia Spacks, *The Female Imagination* (New York: Avon, 1972) p. 171; Gilbert and Gubar, p. 293.

21. A similar point is made by Arnold Kettle, *An Introduction to the English Novel* (New York: Harper and Row, 1967), pp. 135, 143, and Inga-Stina Ewbank, *Their Proper Sphere: A Study of the Brontë Sisters as Early Victorian Female Novelists* (Cambridge MA: Harvard University Press, 1966), pp. 88–89.

22. See Showalter's use of these terms in "Criticism in the Wilderness," in *Writing and Sexual Difference*, special issue of *Critical Inquiry* 8 (1981): 199–201. She adapts them from Edwin Ardener, who derives the term "the wild" from his analysis of Bakweri tribal customs involving rites of female maturation in "Belief and the Problem of Women," pp. 6–7, and "The 'Problem' Revisited," p. 23, both in *Perceiving Women: The Nature of Woman in Society*, ed. Shirley Ardener (New York: Oxford University Press, 1977).

23. Garrett insightfully summarizes several of these versions of viewing the text's doubleness on pp. 18–19.

24. See Gilbert and Gubar, p. 265.

25. The significance of this moment can be measured in its uncanny repetition at several other crucial junctures in the plot structure. A close reading reveals that it has *already* been anticipated in the diary entry that Lockwood reads in the pivotal chapter 3, where Catherine announces her and Heathcliff's intention to rebel against Hindley's tyranny by escaping to the moors under the dairymaid's cloak. Heathcliff's reference to the same cloak in his account of the evening's outcome to Nelly, in chapter 6, becomes the reader's one clue linking the two accounts as parts of the same evening's sequence. Catherine indirectly returns to this moment in the pivotal mad scene of chapter 12, as we shall also see.

26. See Gilbert and Gubar on Catherine's Satanic "fall" from a patriarchal heaven, pp. 271–78.

27. T. E. Apter points to the critique of the *Liebestod* theme in "Romanticism and Romantic Love in *Wuthering Heights*," in *The Art of Emily Brontë*, ed. Anne Smith (New York: Barnes and Noble, 1976), p. 109, as do Gilbert and Gubar, p. 284.

28. Heilbrun, *Androgyny*, p. 81.

29. These points are echoed in Carol Ohmann, "Emily Brontë in the Hands of Male Critics," *College English* 32 (1971): 913, and Carolyn V. Platt, "'Their Eyes are Precisely Similar': Androgyny in *Wuthering Heights*," unpublished article (written while author was with the Women's Studies Program, San Diego State University, 1977), p. 12.

30. In turn, this revelation displaces Isabella's version of Heathcliff's brutish behavior on the evening of Catherine's burial (an inserted narrative flashback occurring in chapter 17). In "The Place of Love in *Jane Eyre* and *Wuthering Heights*," *The Brontës: A Collection of Critical Essays*, ed. Ian Gregor (Englewood Cliffs NJ: Prentice-Hall, 1970), pp. 90–92, Mark Kinkead-Weekes demonstrates how these deliberately juxtaposed accounts form a "radical reinterpretation of the whole story," throwing new light on Heathcliff's suffering.

31. With Catherine's death there ensues another fissure in the temporal structure as Nelly muses to Lockwood about Catherine's heavenly reward. Her wishful impression at the time—"I see a repose that neither earth nor hell can break"—gives way to a direct question to Lockwood: "Do you believe such people *are* happy in the other world, sir? ... I fear we have no right to think she is" (pp. 137–38). A disturbing enough reflection by itself, the remark is immediately juxtaposed with Heathcliff's reaction at the (past) time of Catherine's death, "May she wake in torment!" (p. 139). Again, the superimposition of perspectives transports the unresolved disturbances of the past into the present.

32. See, for example, Ewbank's assertion that "We are left at the end with ... two movements [that] are not at any point fused, but remain counterpointed" (p. 126), and Alan Loxterman's argument for "two distinct endings ... which result from contradictory

types of love" that create an "ambiguous suspension" at the text's end, in *"Wuthering Heights* as Romantic Poem and Victorian Novel," in *A Festschrift for Professor Marguerite Roberts*, ed. Freida Elaine Penniger (Richmond VA: University of Richmond Press, 1976), p. 97. Critics typically attempt to assert the priority of one event over the other, sometimes suggesting that they represent antithetical comedic and tragic patterns, at other times suggesting that the one is conventionally "closed" but the other less so.

33. Peter Grudin, *"Wuthering Heights*: The Question of Unquiet Slumbers," *Studies in the Novel* 6 (1974): 396, and Thomas Moser, "Whatever is the Matter with Emily Jane? Conflicting Impulses in *Wuthering Heights*," *Nineteenth Century Fiction* 17 (1962): 15, respectively. Ironically, several feminist critics have joined Moser in reviling the ending, but for opposite reasons: where he sees a symbolic castration of "masculine" creative energy at work, they have criticized the Hareton–Cathy union for emulating Victorian patriarchal values (see Spacks, p. 172, Gilbert and Gubar, pp. 299–301, and Heilbrun, *Androgyny*, p. 82). In counterpoint to both these extremes, Q. D. Leavis in *Lectures in America* (London: Chatto and Windus, 1969), pp. 119, 130, *praises* the ending for normalizing the relation of the sexes by returning male power to Hareton. All these critics err, I believe, in taking Nelly's word at face value. Readings more congenial to my own include Platt, above, whose viewpoint has greatly influenced my own, and, from a less specifically gendered viewpoint, Arnold Shapiro, *"Wuthering Heights* as Victorian Novel," *Studies in the Novel* 1 (1969): 285.

34. On Hareton's symbolic emasculation by "civilization," see Moser, p. 15; Van Ghent, pp. 169–70; and Richard Chase, "The Brontës or Myth Domesticated," in *Forms of Modern Fiction*, ed. William Van O'Connor (Minneapolis: University of Minnesota Press, 1948), p. 108.

35. Platt, p. 22, also makes this point.

36. See Grudin's careful summary, pp. 389, 404, of these folkloric signifiers.

REGINA BARRECA

The Power of Excommunication:
Sex and the Feminine Text in
Wuthering Heights

Nelly Dean [sat] sewing and singing a song, which was always interrupted from within, by harsh words of scorn and intolerance, uttered in far from musical accents.

'Aw'd rayther, by th'haulf, hev'em swearing i'my lugs frough morn tuh neeght, nur hearken yeh, hahsiver!' said the tenant of the kitchen, in answer to an unheard speech of Nelly's. It's a blazing shaime, ut Aw cannut oppen t'Blessed Book, bud yah set up them glories tuh Sattan, unall t' flaysome wickedness ut iver wer born intuh t'warld! ... O, Lord, judge'em, fur they's norther law nor justice among wer rullers!'

'No! or we should be sitting in flaming fagots, I suppose,' retorted the singer. 'But wisht, old man, and read your Bible like a Christian, and never mind me. This is "Fairy Annie's Wedding"—a bonny tune—it goes to a dance.'[1]

'Read your Bible like a Christian and never mind me', is Nelly Dean's reply to Joseph's 'interruption from within'. Nelly will continue to sing. In doing so, she continues to create an alternative, feminine text which forms a parallel to Joseph's punitive, stuttered threats. Nelly's song, like the other texts created by the female characters of *Wuthering Heights*, indicates an appropriation of the power of language which women then use as an instrument of control

---

From *Sex and Death in Victorian Literature*, Regina Barreca, ed. pp. 227–240. © 1990 Regina Barreca.

against the dominant order. They appropriate the power of inscription. They invert the paradigmatic system in which women are absorbed and oppressed by the unavoidably patriarchal nature of language. In other words, it is the female characters of *Wuthering Heights* who create and shape all the language play of the text. Women in Brontë's novel take control of language, in much the same way as they take control of sex—and for the same reasons. They claim the authority of the 'author'—the initiator and the inscriber; they usurp the male prerogative. They create a system of feminine 'excommunication', whereby they appropriate discourse and desire, surrounding the patriarchal text, so to speak and render it ineffective, if not obsolete.

'Excommunication' here has a number of implications: 'ex' indicates the heretical, unacceptable nature of the action, its expulsion by standing order; 'ex' also indicates the idea of formerly belonging to the standing order, but now remaining out of or above the boundaries of that order. I would like to suggest picturing the female characters of *Wuthering Heights* as forming a circle—or frame—outside of but completely around the male characters and, by association, the patriarchal society presented in the text. The system of feminine discourse in this book is expelled from, existing outside of, but more powerful than the traditional script: the female characters are the only ones who have the ability, desire and will to speak, write and sing. Joseph, muttering overseer of the dominant ideology, has his text overwritten by Nelly's song, in much the same way that Catherine writes all over the blanks of her New Testament, creating a much newer, much more personal testament than the one she had been given. Filling up the empty spaces of the one with her own words, she literalises the conventional phrase: 'Catherine Earnshaw, her book'.

It is important to note the strategies women use to control narrative in the text. Wuthering Heights is a place where women possess the means of 'illumination' and the means of access to language, where: 'the females were already astir: Zillah urging the flames up the chimney with a colossal bellows, and Mrs Heathcliff, kneeling on the hearth, reading a book by the aid of a blaze' (pp. 36–7). Gilbert and Gubar see Nelly acting 'throughout the novel as a censorious agent of patriarchy' (Gilbert and Gubar, p. 292) and Kavanagh spends much of his time enlarging on this idea. He argues that Nelly is the primary instrument by which patriarchal law and lineage are kept intact. Using Jane Gallop's theories on the phallic Mother to support his claim, Kavanagh argues that: 'for the woman, the control of language and writing provides a kind of counter-phallic power which surreptitiously ... channels libidinal energies through social ambitions...' (Kavanagh, p. 20), but will identify writing solely with the processes of sublimation. He links Catherine with the 'effete Lockwood' in using 'literacy and sublimation as indicators of a class difference ...' in opposition to Heathcliff whom Kavanagh names the most 'radically disruptive' character (p. 20).

However, an argument can be made that in *Wuthering Heights*, the power to write and speak are evidence of women's power, not women's subjection. The female characters are the subjects, not the objects, of the discourse. They challenge the male characters by creating texts that exist in opposition to the prevailing ideology. They make use of the books they are given, 'though not altogether for a legitimate purpose', as Lockwood notes (Brontë, p. 24) since the 'treasure' of the texts for the female characters are the blanks, the absences, where they can inscribe themselves and therefore alter the texts they have been given. The most important language distinctions in *Wuthering Heights* are not based on class but on gender.

In *Desire and Domestic Fiction*, Nancy Armstrong argues that certain scenes out of *Wuthering Heights* are 'definitely outside of culture' (Armstrong, p. 180). She can in fact find no grounds for the traditional assumption that the Brontës 'found writing a repressive mechanism' (p. 189). Adapting Armstrong's argument for the purposes of this discussion, it can be seen that Emily Brontë's own 'excommunication' from traditional discourse is the source of her power with language:

> Their marginal relationship to the tradition of letters gave the Brontës access to an entirely different body of knowledge that by its very nature disrupted the life of the parlor. (Armstrong, p. 190)

Armstrong continues that 'the Brontës had to dismantle' the language of social behaviour (p. 192) in order to tell a 'tale told by a woman ... a history of sexuality' (p. 197). The prevailing language of *Wuthering Heights* is paradoxically, not the language of the law but the 'not altogether ... legitimate' language of the letter, the song and the story.

Women are always inscribing themselves in Emily Brontë's text. Catherine is characterised by her persistent and disruptive commentary: 'her tongue was always going—singing, laughing and plaguing everybody ... a wild, wick slip she was ...' (Brontë, p. 51). When the curate gives her passages from the scriptures to learn as punishment, Catherine immediately and instinctively turns this punishment to her own advantage since the texts are simple for her to absorb: '... punishment grew a mere thing to laugh at. The curate might set as many chapters as he pleased for Catherine to get by heart...' (p. 57). (Catherine does not, in fact, seem to share the idea that Gilbert and Gubar attribute to Emily Brontë: '... education for Emily Brontë is almost always fearful, even agonizing ...' (Gilbert and Gubar, p. 275). Catherine's daughter

is tellingly described as 'a second edition of the mother' (Brontë, p. 188), and
Cathy effectively inherits her mother's possession of the text. It should come
as no surprise that 'ere the tiny thing could stammer a word' Cathy wields 'a
despot's sceptre in her father's heart' (p. 226). She has 'curiosity and a quick
intellect' (p. 232) and a desire to use language for her own end; she sends
letters to Linton for her own pleasure: 'playthings and trinkets ... transmuted
into bits of folded paper' (p. 274). Cathy defies Hareton who tries to steal
her books by announcing that 'I've most of them written on my brain and
printed in my heart and you cannot deprive me of those' (p. 364). Cathy is
territorial when it comes to her possession of language. She threatens Joseph
by telling him that 'his library should pay for hers' (p. 383) should he tamper
with her books. And Cathy tells stories to the ultimate story-teller, Nelly.
Nelly is often reduced to 'the censorious agent of patriarchy' (Gilbert and
Gubar, p. 292) even though she is acknowledged as having 'a keen literary
consciousness' (p. 291). But Nelly's relationship to the spoken and written
word should not be summarily dismissed. Nelly has herself 'read more than
you would fancy ... You could not open a book in this library that I have not
looked into, and got something out of also ...' (Brontë, p. 78), bringing herself
to the texts, and 'getting out' of them what she desires. Most importantly,
Nelly has in her possession the unwritten, contraband history of folklore,
songs and ballads. Cathy can 'charm' Linton with this feminine inheritance
of songs—'your songs, Ellen' (p. 302), and so control a situation. Even the
less obviously rebellious female characters create texts. Isabella's letters are
vivid documents that serve as revisions of the romances she had been taught
to read and not to question. It can be argued that Isabella married Heathcliff,
as Gilbert and Gubar note, because she 'has been taught to believe in coercive
literary conventions' (Gilbert and Gubar, p. 288). Yet when Isabella learns to
question, however, she begins to narrate her own story in a letter to Nelly
and so reinscribes and dislodges the inherited convention. She learns to use
the power of language against Heathcliff, who resorts to the use of violence
against Isabella. Also using language to fight is Zillah, the servant who, 'not
daring to attack her master ... turned her vocal artillery against' him (Brontë,
p. 21). The passing on of an otherly-inherited language subverts the male
text; an inheritance of 'old songs ... nursery lore' (p. 280) drowns out the
old testaments by writing across their curriculum, so to speak. Women,
having been given only the blanks, fill those blanks with—quite literally—a
vengeance:

> Catherine's library was select, and its state of dilapidation proved
> it to have been well used, though not altogether for a legitimate
> purpose; scarcely one chapter had escaped a pen-and-ink com-

mentary—at least, the appearance of one—covering every morsel of blank that the printer had left. (Brontë, p. 24)

The male characters, in contrast, can barely articulate their simplest thoughts. Although Lockwood, as the nominal narrator, is inevitably associated with the discourse that would link Brontë's novel itself with the production of patriarchal and repressive texts, he in fact can only hand over Nelly's story. Nelly recognises the fact that Lockwood will inevitably misread her 'you'll judge as well as I can, all these things; at least, you'll think you will, and that's the same' (p. 227). As a narrator, he is sadly in need of invention; he is publisher rather than writer. He is a conduit for the true narrative constructed by women, rather than, as Eagleton implies, the powerful voice that can at times 'clearly ... confiscate' not only Nelly's discourse, but Emily Brontë's own voice (Eagleton, p. 118). At the beginning of Chapter X, for example, Lockwood is capable of reducing Nelly's story to the following:, 'I can recollect [the story's] chief incidents, as far as she had gone. Yes, I remember her hero had run off, and never been heard of for three years: and the heroine was married' (Brontë, p. 112). Lockwood must rely on the fact that 'looks have language' since he cannot bring himself to declare his affections in words to the unnamed woman to whom he is attracted (p. 7). Men cannot speak their desire in *Wuthering Heights*: they can barely acknowledge it.

Heathcliff appears entirely separated from language, having, as Stevie Davies notes, 'no mother country and no mother tongue' (Davies, p. 118). Heathcliff enters the Earnshaw household repeating over and over again 'some gibberish that nobody could understand' (Brontë, p. 44) and he grows up little minding 'what tale was told' as long as he 'had what he wanted' (p. 49). Heathcliff, 'deprived ... of the instructions of the curate' (p. 56), cannot keep pace with Catherine's learning: 'He struggled long to keep up an equality with Catherine in her studies and yielded with poignant though silent regret; but he yielded completely ...' (p. 84). Catherine is impatient with his silence, and lets him know that 'It is no company at all, when people know nothing and say nothing' (p. 86). Even as an adult, Heathcliff is given to garbled, guttural responses; Isabella can only 'guess' that he utters certain words because 'his voice was hardly intelligible' (p. 223).

Perhaps the most telling incident involving Heathcliff and language occurs when Heathcliff 'is impatient and proposes' that he and Catherine 'should appropriate the dairy woman's cloak, and have a scamper on the moors ...' (p. 26). It is not coincidence that Heathcliff proposes this, as Catherine's diary indicates, right after she 'reached this book, and a pot of ink from a shelf, and pushed the house-door ajar to give me light, and I have got the time on with writing for twenty minutes; but my companion is impatient

...' (p. 26). While Kavanagh believes this scene shows that Heathcliff pulls 'Catherine away from her own book ... pulling her from sublimation ... to her own sexuality' (Kavanagh, p. 19), I believe we can more accurately read this scene as providing an outline of Heathcliff's fear and frustration at Catherine's desire and ability to write. This scene represents Heathcliff's struggle to have Catherine 'appropriate' a proper feminine garment to replace her inappropriate appropriation of the masculine text.

It is true that, in contrast to Heathcliff, Edgar Linton is often associated with books. Yet Edgar remains separated from the texts he owns; unlike Nelly, who steals his language and makes it her own, the owner of the library simply 'shuts himself up among books that he never opened'. He is emblematic of the commodification of literature that identifies libraries as evidence of conspicuous consumption rather than evidence of imagination or intelligence. Like Lockwood, he is the nominal owner, rather than the creator or 'true' possessor of texts. Edgar will not write; he refuses to correspond with Isabella despite his sister's earnest plea, or Nelly's request (Brontë, p. 147). Edgar, like Joseph, is purveyor of inert texts, of little use to Catherine who has a far more active relationship with language than her husband.

Unlike his father Hindley, who is at least understandable, Hareton Earnshaw speaks to Isabella 'in a jargon' she 'did not comprehend' (p. 167), and he can barely comprehend Cathy's language when he first meets her: '... comprehending precious little of the fluent succession of remarks and questions which her tongue never ceased pouring forth' (p. 237). Hareton is 'too awkward to speak' (p. 238) and he must be told to 'say your words slowly and keep your hands out of your pockets' (p. 266). Hareton has no ability to read 'damnable writing', while of course Cathy can not only read it but also wants to know 'why it's there' (p. 268). Hareton is finally taught to read by Cathy, who trains him to sound words properly the way you might teach a dog to beg: by offering him attention when he comes close to completing the act effectively. She teaches him the letters of his own name. Could it not be argued, in fact, that Hareton's inability to name himself through writing is in direct contrast to the elder Catherine, who named herself over and over again by writing various surnames in the wood of the windowsill? In any event, young Cathy is keeping close watch over her language. Cathy does not want Hareton to 'appropriate what is mine, and make it ridiculous ... with his vile mistakes and mispronunciations' (p. 365). She claims language, 'damnable writing', as her own. Linton Heathcliff, it is true, does write, but Nelly, with her finely critical response, reads and dismisses Linton's prose as 'very worthless trash' by 'decomposing' it in a detailed textual analysis, declaring that his letters to Cathy are: 'odd compounds of ardor and flatness; commencing in strong feeling and concluding in the affected, wordy way

...' (p. 275). Linton complains to Cathy that 'it tired me dreadfully, writing those long letters...' (p. 288) in much the same way as he says, 'No—don't kiss me. It takes my breath ...' (p. 288). For Linton, the kisses and composition desired by Cathy are equally fearful and unappealing. He equates feminine inscription with feminine sexuality and fears both. In fact, he fears, as well he might, that Cathy has the power to kiss him—or write him—to death.

Joseph is the primary instrument behind the 'fouling of language' that annoys Cathy. He is the self-proclaimed agent of patriarchal discourse which, of course, pretends to be a totalising and just system. He is fiercely didactic and unrelentingly unintelligible: a combination that suggests that the dominant ideology is hardly to be respected. Joseph believes in the Bible, in sermons and in the laws of inheritance. He is terrified of women. They represent the refusal of his dogma; they are inherently dangerous. They can, as Catherine did, tear 'th'back off "The Hemut uh Salvation"' (p. 26). Yet it is her language, written and spoken, that is impeccable; he is barely intelligible. In the first chapter, Joseph accuses Cathy of witchcraft; she laughing agrees that she is indeed a sorceress. Calling him 'a scandalous old hypocrite', the first action she uses to verify his verdict is to reach for a book:

> 'Stop, look here, Joseph,' she continued, taking a long, dark book from a shelf. 'I'll show you how far I've progressed in the Black Art—I shall soon be competent to make a clear house of it. The red cow didn't die by chance; and your rheumatism can hardly be reckoned among providential visitations!'
>
> 'Oh, wicked, wicked!' gasped the elder, 'may the Lord deliver us from evil!'
>
> 'No, reprobate! you are a castaway—be off, or I'll hurt you seriously! I'll have you all modelled in wax and clay; and the first who passes the limits I fix, shall—I'll not say what he shall be done to—but, you'll see! Go, I'm looking at you!' The little witch put a mock malignity into her beautiful eyes, and Joseph, trembling with sincere horror, hurried out praying and ejaculating 'wicked' as he went. (p. 18)

In a carefully constructed inversion of the patriarchal code, Cathy sets the limits beyond which Joseph cannot go; she laughs at his 'ejaculation' of curses. She joyfully accepts excommunication from his domain and sets up her own.

She looks him in the eye and steals his definition of her, embracing rather than refusing his condemnation, and so usurping his power to name and thereby confine her. Looking him in the eye doubles her act of defiance; Armstrong notes, in obvious reference to Lacan, that the female characters of *Wuthering Heights* profoundly, disturb the male characters by returning their gaze, and 'so violate the aesthetically grounded notion of desire as they become the signs of the active female self' (Armstrong, p. 196). Cathy's response to Joseph echoes a gesture made by her mother, Catherine, years before: when chastised by Joseph for not seeing that there are 'good books enough if ye'll read 'em' (Brontë, p. 26), Catherine immediately goes to her own book and writes. Women reach for pots of ink and paper when men threaten them. The ghostly figure of the child Catherine pushes her books on to Lockwood even though he had 'hurriedly piled the books in a pyramid against' her. He might believe he is protected by these volumes, but he is mistaken: 'the pile of books moved as if thrust forward' (p. 31). Catherine controls the texts.

Men reach for weapons or clench their hands into a fist rather than around a pen. Heathcliff hits Cathy so hard in Chapter XIV that, in a bloody echo of the ghostly Catherine in Lockwood's dream, Cathy goes to the window, her 'mouth filling with blood' (p. 341). In another act of violence meant to silence her or drive her to submission, Hareton hits Cathy, 'a manual check given to her saucy tongue' that Lockwood hears 'not altogether disapprovingly' (p. 366) because 'the little wretch had done her utmost to hurt her cousin's ... feelings, and a physical argument was the only mode he had of balancing the account ...' (p. 366). Yet Cathy still manages to hurl a retort at Hareton; he has not, in fact, silenced her. She has not surrendered.

In a similar act of defiance of the 'law', Nelly refuses to surrender to Hindley. She employs language to control the situation even when her mouth is being violated in a manner that cannot but suggest a sexual violation:

> 'You'd rather be damned!' he said, 'and so you shall—No law in England can hinder a man from keeping his house decent, and mine's abominable! open your mouth.'
> He held the knife in his hand, and pushed its point between my teeth: but, for my part, I was never much afraid of his vagaries. I spat out, and affirmed it tasted detestably—I would not take it on any account. (p. 92)

Hindley's weapons, like the one he shows Isabella (p. 170), are quite useless, unless they are used against him.

By inscribing the action, the women in the text can exert control and contain action, resetting boundaries through narration of the event. Rather than reduce Brontë's novel to offering only 'the subordination of the rebellion within the ideological order' (Kavanagh, p. 91), rather than forever locking women into silence by damning all their inscription as mimicry, we should look at the way words free rather than bind women. Writing and reading are not symbolic of repression in the context of this novel; like Catherine's 'faded hieroglyphics', they encode a decipherable text of resistance (p. 24). In *Wuthering Heights* reading and writing are forms of engendered 'excommunication' that defy the sanctity of the atrophied social, religious and domestic order. Women's narrative in this text is not concerned with good books; it is concerned with control and with the will to possess the page—insofar as the page represents power.

In what Kavanagh calls the 'standard statement on the book image in *Wuthering Heights*' (p. 106), Robert C. McKibben writes that the 'book is used to sustain a shallow view of the world, a view rendered false by its omissions ...' (McKibben, p. 163) and sees the book as the representation of the difference between the Heights and the Grange. According to McKibben's essay, Catherine's downfall is caused by 'the overestimated power of her will' (p. 168), and her daughter's superior 'accomplishment' is not in 'the glorification of the will, but within ... the modification of the will' (p. 168). Because Cathy can modify her will, 'Hareton in his turn endows her existence with a purpose' (p. 168). He can endow her existence with a purpose, it seems, only after he has destroyed the 'prose and verse' she has called 'consecrated' (Brontë, p. 365). Out of Hareton's burning of Cathy's books McKibben makes heaven: 'the fire has returned things to themselves, to the paradise of normalcy: Cathy and Hareton are ready to resume their rightful places ...' (McKibben, p. 168). He claims that 'Emily Brontë's conception of the effectiveness of the book and its rightful use' was 'a world of eternal summer where the individual is reconciled to himself and to reality' (p. 169). This seems, to me, to be a key problem in McKibben's argument. It ignores completely the idea of language as power, even given that McKibben does not consider any gender-related issues in his discussion except where he apparently indicates that only a man can endow a woman's life with meaning.

It seems reasonable to claim, in contrast to these earlier observations, that the image of the book in Brontë's novel is not one of the passive recycling of a dominant curriculum, or of feminine resignation to the standing order. The engendered acts of reading and writing that structure Brontë's novel are aligned both with the feminine excommunication of story-telling and singing, and indicative of the power of language to rupture and dislodge the dominant discourse, as embodied by Joseph, Edgar and other male figures in the text. 'When women claim authorship', argue the editors of *The (M)other Tongue* in the introduction to that volume, they subvert the paradigm wherein 'women may be spoken of, spoken through, but may not bespeak themselves' and they raise questions concerning 'priority and the stories by which it is maintained and conferred' (Garner *et al.*, p. 24).

And finally, these acts of feminine inscription are linked to another important inversion of the patriarchal code that forms the excommunicated structure of Brontë's novel: it is the female characters who initiate and control sexual activity. Armstrong, in fact, comments on the 'curiously tenacious belief that writing and desire are ontologically different and ideologically opposed' that forms the basis for much Brontë criticism (Armstrong, p. 189). It is interesting to note that a number of critics do not see sexuality as an important narrative force. A. O. J. Cockshut, for example, claims that Catherine's love for Heathcliff 'is not sexual, and does not conflict with her love for her husband ...' (Cockshut, p. 108) and Arnold Kettle argues that theirs is 'not primarily a sexual relationship' (Kettle, p. 31). But to trace the primary relationships between men and women in *Wuthering Heights* is to trace an outline of women's desire.

Women's desire in *Wuthering Heights* is explicit and catalytic. Women speak their desire and act on it. Catherine can articulate quite clearly her attraction to Linton as well as to Heathcliff; some critics seem remarkably surprised by the very idea that she can desire two men simultaneously. Albert Guerard, in a preface to *Wuthering Heights*, suggests that 'the oddity is that Cathy expects to "have them both", finds this expectation entirely "natural", and is enraged because neither Heathcliff nor Edgar will consent to such a menage-à-trois' (Guerard, p. 66). I find that Armstrong once again supplies the most convincing observations in this matter when she writes that 'the new territories of the self that the Brontës sought to represent were the unseen desires of women' (Armstrong, p. 192).

In the explicitly sexual encounter between Catherine and Heathcliff (and I find it impossible to see their relationship as founded on anything apart from sexual desire) 'he bestowed more kisses than he ever gave in his life before ... but then my mistress kissed him first ...' (Brontë, p. 194). In an interesting comment on what can be regarded as a scene central to the idea of excommunication in *Wuthering Heights*, Davies notes that this 'meeting is the conscious violation of a taboo, a sacrament celebrated through the communion of two spirits in vehement contradiction of the church service which is going on simultaneously' (Davies, p. 112). In one of her final actions, Catherine 'springs' at Heathcliff so that he might hold her (Brontë, p. 199). It is Cathy who expresses her desire to 'hold' Heathcliff 'until we were both dead' (p. 195), with physical desire overriding any spiritual context for that remark. It is her ghost that seems to seek him even after death to make good her desire to lie beside him. She seems to kill Heathcliff by her hauntings; she kills him the way Linton is afraid Cathy will kill him. Heathcliff twice attempts to dig up Catherine's corpse and he wishes to be united with her physically in death (pp. 349–50). When he sees her body, he finds that Catherine has not 'decomposed' at all.[2]

Isabella also pursues Heathcliff; Heathcliff explains his relationship with Isabella to Catherine in the following terms: 'I have a right to kiss her, if she chooses ...', acknowledging Isabella's power to choose (p. 137). After they are married, it is Isabella who demands the key to their bedroom from Joseph, who seems surprised to hear that she intends to sleep with his master: '"Oh! It's Maister Hathecliff's yah're wenting?" he cried, as if making a new discovery ...' (p. 174). Heathcliff refuses to acknowledge that, as Isabella claims, it is her room now: 'He swore it was not nor ever should be mine ...' (p. 176). Heathcliff apparently refuses to submit to her desires in what John Hewish has called 'a sadistic denial of conjugal rights' (Hewish, p. 151). Obviously, since Isabella becomes pregnant very soon after her marriage, Heathcliff does submit at some point.

As we have seen, young Cathy pursues Linton with letters and books. He, on their wedding night, 'screams for vexation that he can't sleep' (Brontë, p. 339) and calls his father in to quiet his wife. Heathcliff does this by threatening to strangle her. Linton reclines on the settee and sulks, after his marriage to Cathy, occupied by 'sucking a stick of sugar-candy' (p. 338).

After Linton dies, Cathy initiates the relationship with Hareton, declaring 'Come, you shall take notice of me ...' (p. 379). Despite the fact that he has thrown her books into the fire, having been frustrated in his attempts to win her approval and in doing so only managing to have 'produced the contrary result' (p. 366) to his wishes, Cathy is relentless in her pursuit of Hareton. She acts out her own scene of temptation by offering texts that are strewn suggestively throughout the house, their open pages seducing the illiterate boy almost against his will: '[w]hen Hareton was there, she generally paused in an interesting part, and left the book lying about—that she did repeatedly' (p. 377). They are seen together, finally, with Cathy attempting to teach Hareton how to pronounce 'contrary' (p. 371). At one point, in trying to win Hareton over, Cathy 'impressed on his cheek a gentle kiss' and then directly wraps 'a handsome book neatly in white paper' (p. 381) to give to Hareton as a gift.

Cathy and her books must battle. with Joseph and his texts—Bible and bank-notes—for the 'possession' of Hareton. That books are the final analogue for feminine desire and triumph, as outlined in the following exchange, exemplifies the place of the female text and the power of excommunication in *Wuthering Heights*:

> [Joseph], poor man, was perfectly aghast at the spectacle of Catherine seated on the same bench with Hareton Earnshaw, leaning her hand on his shoulder; and confounded at his favourite's endurance of her proximity ... His emotion was only

revealed by the immense sighs he drew, as he solemnly spread
his large Bible on the table, and overlaid it with dirty bank-notes
from his pocket-book, the produce of the day's transactions ...

'Tak these in tuh t'maister, lad,' he said, 'un'bide theare ... This
hoile's norther mensful nor seemly fur us ...'

'Come Catherine,' [Nelly] said ...

'Hareton, I'll leave this book upon the chimney-piece, and I'll
bring some more to-morrow.'

'Ony books ut yah leave, Aw sall tak intuh th'hahse,' said Joseph,
'un' it'ull be mitch is yah fine 'em agean; soa, yah muh plase
yourseln!'

Cathy threatened that his library should pay for hers; and smil-
ing as she passed Hareton, went singing upstairs... (pp. 384–5)

If the system of patriarchal discourse is upheld by the likes of Joseph, then it is
obvious that this system fails to remain dominant in *Wuthering Heights*. The
voices of Nelly and Cathy sing over Joseph's muttered threats. If patriarchal
discourse exists in part through an ability, to prevent the illegitimate, feminine
use and creation of texts, then patriarchal discourse in *Wuthering Heights* is
over-written/written-over and undermined by the strength and energy of
feminine 'excommunication'.

NOTES

1. Extracts from *Wuthering Heights* are all taken from the edition given in the
Bibliography at the end of these notes. I would like to thank the following colleagues and
friends for their comments and suggestions on the idea for this paper: Carol MacKay, Jane
Marcus and Mary Ann Caws.

2. *Wuthering Heights* is a book where sex and death are often allied; Gilbert and
Gubar argue that 'funerals are weddings, weddings funerals' (p. 259). There are so many
death/birth scenes in the book that it is difficult to see these comings and goings as coincidental. The births and deaths, weddings and funerals form equations: Heathcliff arrives;
Mrs Earnshaw dies. Hindley marries Frances; Mr Earnshaw dies. Hareton Earnshaw is
born; Frances Earnshaw dies. Catherine goes to the Grange; Mr and Mrs Linton die.
Cathy is born; Catherine dies. Linton Heathcliff born; Hindley Earnshaw dies. Cathy
meets Hareton; Isabella dies. Cathy and Linton marry; Edgar dies. Cathy befriends
Hareton; Heathcliff unable to eat. Heathcliff dies; Cathy and Hareton will marry. While
these events cannot inevitably be charted on a cause/effect basis, they do follow closely
enough on the heels of one another to give us pause. It is important, then, to see which
characters control sexuality in this novel.

SUSAN MEYER

"Your Father Was Emperor of China, and Your Mother an Indian Queen": Reverse Imperialism in Wuthering Heights

Emily Brontë's *Wuthering Heights* was published in December 1847, two months after the publication of Charlotte Brontë's *Jane Eyre*. The two writers created their novels sitting side by side in the Haworth evenings around the dining room table, with their sister Anne, who was composing *Agnes Grey* and *The Tenant of Wildfell Hall*, the three sometimes pausing to read each other passages and to comment on each other's manuscripts.[1] The sisters' imaginative origins in childhood had also been parallel: while Charlotte, with Branwell, wrote about Glass Town, the imaginary African colony, Emily, after an initial five years of participation, broke away, with Anne, to create a separate literary world also structured around a situation of imaginary imperialism. Indeed, even during the years in which she was composing *Wuthering Heights* and a second, never completed novel, Emily Brontë continued to write about Gondal, an imaginary North Pacific island with a climate much like that of England's Yorkshire, and its tropical colony Gaaldine, which Anne described, in her penciled additions to the family's copy of Goldsmith *A Grammar of General Geography*, as "a newly discovered island in the South Pacific."[2] Although Emily Brontë continued, rather astonishingly, to write about Gondal and Gaaldine until her death at the age of thirty in 1848, none of the prose fiction she wrote about either her first or her second imaginary colonial world has survived. The surviving Gondal/Gaaldine lyrics are tantalizing, in

From Imperialism at Home: Race and Victorian Women's Fiction, pp. 96–125. © 1996 by Cornell University.

their references to a golden-haired girl linked with a dark "boy of sorrow," but any narrative one might attempt to derive from them remains fragmentary and speculative.[3] Yet the extent to which for Emily Brontë, as for Charlotte, the idea of race was a powerful preoccupation—and a powerful metaphor—is evident in her one completed novel, *Wuthering Heights*.

I

When Catherine and Heathcliff are captured by the Lintons in *Wuthering Heights*, after gazing in at their opulent splendor through the "great glass panes" of Thrushcross Grange, Heathcliff is subjected to a visual scrutiny that relegates him to what is to be his place in the social order. "Oh, my dear Mary, look here!" exclaims Mr. Linton:

> "'Don't be afraid, it is but a boy—yet, the villain scowls so plainly in his face, would it not be a kindness to the country to hang him at once, before he shows his nature in acts, as well as features?'
>
> "He pulled me under the chandelier, and Mrs. Linton placed her spectacles on her nose and raised her hands in horror. The cowardly children crept nearer also, Isabella lisping—
>
> "'Frightful thing! Put him in the cellar, papa. He's exactly like the son of the fortune-teller, that stole my tame pheasant.'"[4]

Pulled under the chandelier, scrutinized through spectacles, and pronounced upon as if he were a specimen of some strange animal species, Heathcliff is subjected to the potent gaze of a racial arrogance deriving from British imperialism. In Heathcliff's dark face, the Lintons read his nature and his destiny, and they find in it a license to punish him for crimes of property putatively committed by others of similar appearance. Isabella first describes Heathcliff as a gypsy, giving him the generic designation for a dark-complexioned alien in England which is attributed to him throughout the novel. But in a moment Mr. Linton's gaze becomes more historically specific, as he recognizes in Heathcliff "that strange acquisition my late neighbour made, in his journey to Liverpool—a little Lascar, or an American or Spanish castaway." He speculates that the boy is of a race subject to European imperialism: Heathcliff may be the child of one of the Indian seamen, termed lascars, recruited by the East India Company to replace members of the British crews who died on exposure to disease in India or in military encounters with the Indians. Discharged at the end of the voyage, the lascars remained unemployed and starving in England's port cities for several months before their return journey home.[5]

Or perhaps, Mr. Linton hints with his second, ambiguous designation, the dark-skinned child arrived in Liverpool as a result of the trade for which the city was most famous in the late eighteenth century. In 1769, the year in which Mr. Earnshaw found Heathcliff in the Liverpool streets, the city was England's largest slave-trading port, conducting seventy to eighty-five percent of the English slave trade along the Liverpool Triangle, exchanging manufactured goods from the Mersey region for West African slaves, who were exchanged for plantation crops in the American and the Spanish American colonies.[6] Perhaps the young Heathcliff, Linton suggests, is the cast-off offspring of one of those slaves, or "an American or Spanish castaway." Thousands of black slaves were living in England itself in the late eighteenth century, concentrated particularly in the port cities of London, Liverpool, and Bristol, to which they had been brought by captains of slaving vessels and planters, government officials, and military officers returning from the West Indies.[7] Black slavery within England did not come to an end until 1834, when the English slaves were emancipated by the same legislative act of Parliament that (gradually) put an end to slavery in the English colonies.[8] In 1764, the *Gentlemen's Magazine* estimated that there were more than 20,000 black slaves in London alone. A street in eighteenth-century Liverpool was nicknamed "Negro Row," and slaves were sold in the city at public auctions held in warehouses, coffee houses, and shops, and outside the custom house.[9] Newspapers ran advertisements announcing the sale of slaves, giving notice of their escape, and offering rewards for recapture. In 1768, for example, the *Liverpool Chronicle* advertised the sale of "A fine Negroe Boy, of about 4 Feet 5 Inches high. Of a sober, tractable, humane Disposition, Eleven or Twelve Years of Age, talks English very well, and can Dress Hair in a tolerable way."[10] When Mr. Earnshaw finds the dark Heathcliff in the streets of Liverpool in 1769 and inquires for "its owner" (78), he is simply following the dictates of contemporary English property law. By taking Heathcliff into his home and giving him the name (although not the surname or the property) of a son, Mr. Earnshaw attempts to give him a more favorable social status. But as the Lintons inspect the adolescent Heathcliff and describe him as "an American or Spanish castaway," they return him, with the power of the gaze of empire, to the status of racial property—he is the late Mr. Earnshaw's "acquisition"— and fix him into the role of inferior racial outsider, a thoroughgoing outsider, as the servant's derogatory phrase, "an out-and-outer," suggests, or, in Mrs. Linton's terms, "a wicked boy ... unfit for a decent house" (91).

Catherine's laughter on hearing the Linton's horrified commentary alerts us to Emily Brontë's satirical attitude toward the Lintons' literal and moral myopia, as they peer through spectacles at Heathcliff, and toward their exploitative racial arrogance. In this passage Brontë only slightly exaggerates the sublime irrationality of nineteenth-century British racism, a typical, and similar, example of which could be found in an essay in the Brontës' favorite periodical, *Blackwood's*, in which the writer, meditating upon the scenes of his boyhood in Scotland, chances upon a gang of gypsies, and comments: "I should not be surprised to read some day in the newspapers, that the villain who leads the van had been executed for burglary, arson, and murder. That is the misfortune of having a bad physiognomy, a side-long look, a scarred cheek, and a cruel grin about the muscles of the mouth...."[11] In describing the Linton's simultaneously frightened and arrogant inspection of Heathcliff's dark face, Emily Brontë satirizes the British desire to contain and control the "dark races" through a reductive and predictive reading of physiognomy.

Yet at the same time, in this passage Emily Brontë reveals the force of the imperialist gaze wielded against Heathcliff. In the moment of inspection itself, the various participants in the scene behave in a manner that would seem to bear out the Lintons' assumptions about the brutelike, dumb character of people with dark skin. But Brontë reveals the way in which the power dynamics of the imperialist encounter artificially distribute the agency of language by having Heathcliff himself tell the story of his own capture and silencing to Nelly, fully revealing his capacity to form judgments about his captors and to give an account of the imperialist encounter from his own perspective. In the moment of inspection, however, he is, as when first brought home and examined by the Earnshaws, "as good as dumb" (78). In that first appearance in the novel Heathcliff is incapable of communication because he speaks a foreign language—"some gibberish that nobody could understand," as Nelly puts it (77)—but here he is silenced by the relentless gaze and commentary of the Lintons. They react to him as if he is a visual object only, or an animal, incapable of speech. First termed "foul-mouthed" and told to hold his tongue by the servant, and then heard only in the style rather than the substance of his speech—"Did you notice his language, Linton?" asks his wife, "I'm shocked that my children should have heard it"—Heathcliff might say, with Caliban, "You taught me language, and my profit on't / Is, I know how to curse."[12]

In *Wuthering Heights*, Emily Brontë makes an extended critique of British imperialism.[13] She does so in part by exploring what would happen if the suppressed power of the "savage" outsiders were unleashed. Brontë relentlessly explores the nature of forces external to, subordinated to, marginalized by, or excluded from the British social order. And like her sister Charlotte, Emily Brontë invokes the metaphorical link between white women and people of nonwhite races as she explores energies of resistance to the existing social structure. In *Wuthering Heights* these energies have a universal resonance—they suggest the external, untamable energies that forever threaten the cozy domestic internal. But the novel also gives them a local specificity, associating them with nineteenth-century social issues of topical significance.

Critics such as David Wilson, Arnold Kettle, and Terry Eagleton have accounted for the threatening power of *Wuthering Heights* by reading Heathcliff as a representative of the discontented working class of the "hungry forties," rising in rebellion against an oppressive society and learning himself to wield the oppressive tools of capitalism.[14] As Eagleton puts it, Heathcliff's "rise to power symbolizes at once the triumph of the oppressed over capitalism and the triumph of capitalism over the oppressed."[15] The issue of economic injustice is certainly central to *Wuthering Heights*. But the novel is most powerfully concerned, I would argue, not with economic injustice within the domestic class system, but with the economic injustice imposed by British imperialism on the "dark races" of the world. To read Heathcliff simply as a working man within a domestic context does not sufficiently account for the novel's threatening power. Read as a discontented worker, Heathcliff does not behave in a particularly dangerous manner. He does not form alliances with other workers (Nelly, Joseph, or Michael, for example), as the middle class most feared discontented laborers would. Instead, Heathcliff simply makes an individual rise, enacting, although in a vengeful form, the individualistic rags-to-riches plot, a plot that in fact reinforces the values of capitalism. Such a reading thus fails to explain what remains menacingly resonant in the novel. Considered in the interpretive context of imperialist history, however, Heathcliff suddenly looks, as it were, collective—accruing associations with India, China, Africa, and the West Indies. Reading the novel in this context, one also linked with the discontents of gender, helps to explain its potently disruptive and threatening energy. This is not to say that the novel is not concerned with class inequality—it obviously is—but that it locates the energies of resistance to social inequality not so much in the English working class as in the "dark races" beyond the margins of England.

Heathcliff, with his dark skin and indeterminate, widely suggestive colonial origins, is at once the novel's "ghoul" or "vampire"—its "incarnate demon" (359)—and its incarnation of the resistant energies of those subjected to British imperialism, those made, as entire peoples, into a servant class for England. The other, most potent asocial energies in the novel are located in Catherine, in the "savage" free child trapped within her adult ladyhood. Again in this novel these resistant energies are linked, here through the passionate sense of identity that Catherine feels with Heathcliff. And yet the novel does not simply, or primarily, represent the discontents of gender and class through the racial metaphor, as does Charlotte Brontë's *Jane Eyre*. In *Wuthering Heights* the energies embodied in the dark-skinned Heathcliff have a potency that exceeds the role of metaphor. In *Jane Eyre* the representative of the "dark races" is killed off as the heroine lives on. But Heathcliff lives on, in *Wuthering Heights*, long after the white woman who claims identity with him, and his fictional longevity suggests his greater-than-metaphorical status in the novel. The ending of *Jane Eyre* symbolically represents a reformed society, an imaginative act of social reform that requires purging the novel of the character who represented rebellion against the social order. *Wuthering Heights* makes no comparable attempt to represent a reformed social order: this novel instead persists through its ending in affirming transgression against British social structures. In so doing, *Wuthering Heights* also suggests the ways in which traditional moves of fictional closure act to suppress energies of social resistance.

Emily Brontë's mockery of the adolescent Isabella, whose own access to language, distorted by the lisping, child-like affectations of femininity, is immediately used to command that Heathcliff be locked in the cellar, suggests Brontë's attitude toward those novelists, like her sister Charlotte, whose inclination is for the most part to lock such transgressive energies in the attic. Charlotte Brontë certainly was made uneasy by the energies released by *Wuthering Heights*, an uneasiness with which her sister had little sympathy. In her preface to the novel, Charlotte, referring to the sisters' habit of reading their novels in progress to each other, writes: "If the auditor of her work, when read in manuscript, shuddered ... if it was complained that the mere hearing of certain vivid and fearful scenes banished sleep by night, and disturbed mental peace by day, Ellis Bell would wonder what was meant, and suspect the complainant of affectation."[16] Unlike *Jane Eyre*, in which dangerous energies are tamed or suppressed in the novel's ending, as Bertha Rochester leaps to her death, *Wuthering Heights* relentlessly pursues its exploration of the "fearful" and "disturbing" energies of social transgression.

II

The yoking of the rebellious Catherine with Heathcliff, the novel's representative of the "dark races," is central to *Wuthering Heights* and is established early in the novel. *Wuthering Heights* tells the story of a preadolescent girl, "half savage and hardy, and free" (163), whose desire to resist a constraining female social role is figured through her identity with the "dark races."—"I *am* Heathcliff," Catherine proclaims (122). Maggie Tulliver in George Eliot *The Mill on the Floss*, who is "like a gypsy, and 'half wild,'" perhaps owes something to Brontë's Catherine Earnshaw, and certainly follows in the same metaphorical tradition.[17] When Maggie Tulliver makes her entrance in *The Mill on the Floss*, she is immediately chastised by her mother for dragging her sunbonnet along the floor. Maggie's reluctance to wear a hat simultaneously suggests her rejection of the rules and constraints of feminine behavior, her unwillingness to accept barriers between herself and nature, her mildly scandalous approximation, in Victorian terms, to the relative nakedness of "savages," and her lack of interest in protecting the whiteness of her skin. The young Catherine Earnshaw's wildness and rejection of the female role are represented similarly in *Wuthering Heights*: before she is tamed and whitened by her confinement at the Lintons, Catherine is, according to Nelly, a "wild, hatless little savage" (93).

But while Maggie's wildness will be represented through her brown complexion and her relatives' frequent descriptions of her as resembling a gypsy (or a mulatto), Catherine Earnshaw's resistance to female acculturation, her "half savage" nature (163), is metaphorically represented not on her own body but associatively, in the companion from whom in her childhood she is inseparable: the dark-skinned gypsy Heathcliff. Since Catherine's resistance to acculturation is represented externally, in a vividly realized character, *Wuthering Heights* gives these energies a more forceful, more independent reality than does *The Mill on the Floss*. When Maggie Tulliver reaches adolescence, and, for the most part, assimilates to proper female behavior, her transgressive, gypsy nature will be driven underground, emerging only as the "savage" impulses that she will attempt, in adulthood, to beat down. When Catherine Earnshaw enters adolescence, on the other hand, Brontë explores the way in which the constraining life of adult womanhood splits her off from what for Brontë are her most vital energies, energies that remain fully present in the novel, yet painfully divided from Catherine, in the character of Heathcliff.

It is possible that Emily Brontë's Heathcliff owes something to the African Quashia Quamina of the Glass Town stories. The Brontë children collaborated on these juvenile tales in the beginning, and later, even after Emily and Anne separated from their older sister and brother to create an imaginary world of their own, all four children may well have discussed their imaginative creations or read them to each other. Brontë biographer Winifred Gérin believes that Quashia finds an echo "not only in the enigmatic figure of the dark-haired orphan boy, of 'the iron man,' the 'accursèd man' of the Gondal poems, but preeminently in the conception of Heathcliff, the louring 'gypsy brat' whose origins ... Emily deliberately left undefined."[18] Some of the imagery surrounding Heathcliff in *Wuthering Heights* does seem strikingly similar to that in the early tales, particularly the imagery of glass structures of privilege and racially alien outsiders. Particularly reminiscent of the juvenilia is the episode in which the two children are discovered peering in through the enormous windows of Thrushcross Grange: Catherine is seized and entrapped by the world inside the glass structure of British civilization—much like the "diamond House with golden windows" through which the African Quashia sees the image of his own exclusion in the Glass Town stories.[19] Meanwhile Heathcliff, left outside because of his dark features, remains excluded from the world within what he calls those "great glass panes" (91), and thus uncivilized and unacculturated.

At Thrushcross Grange, Catherine is inserted into a social role internal to the domestic civilization of Britain. While Heathcliff, at this determining moment in their adolescence, becomes fixed into the external role of "out-and-outer," Catherine becomes civilized in the British fashion—she becomes, as Hindley exclaims in delight, "a lady" (93). In the scene of her return, Brontë concisely demonstrates the way in which Catherine's enclosure in this role is accompanied by a painful splitting of herself, a division of herself from her earlier "savage" energies. As an adult woman, Catherine is separated from her former physical vitality and emotional immediacy: instead of "jumping into the house, and rushing to squeeze us all breathless" (93) as Nelly expects, she arrives attired in cumbersome clothes, which hamper her movement and her emotions. She is obliged to hold up her new riding habit "with both hands" in order to walk (93). Her new social role also breaks her bond with the natural world: Nelly reports that "while her eyes sparkled joyfully when the dogs came bounding up to welcome her, she dare hardly touch them lest they should fawn upon her splendid garments" (93). Catherine's attire creates a new division between her and the servants—"I was all flour making the Christmas cake," Nelly reports, "and it would not have done to give me a hug" (93)—and causes her to require waiting on for things she could once do by herself. "Ellen, help Miss Catherine off with her things," commands Hindley's wife (93). This new need for service both renders Catherine physically helpless and enforces social distinctions: "little Cathy" (77) becomes "Miss Catherine."

Most painfully, of course, Catherine's insertion into the social structure, her restrictive, isolating attire of "ladyhood," splits her off from Heathcliff, who is now divided from her by "great glass panes" at once as transparent and as deadly as the jagged window glass into which Lockwood forces the flesh of the ghostly Catherine's bare wrist. Catherine for the first time sees Heathcliff from the perspective of the inside: he looks "dirty" and startlingly "black and cross," now that she is divided from her own "savage" anger and resistance (94). Heathcliff's fingers, as she sees when she takes them in her own, are "dusky" (95), while her own are "wonderfully whitened with doing nothing and staying indoors" (94). Brontë's phrase at once marks the new racial divide between Catherine and Heathcliff and mocks the association of dark skin with dirt by associating white skin with a "civilized" indoor idleness and physical frailty.

Catherine is at first able to connect with the split-off part of herself. When Hindley locks Heathcliff in the garret, much as Bertha is imprisoned in *Jane Eyre*, instead of existing separately from this angry, revengeful aspect of herself, as Jane does, Catherine climbs in through the skylight to join him and later takes him out with her the same way. But the two are soon at odds: Heathcliff complains of the "silly frock" that divides Catherine from him (109), while Catherine objects to the absence of speech that marks Heathcliff's mutilation by the social order: "You might be dumb ... for anything you say to amuse me" (110). Catherine's lamenting protestations of her bond with Heathcliff are eulogistic, as if she needs to assert the connection verbally only when it is being broken. Yet Catherine's protestations are at the same time accurate: struggling to resist the loss of her unacculturated, free self as she discusses her engagement to Linton with Nelly, she says of Heathcliff: "He's more myself than I am" (121). As Catherine conforms to the constraining role of womanhood, and as Heathcliff remains energized by resistance, this statement rings increasingly true.

When Catherine makes her famous assertion in the same exchange— "Nelly, I *am* Heathcliff—he's always, always in my mind—not as a pleasure, any more than I am always a pleasure to myself—but as my own being" (122)—Brontë clearly establishes the metaphorical bond between these two characters. But Emily Brontë's use of the metaphor in this novel is in several respects unusual. The construction of the metaphor in *Wuthering Heights* gives Heathcliff, and through him the "dark races," an exceptionally fully realized status. After Catherine dies, sickening from being split off from the most vital part of herself, Heathcliff lives on, embodying energies of resistance that persist after his original figurative role seems over. The novel is indeed not so much the story of Catherine as it is the story of Heathcliff: the need for the narration of a story is evoked by his arrival and ends with his death. The anger Heathcliff expresses in the course of the novel does imply some resistance to the social constraints imposed on women, since he is linked early on with Catherine's "half savage" energies, and since he passionately wants, when she is an adult, to enable her to escape from the constricting social role she has assumed. But as the novel goes on, Heathcliff increasingly escapes the bounds of metaphor. The contrast in this respect with *Jane Eyre* is striking. *Wuthering Heights* becomes so interested in the dark character's position in and of itself, rather than in its figurative capacity, that in the latter part of the novel Heathcliff himself becomes, in an apparent paradox, one of the novel's most horrific oppressors of women. The dark character's role in *Wuthering Heights* so much exceeds the metaphorical that as the novel proceeds, it virtually loses the concern with women's oppression so important in its earlier chapters, while Heathcliff's rage becomes an increasingly literal response to the oppression of the "dark races" themselves.

III

In the early chapters of *Wuthering Heights*, Emily Brontë explores the rationale for the association of white women with colonized races by suggesting that white women and races subject to imperialism both experience an oppressive disempowerment. Brontë even subtly suggests that the situation is harsher for colonized peoples. As Heathcliff says, on being thrust out of Thrushcross Grange, "She was a young lady and they made a distinction between her treatment and mine" (92). One of the forms of mutual disempowerment with which the novel is most concerned is economic. Catherine's only access to money is through marriage, for apparently her father, following patriarchal tradition, has bequeathed all his property to his oldest son. "Did it never strike you that, if Heathcliff and I married, we should be beggars?" (122) Catherine asks Nelly. Hindley forces Heathcliff into the role of servant—probably an unpaid one, to judge from Heathcliff's later recreation of his own situation in Hareton, whom he "deprive[s] of the advantage of wages" (223). Forced to labor in the fields, deprived of literacy, and beaten by his "master" (one who certainly, despite their upbringing, never treats him as "a man and a brother"), Heathcliff is little better off than if he had remained on a Liverpool slave ship. The novel reveals the constraining economic situation of women, while demonstrating that the economic situation of the colonized peoples who are made into a servant class for England is even worse.

Wuthering Heights also emphatically demonstrates the mutual exclusion of women and of colonized races from the language of power, from the "good books," like the ones Catherine and Heathcliff cast into the dog kennel, that embody law and authority in British society. Catherine and Heathcliff's mutual exclusion from the central texts of the culture is made evident in Heathcliff's complaint to Nelly that, as a punishment for incorrectly answering questions about Joseph's sermons, he and Catherine are "set to learn a column of scripture names" (88). The two children are forced to learn a text explicitly constructed so as to exclude them: neither has any part in such self-authorizing genealogies, lists of ancestral names that establish a current generation's claim to sanctity and to the land. Heathcliff's missing surname marks his unknown ancestry: deprived of his history by British imperialism, he is simultaneously deprived of the authority and the claim to ancestral ownership of the land that such a list of names establishes. Catherine also has no place in the genealogy: as a woman she would exist in such a list usually as an unmentioned link. Like Heathcliff, she is also essentially without a stable name and a solid identity and place in the succession of generations, as her scratching of multiple surnames for herself on the window sill of Wuthering Heights makes clear.

More critical attention has been paid to Catherine's relation to language and writing than to Heathcliff's, but the novel is equally concerned with Heathcliff's marginal position in relation to the dominant stories the culture tells itself, with the way in which he too, indeed more extremely than Catherine, is silenced and suppressed by them.[20] Although Lockwood piles up books against the broken window in his dream to keep Catherine out, she has already demonstrated, through her marginal writing, that she can use those books to create a defiant and destructive telling of her own story. The terrified Lockwood, screaming in his sleep, realizes that the books will not serve as an impenetrable barrier to her. Her marginal writing in the religious texts simultaneously mocks the patriarchs (as in her caricature of Joseph), asserts her own, contrary experience, and, in so doing, damages the dominating text. In his childhood, Heathcliff has been able to follow Catherine's lead in aggressively fighting with that text. As Catherine reports in the destructive diary itself, when the children rebel against the "good books" he forces on them, Joseph cries out in despair that Catherine has "riven th' back off 'Th' Helmet uh Salvation,'" and that Heathcliff, kicking his book after Catherine's, has "pawsed his fit intuh t' first part uh 'T' Broad Way to Destruction!'" (63). His outraged wording suggests that Catherine has damaged more than simply the material book: one might say that the whole armor of the Lord emerges from its confrontation with her a bit the worse for wear. But Heathcliff's relation to the text, Joseph's words suggest, is quite different: even in violently rejecting the text, he seems to be drawn into the deleterious plot within which it would insert him. Heathcliff's foot is already on the broad way to destruction.

On his own, Heathcliff has yet more difficulty with the language of power. When he is first brought home to Wuthering Heights, he is about seven years old—his face looks older than that of the six-year old Catherine— and he can of course already speak his native language. But nothing that he has experienced in that language, which Nelly dismissively terms "gibberish" (77), ever makes its way into the cognitive space of the novel. Oddly, no one ever even seems to ask Heathcliff, once he can speak English, where he is from or who his parents are, and he does not seem himself to remember. It is as if everything he has experienced in his native language is somehow untranslatable into the language of the colonizer. Already as a child, when he learns that language, Heathcliff is subdued by it: he speaks "precious little,"

Nelly reports, ("and that generally the truth," she comments [79]). As an adolescent, Heathcliff is deprived of instruction in literacy: he is forced into what Nelly terms '"savage sullenness" and ignorance by Hindley's attempts to make him into his idea of a savage (106). Told that "the first word he spoke to Miss Catherine should ensure a dismissal" (92), he becomes "dumb" with her, thus earning her annoyance and exacerbating the separation between them. Even when Heathcliff returns to Wuthering Heights after his absence, newly in control of economic power, his marginal relation to the English language is immediately indicated in the text: his newly deep voice, Nelly notes, is "foreign in tone" (132). Gilbert and Gubar note that "the power of the patriarch, Edgar's power, begins with words.... Edgar does not need a strong, conventionally masculine body, because his mastery is contained in books, wills, testaments, leases ... languages, all the paraphernalia by which patriarchal culture is transmitted from one generation to the next."[21] It is telling then that the feeble Edgar Linton lands his one blow on Heathcliff in his point of greatest vulnerability, the same place that his culture has been striking Heathcliff—"full on the throat" (154). When Heathcliff mourns for Catherine, later, his voice is again "strangled in his throat" (210).

Heathcliff does achieve some control over authoritative language at the apex of his power: he is able to prevent Edgar Linton from altering his will by paying off the lawyer. But his linguistic power in this case is, interestingly, only negative: he is able to prevent Edgar Linton from exercising the power of language, but never fully wields it himself. The second Catherine, obviously without comprehension of his reasons, complains that Heathcliff has taken it into his head to burn all the books in the house. Even when Heathcliff owns Wuthering Heights, that structure itself marks the tenuousness of his occupation: the name of Hareton Earnshaw is the one written over its door. Catherine may self-assertively (and with mild destructiveness) scratch her name on the window sill of the house, but Heathcliff's name is never written, except as part of Catherine's exploration of her own identity, anywhere on Wuthering Heights. The name of Earnshaw engraved over the door marks the genealogy, the tradition, the culture, and the class, as well as the race, from which Heathcliff is permanently excluded.

Heathcliff's namelessness is emphasized at the beginning of the novel, and again, as the novel draws to a close, Brontë reminds the reader of Heathcliff's anonymity and his status as racial and linguistic outsider.[22] Nelly has a dream, in the novel's final pages, which exposes Heathcliff's problematic relation to the language of the colonizer; it is parallel to Lockwood's dream about Catherine's relation to language in the novel's opening. "Where did he come from, the little dark. thing, harboured by a good man to his bane?" muses Nelly. Half-asleep, she wearies herself "imaging some fit parentage for him," and recalling the course of his existence (360). In the ensuing dream, she has the vexing task of dictating the inscription on his gravestone. She cannot, of course, tell his surname or his age, and in the end dictates only "the single word, 'Heathcliff.'" ("That came true," she adds [360].) Even Heathcliff's final mark in the world, the writing his existence inscribes on the blank page of his tombstone, is suffused more with absence than with presence. Even the one word written on the stone denotes his tangential relationship to the colonizing language into which he has been inserted. It is the name of a son already dead, a used name, empty and waiting for an occupant, and a name to which he has only a fragile and secondary claim. His claim is more secondary, than, for example, the claim of the second Catherine to the name of her mother, because this is a name already used within his generation: this Heathcliff, who was given some other, untranslatable name at birth, will always remain, in relation to his belated English name, only a shadow Heathcliff. His relation to even the one word with which his gravestone is marked is as tenuous as his temporary claim to the building of Wuthering Heights. The gravestone of Heathcliff denotes his exile from history, genealogy, and property through his exile from the language of the colonizing race, and reveals the effect of that exile in erasing his identity.

IV

Both Catherine and Heathcliff are excluded from the dominant language, from the central stories of the culture, and both Catherine and Heathcliff are economically disempowered. But Catherine, whose exclusion is less extreme, assimilates to the oppressive society, assuming her designated social role and essentially, although with outbursts of now self-destructive fury, accepting her limited position. This one "wild, hatless little savage" is successfully colonized. Now "more [her]self than [she]," however, Heathcliff, remains an angry outsider who continues to express all the energies of resistance to subjugation that he once shared with Catherine. Indeed as the novel proceeds and the character of Heathcliff gathers energy, the novel seems largely to lose its interest in women's social subjugation. Emily Brontë gleefully unleashes Heathcliff's energies of social resistance, and that resistance takes the form of the worst nightmare of the imperialist power: reverse colonization. As Heathcliff takes this revenge on an oppressive British society, however, he himself becomes a subjugator of women.

That Heathcliff will enact the drama of resistance in this form is already predicted in his childhood. Nelly, helping Heathcliff to wash and comb, and encouraging him to join Catherine and the Linton children, offers a reading of the colonial dynamics written in his face quite different from that given by the Linton family. "You're fit for a prince in disguise," she tells him:[23]

> "Who knows, but your father was Emperor of China, and your mother an Indian queen, each of them able to buy up, with one week's income, Wuthering Heights and Thrushcross Grange together? And you were kidnapped by wicked sailors, and brought to England. Were I in your place, I would frame high notions of my birth; and the thoughts of what I was should give me courage and dignity to support the oppressions of a little farmer!" (98)

Nelly's reconstruction of Heathcliff's history turns from the speculative to the definite, as indicated by the punctuation, at a telling place: Heathcliff may have an impressive parentage, but he was more certainly brought unwillingly to England by "wicked sailors." But Nelly's speculations about Heathcliff's parentage offer him a fantasy of retribution for his unwilling colonization. In this predictive moment, Nelly associates Heathcliff with the appropriation of English land and property by countries subject to British imperialism, that is, with the reverse colonization of England.

Brontë has Nelly imagine for Heathcliff a particularly telling royal colonial lineage, one that would have evoked specific forms of political anxiety in a British audience in 1847. When Emily Brontë published *Wuthering Heights*, the British were on their way to establishing solid political control in India, governing directly and through subordinate princes. But a reference to the Chinese emperor would have been fraught with more political uncertainty in Britain in 1847. China was by no means under such strong British control as India, although it had recently had an encounter with the might of British imperialism during the first Opium War of 1840–42. As the nineteenth century began, Britain had been purchasing increasingly large quantities of tea from China, yet was unable to develop much Chinese interest in the products it had to offer in exchange. The resulting drain of British silver into China made the British uneasy, and, to prevent it, British merchants began a triangular trade, using India's exports of opium and cotton to pay for the tea Britain bought from China. As this resulted in a drain of Chinese silver from the economy and increasing Chinese addiction to opium, the Peking court banned the opium trade. The British continued to smuggle opium into China, but in the late 1830s Chinese authorities began to enforce the ban more successfully. In June 1840, British warships arrived in Hong Kong, claiming the principle of free trade, and began the first Opium War. In 1842, China yielded and was forced to sign a treaty opening five ports to the British, limiting import and export duties, and ceding Hong Kong to Britain. For a few years, the British were able to congratulate themselves on their relatively easy dissolution of the mighty, ancient Chinese empire by their own.[24]

Yet despite Britain's military triumph, China was still able to resist its forcible opening with some success. The British were disappointed to find their trade with China dropping off after 1846. The Chinese also succeeded in keeping the British out of the important walled city of Guangzhou (Canton), and the economically self-sufficient communities in China proved more resistant than those in India to British control. When Emily Brontë published *Wuthering Heights* in 1847, the British were feeling less confident about their success in dissolving the Chinese empire. When Nelly asks Heathcliff to consider that his father may be the Emperor of China, able to buy up the two English houses with "one week's income," she hints at a possible relationship between the Chinese and the British empire in which the British might not find themselves so easily triumphant. While Indian exports had been used by the British as a way of wielding their economic power over China, Nelly's imaginative recreation of Heathcliff's ancestry suggests, in fantasy, the prospect of an alliance between the two countries—a marriage between an Emperor of China and an Indian queen—and the possibility of their joint economic occupation of Britain. Together they might readily buy up, as trifles, pieces of England—the Heights and the Grange. In restoring to Heathcliff a history, Nelly suggests to the nineteenth-century British reader a way in which dark-skinned people like Heathcliff might be able to take revenge for the subjugation they have suffered at British hands.

In addition, Brontë situates the three years of Heathcliff's absence from Wuthering Heights, from which he returns with a new bearing, money, and a sense of his own power, at a historical moment that associates him with precisely such colonial insurrection. The novel is set in a historical period, the late eighteenth century, which enables the expression of mid-nineteenth-century political anxieties about loss of empire. Lockwood speculates that Heathcliff has "escape[d] to America, and earn[ed] honours by drawing blood from his foster country" (130–31), and his theory seems to be borne out by Nelly's comments that Heathcliff seems to have "been for a soldier" (133) and that his "upright carriage suggested the idea of his having been in the army" (135). Heathcliff's absence, as a calculation of dates in the novel reveals, takes place between 1780 and 1783, the last three years of the American Revolutionary War.[25] By suggesting that Heathcliff has been in the American army in the years he was away, Brontë associates him with the archetypal war of successful colonial rebellion, one in which England was even at one point in fear of invasion. The revolution of the American colonies, accompanied by Canadian discontent and disturbances in the West Indies, demonstrated to the British the possibility of the loss of their colonies and the dissolution of their empire. Because the West Indies were dependent on the American colonies for food, at some points during the Revolutionary War it seemed likely that they would join the American colonies in the revolt against Britain.[26] An 1833 article in *Blackwood's* commented on the remarkable growth and progress of the East India Company and its ability to win "the native affections" at this very time, the time "when the Colonies of England, under the direct control of the mother country, were brought into such a state of discontent, as led to the dismemberment of a large portion of the empire, and threatens soon to sever from the parent state its colonial possessions."[27] Heathcliff, gaining a new sense of power by "drawing blood from his foster country," is the disconcerting representative of all the British colonies that, however subtly, may threaten to turn against the "parent state"—a parent state that, like Mr. Earnshaw, may turn out to have "harboured" them "to [its] bane."

The American Revolutionary War had other detrimental effects on the British empire as well. The war brought the trade with Africa to a standstill, and, with America and the West Indies ruled out as markets, completely cut off the slave trade, threatening to put a permanent end to it. As Liverpool's shipping industry was hit even harder than London's by the destruction of these two forms of trade, Brontë's subtle association of Heathcliff with the Revolutionary War hints at the beginnings of his revenge on the "wicked sailors" of Liverpool who brought him to England.[28] If Heathcliff has indeed "been for a soldier" during these three years, "drawing blood from his foster country," he has begun his retribution by impeding and threatening the business of the British empire.

And on his return from those three years away, Heathcliff immediately proceeds with the revenge Nelly had hinted at, as he begins to appropriate English land and wealth. He takes possession of Hindley's land, piece by piece, and soon installs himself as the master of Wuthering Heights, easily acquiring the estates Nelly had once suggested his father and mother, as Emperor of China and Indian queen, could readily buy up. He simultaneously drains Hindley's silver and encourages his self-destructive addictions (to drink and gambling), in a way reminiscent of the demoralizing effects of the British opium trade on the Chinese—but in reverse.[29] He sexually appropriates, imprisons, and beats British women, and subjects them to sexual and economic coercion. He creates a world in which physical force and economic power—coming from a mysterious external source—take the place of law or local standards of morality. His actions hideously mimic the ugly brutality of British imperialism.

Heathcliff's first indication of his intent to engage in reverse colonization takes place in a scene that recalls his subjection to the imperialist gaze on his capture by the Lintons. In a reversal of that earlier scene, Catherine and

Heathcliff now wield the imperialist gaze, bringing it to bear on the captive Isabella Linton and treating her, as she and her family had once treated Heathcliff, as an object to be scrutinized and commented on, rather than spoken to, as an exotic, subhuman creature. When Catherine, after her marriage and Heathcliff's return, torments Isabella by telling Heathcliff, in her presence, that Isabella has been pining for him, she holds the young woman fast, just as Heathcliff was once held by the Lintons, so that Heathcliff can fix his eyes upon her in her humiliation and confusion. Heathcliff gazes at Isabella, as she had once at him, in a way that deprives her of human status, and he comments on her as if she now were incapable of speech:

> "I think you belie her," said Heathcliff, twisting his chair to face them. "She wishes to be out of my society now, at any rate!"
> And he stared hard at the object of discourse, as one might do at a strange repulsive animal, a centipede from the Indies, for instance, which curiosity leads one to examine in spite of the aversion it raises.
> The poor thing couldn't bear that; she grew white and red in rapid succession, and, while tears beaded her lashes, bent the strength of her small fingers to loosen the firm clutch of Catherine. (144)

Heathcliff, who had once been denigrated as colonial detritus, as "an American or Spanish castaway," looks at Isabella as one might at a centipede crawling out of a hogshead of West Indian sugar. And Catherine, holding Isabella captive as she and Heathcliff were once held, participates in the reversal of the imperialist gaze by describing the young woman, who is using her fingernails to free herself, as another exotic, colonial animal: she shakes Isabella off, exclaiming, "There's a tigress!" (145).[30] Isabella, unable to speak under such tormenting scrutiny and commentary, is silenced, like Heathcliff before her, and becomes the object, rather than the subject, of imperialist discourse.

In Heathcliff's childhood, Nelly had coaxed him, rather inanely, in ways of making his face look more white: he must smooth his forehead and learn to change his "black fiends" of eyes into "confident, innocent angles" (97). Heathcliff, decoding the impossible agenda of racial transformation in her beauty advice, comments wryly that in other words he must "wish for Edgar Linton's great blue eyes, and even forehead." "I do," he says, "and that won't help me to them." Nelly insists, however, that "A good heart will help you to a bonny face, my lad ... if you were a regular black" (97–98). Nelly evidently believes that washing will turn the gypsy white, and that such a transformation is to be desired. When Heathcliff acquires power, in his years away from Wuthering Heights, however, he threatens to make the attempted racial metamorphosis work in the opposite direction, as he proposes to take his revenge on the white skin and blue eyes that have tyrannized over him. He tells Catherine: "You'd hear of odd things, if I lived alone with that mawkish, waxen face; the most ordinary would be painting on its white the colours of the rainbow, and turning the blue eyes black, every day or two; they detestably resemble Linton's" (145). When Heathcliff, now "master" at the Heights, describes Isabella as an animal—"a mean-minded brach"—and terms her "slavish" (188), the reversal is accomplished and his imperialist power over her is complete.

As Heathcliff was once himself locked up in Wuthering Heights, he locks up Isabella, the younger Catherine, and Nelly. And as Heathcliff was once kept from education and language, he deprives Hareton of literacy to the point where, in the ultimate metaphor of disinheritance, he cannot read his own name over the door of Wuthering Heights. Hareton himself, with his animal-like appearance—"his whiskers encroached bearishly over his cheeks"—and his "embrowned" skin, is Heathcliff's reverse enactment of his own colonization (53–54).

The "vivid and fearful" scenes in *Wuthering Heights*, of which Charlotte Brontë complained, are primarily scenes in which the ugliness of starkly wielded colonial power, usually exercised in areas remote from the reach of British law or putative moral standards, is enacted through Heathcliff's fearful reversals. Here too British law seems strangely powerless, and Heathcliff's actions, as he reverses the colonizing process, take on the quality of nightmare. The shifting white shape espied by Nelly outside Thrushcross Grange, "moving irregularly, evidently by another agent than the wind" (167), gasping for breath in the last throes of hanging, is a sinister reminder and reversal of Mr. Linton's suggestion that Heathcliff should be hanged simply on account of his dark complexion. The gasping, dangling white shape turns out to be only a dog, but Heathcliff's implicit threat is clear.

In *Wuthering Heights*, Emily Brontë gives imaginative life to the colonial "other" who is kept outside the "great glass panes" surrounding the prosperity of the colonizing power, and empowers him to shatter those barriers surrounding and protecting the secure domestic prosperity of Britain. Isabella and Hindley attempt to prevent Heathcliff from entering Wuthering Heights after his vigils over Catherine's body, repeating the scene in which he looked in the windows of Thrushcross Grange as a child. Isabella describes their attempt to lock Heathcliff out: "The casement behind me was banged on to the floor by a blow from the latter individual; and his black countenance looked blightingly through. The stanchions stood too close to suffer his shoulders to follow; and

I smiled, exulting in my fancied security. His hair and clothes were whitened with snow, and his sharp cannibal teeth, revealed by cold and wrath, gleamed through the dark" (212). Much like the African Quashia of the Brontë children's juvenilia, lurking outside the fragile imperial palaces of Glass Town, Heathcliff represents the return of the colonial repressed. In Emily Brontë's novel, he enacts the worst nightmare of empire: he gets in. Isabella is "unnerved by terror for the consequences of [her] taunting speech" when Heathcliff, with his "black countenance" and "sharp cannibal teeth" easily takes a stone, "[strikes] down the division between two windows" (213), and, with preternatural energy, forcibly enters the "decent house."

The repeated motif of Heathcliff's cannibalism is yet another image of the imperialist's nightmare of being subjected to reverse colonization. A cannibal treats other men—in the nightmare of empire, the colonizers—as if they were animals, and then takes this metaphor literally. Cannibalism is also the ultimate manifestation of the violation of boundaries, and represents the fear, on the most immediately horrifying personal and bodily level, of being invaded and used by another for his own purposes. Heathcliff, who Catherine suspects will "devour" Isabella (145), whose mouth waters, according to Isabella, to tear Hindley "with his teeth" (216), who claims that had he been born "where laws are less strict, and tastes less dainty" he would have treated himself to the "slow vivisection" of the younger Catherine and Isabella's son Linton (302), is the imperialist's horrific image of retribution for having treated colonized peoples like animals. This treatment of the "dark races" as animals rarely reached the extreme it did on a nineteenth-century hunting expedition in Southern Africa, where a group of Dutch settlers shot and killed a Bushman and then cooked and ate him, thinking him an orangutan, but this incident suggests why being eaten by cannibals was one of the deepest fears of empire.[31] This horror is evoked in *Jane Eyre* through Bertha Rochester, who has bitten, and to the physician's horror, *chewed* the shoulder of Richard Mason: "She worried me like a tigress," he murmurs. "She sucked the blood: she said she'd drain my heart."[32] But while the resolution of *Jane Eyre* controls these fearful energies of resistance to empire, the impulse of *Wuthering Heights*, even in its ending, is to let these energies loose. Even at the novel's end, when Heathcliff dies, Nelly is horrified by the "sarcastic, savage face" of the corpse, horrified that she cannot compose the face and get the lips to close over the threatening "sharp, white teeth" (365).

V

By the time *Wuthering Heights* comes to its own ending, the novel has already satirized some common moves of narrative closure in nineteenth-century fiction. In doing so Brontë mocks the sensibilities of novelists like her sister Charlotte, who would use just such moves to come to a resolution to the complicated metaphorical maneuvers of *Jane Eyre*. *Wuthering Heights* points out that marriage need not lead to permanent domestic happiness, as nineteenth-century novel closures commonly suggest, and as Charlotte Brontë, for example, will indicate that it does for Jane and Rochester. Instead Emily Brontë shows in Isabella's story what happens *after* an innocent girl marries a surly, difficult hero. The tradition of the blissful deathbed of the saintly man is also ferociously mocked in *Wuthering Heights*. The novel unmasks the horrible truths that may lurk beneath the surface of such scenes when, in order that Edgar Linton may die in tranquility, Nelly instructs young Cathy to tell her father that she will be very happy with her whining, malicious husband, Linton Heathcliff, whom she has been forced to marry. Nelly knows how the good are supposed to die. But storytellers with Nelly's narrative conventionality, Emily Brontë demonstrates, must suppress a great deal in order to force a plot into traditional shape. It is the evil man, not the good one, who dies joyfully in *Wuthering Heights*. The artificiality of Edgar's happy passing is all the more evident when Heathcliff dies, taking a wild, ferocious joy in the event and so disconcerting Nelly with the "frightful, life-like gaze of exultation" on his corpse that she tries earnestly, like a good nineteenth-century narrator, to extinguish it (365).

The inevitable gestures of nineteenth-century fictional closure, marriage and death, both of which will be crucial to the resolution of *Jane Eyre*, are unsettled in *Wuthering Heights*: they begin to look like artificial fictional impositions, intended to quiet troubling yet uncontainable passions and energies. The duality in the ending of *Wuthering Heights* itself works similarly to reveal that such closures suppress the energies of social resistance. The passion of Heathcliff and the first Catherine ends in Heathcliff's sneering death, but *Wuthering Heights* provides an alternate, more socially acceptable ending, as the second Cathy and Hareton reenact Catherine and Heathcliff's passionate bonding as a love story with a happy, traditional consummation. With this alternate ending, the resolution to the second Cathy/Hareton plot, rather than to the first Catherine/Heathcliff plot, Brontë writes a double ending to mock the expectations of her readers and to satirize the conventional conclusion of the domestic novel. Charlotte Brontë's *Jane Eyre* (like her earlier *The Professor*) ends in happy, if slightly uneasy, self-enclosed domesticity; Emily Brontë mockingly provides her novel with a faux version of this kind of fictional conclusion with a courtship at Easter, time of rebirth, a marriage and a new start on New Year's Day, plans for domesticated gardens, and a removal to the "civilized" domestic sanctuary of Thrushcross Grange.

The marriage of Hareton and the second Cathy may indeed at first seem like an adequate resolution to the problems of social marginality and oppression experienced by Heathcliff and Catherine. Their marriage brings an end to class inequality, as Hareton, the former servant, marries the once pampered and wealthy young Cathy. The image of the second Cathy's "light, shining ringlets blending, at intervals, with [Hareton's] brown locks" (338) reminds the reader of a crossing of racial barriers, Hareton's reading lessons suggest the process of decolonization, and the two heads bent avidly over the book they are jointly reading suggest a mutual access to the language of power.

But closer attention reveals the inadequacy of this resolution. The marriage between Hareton and Cathy is an instance neither of true class mobility nor of racial rapprochement. Hareton, although transformed for a while into a "boor," is not truly of another class or race from the second Cathy, and therefore can be incorporated into the British middle class in a way that Heathcliff never can. Hareton is readily civilized: when he washes, *his* dusky skin lightens, although washing will never turn Heathcliff white. The second Cathy, too, has little of the socially resistant energy of the first Catherine. When Cathy and Hareton read the book together, although they pause on the word "contrary," they are at quite a remove from the first Catherine's carelessly blasphemous marginal commentary (338).

Brontë's dual ending mockingly draws attention to the type of conclusion she is not giving her novel. It reveals who is excluded from such endings, what energies they tame and dilute, what they cannot imagine. The last images in the novel ironize the exclusive, walled-in domestic bliss of the Cathy/Hareton ending, which assumes a position only slightly "contrary" to the dominant culture. After showing us, through Lockwood's eyes, the young couple entering the house, the novel moves on to an image of a badly decayed building, the kirk, with its broken windows and collapsing roof. Outside forces have invaded and destroyed this central structure of British society, leaving only "black gaps" where windows, "glass panes," once successfully kept the outside—and the outsiders—out (367). Last, the novel shows us the three headstones above the graves, where, even as Lockwood watches unseeingly, a radical merging is taking place. Catherine and Heathcliff, divided since adolescence by the "great glass panes" of British civilization, return in their deaths to a unity in social transgression: Heathcliff has arranged to have his coffin constructed with a removable panel, and has already knocked the side of Catherine's loose, so that their bodies, no longer artificially divided, will dissolve together, finally consummating their passionate sense of identity. In the context of nineteenth-century British culture, Emily Brontë's image of the two bodies uniting in dissolution, the barrier lifted between the white woman and the dark colonial outsider, has a dramatically defiant power.[33] Lockwood, a civilized narrator and a violent defender of British social boundaries against transgression, can see only what is above the ground and denies the possibility of "unquiet slumbers, for the sleepers in that quiet earth" (367). But by returning us to the novel's first plot, in that final image of a radical unity in marginality, Emily Brontë points out what is suppressed by the type of literary imagination that curbs troubling energies with quiescent endings. At the same time she intimates that the invisible barriers separating those within the glass house of British imperialist civilization from the wrathful dark faces outside are hardly as impenetrable as they might at first seem.

If *Wuthering Heights* is more convincing than *Jane Eyre* in according an independent, more fully realized status to the people of the "dark races" to whom it compares white women, and in calling into question the oppressive might of the British empire, it is less convincing than *Jane Eyre* in following through on its critique of the forces exerting constraints on women's lives. The novel invites us to feel sympathy for Catherine, as she writes her story in the margins of a dominating religious text, or scratches her name on a windowsill, since the name over the door does not belong to her, but it does not invite nearly such an unambivalent response to the women subjected to a much more violent and literal oppression later in the novel—Isabella, Nelly, and the second Cathy—whom Heathcliff imprisons, beats, and forces into unwanted sexual relationships or unequal marriages, as he enacts his reversals of power in relation to British society. Though the novel does not morally endorse Heathcliff's actions, and indeed it suggests the brutality of the imperialist project in part through them, the energy it unleashes in the character of Heathcliff has an irresistibly compelling force. Indeed once the novel proceeds beyond the life of the first Catherine, as I comment earlier, it seems to have repressed the problems of women's oppression so powerfully and subtly expressed in her story. It does this in the interest of exploring Heathcliff's situation as it moves beyond the status of metaphor, an interest that then leads Brontë into the transgressive pleasure of imagining a reversal of imperialist power.

The question of the implications of the rhetorical strategy of reversal as political critique arises in Tania Modleski *Feminism without Women*, in a discussion of Jean Renoir film *Sur un air de Charleston*. The problems she has with the film's rhetoric have some bearing on what I have described as the representation of reverse colonization in *Wuthering Heights*. In Renoir's film a black man discovers a post-holocaust Europe in which he finds a wild white woman cavorting lasciviously with an ape companion. Modleski notes that Henry Louis Gates has praised this film for its critique of racist discourse through masterful irony, through the "fairly straightforward ... reversal ... of common European allegations of the propensity of African women to prefer the company of male apes." Gates's praise of the film, Modleski writes, suggests that he is blind to "the way the female Other, regardless of race, has been frequently consigned to categories that put her outside the pale of the fully human"; she goes on to question the "viability of 'straightforward reversal' as political critique."[34]

The reversal of the actions of colonization in *Wuthering Heights* has effects in some respects similar to those Gates and Modleski describe in their analyses of Renoir. The direct reversal of the actions of empire in *Wuthering Heights* gives powerful emphasis to the brutality of empire and to the possible insurrection of the subject "dark races." It gives a startlingly vivid reality to the anger, and to the individuality, of a dark-skinned character. Yet Brontë's rhetorical strategy also has the effect of deflecting attention from the fully human status of female characters like Isabella, and more generally from women's problems in relation to the unjust distribution of social power, although the reminder at the novel's close that under the tombstones Catherine's and Heathcliff's bodies are disintegrating together to some extent does recall the novel's early exploration of the two characters' mutual marginality. It is as if the metaphor linking white women with people of the "dark races" has taken on a life of its own as Emily Brontë deploys it in *Wuthering Heights*, moving beyond its initial function in elucidating the debilitating effects of the social constraints on British women. This is a surprising phenomenon to encounter in the work of a British woman writer of this period, considerably more surprising in its political emphasis than the ending of *Jane Eyre*. The anti-imperialist but not as powerfully feminist politics of *Wuthering Heights* provide another example of the unpredictable consequences of a British woman writer's complex transformations of the metaphor linking gender and race.

NOTES

1. See Winifred Gérin, *Charlotte Brontë: The Evolution of Genius* (Oxford: Clarendon Press, 1967), 338, 340, 318.

2. Fannie Elizabeth Ratchford, ed., *Gondal's Queen: A Novel in Verse by Emily Jane Brontë* (Austin: University of Texas Press, 1955) app. 2, 185.

3. See Fannie Elizabeth Ratchford, "Emily Brontë's Poems Arranged as an Epic of Gondal," in *The Complete Poems of Emily Jane Brontë*, ed. C. W. Hatfield (New York: Columbia University Press, 1941), 17–19; Ratchford, *Gondal's Queen*.

4. Emily Brontë, *Wuthering Heights*, ed. David Daiches (New York: Penguin, 1988), 90–92. Subsequent references will be included in the text.

5. See Peter Stallybrass, "Marx and Heterogeneity: Thinking the Lumpenproletariat," *Representations* 31 (1990): 76–77.

6. Suzanne Miers, *Britain and the Ending of the Slave Trade* (New York: Africana Publishing, 1975), 4. For accounts of the Liverpool slave trade, see C. Northcote Parkinson, *The Rise of the Port of Liverpool* (Liverpool: University Press of Liverpool, 1952), especially 86–101; Gomer Williams, *History of the Liverpool Privateers and Letters of Marque with an Account of the Liverpool Slave Trade* (London: William Heinemann, 1897). I calculate the date to be 1769 based on the following information. Nelly says (103) that in the summer of 1778 Catherine is fifteen and Heathcliff about sixteen. We are told (77) that Catherine is "hardly six" when Heathcliff is brought home, which makes him about seven and the date nine years earlier, or 1769.

7. F. O. Shyllon, *Black Slaves in Britain* (New York: Oxford University Press, 1974), 3–4.

8. Shyllon points out that there has been considerable misunderstanding about the results of Lord Mansfield's decision of 1772 that a slave, upon setting foot in England, is legally free. This decision did not bring slavery in England to an end. An 1827 ruling in the case of Grace Jones declared that a slave brought into England did not become free unless she had proof of having been manumitted by her master. Not until 1834, with the legislative act of Parliament, were all English slaves emancipated. Shyllon, ix–xi, 230–31.

9. Gomer Williams, 474.

10. Quoted in Shyllon, 6.

11. "May-Day," *Blackwood's Edinburgh Magazine* 21, no. 125 (May 1827): 517.

12. Shakespeare, *The Tempest*, 1.2.363–64.

13. Two other critics discuss race as a central issue in *Wuthering Heights*. See Emmanuel Bazze-Ssentongo, "Heathcliff's African Brothers," *Dhana* 4, no. 1 (1974): 79–81; Elsie Michie, "From Simianized Irish to Oriental Despots: Heathcliff, Rochester, and Racial Difference," *Novel* 25 (1992): 125–40. In his brief comment on the novel, Bazze-Ssentongo describes Heathcliff as a dark-skinned gypsy who has "millions of brothers and sisters in Africa and the United States who are suffering from unjust humiliation created by the oppressive racist social systems they happen to live under" (Bazze-Ssentongo, 79). For Bazze-Ssentongo Heathcliff is no "angelic victim of oppression"; instead he is so "pushed to extremes by the system that he almost alienates our sympathy for him in the end" (79). Yet in representing Heathcliff and the results of his oppression "without bias," Emily Brontë "speak[s] the conscience of the just society" (79–80). For Michie, behind the references to blackness and orientalism in *Wuthering Heights* "lie details that implicitly link Heathcliff ... to contemporary stereotypes of the Irish" (Michie, 129). When Heathcliff is poor his blackness is emphasized (133); when he achieves a position of dominance "he continues to be characterized in terms that link him to non-white stereotypes, specifically to the figure of the oriental despot" (134). For Michie, the novel ends with a "comfortable representation of missionary work" (139) as Hareton is civilized, an ending which, in masked form, represents the English relation to Ireland in the 1840s (140). Peter Miles similarly suggests that Heathcliff, found in industrial Liverpool, would have evoked the Irish immigrants arriving there in the days of the Irish famine of 1845–46 for Brontë and her earliest readers, although, Miles points out, as the novel is dated he is a child in the 1760s rather than the 1840s. Peter Miles, "Wuthering Heights" (London: Macmillan, 1990), 54. For Nancy Armstrong "Imperialist Nostalgia and Wuthering Heights," in *Wuthering Heights*, by Emily Brontë, ed. Linda H. Peterson (Boston: Bedford Books, 1992), 428–49, the novel is not about global imperialism but about the "internal colonization" of the rural, less advantaged areas of England by an urban "English core" (446). Like the contemporary collection of folklore or the appropriative photographic representation

of rural people, Armstrong argues, Brontë's novel nostalgically represents a primitive native culture which is being lost.

14. David Wilson, "Emily Brontë First of the Moderns," *Modern Quarterly Miscellany* 1 (1947): 94–115; Arnold Kettle, "Emily Brontë: *Wuthering Heights*," in *An Introduction to the English Novel* (1951; reprint New York: Harper, 1968), 130–45; Terry Eagleton, *Myths of Power: A Marxist Study of the Brontës* (London: Macmillan, 1975). Raymond Williams, *The English Novel from Dickens to Lawrence* (London: Chatto, 1970), 50–61, contends that the historical problems of the 1840s are not so much directly represented as displaced into psychological events in the novel; Nancy Armstrong similarly suggests that although Heathcliff comes from Liverpool and appears "around the time of the provincial hunger riots (1766)," by the end of the novel "he has become a phantasm of unfulfilled sexual desire." Nancy Armstrong, *Desire and Domestic Fiction: A Political History of the Novel* (New York: Oxford University Press, 1987), 187.

15. Eagleton, 112.

16. Charlotte Brontë, "Editor's Preface to the New [1850] Edition of *Wuthering Heights*," in *Wuthering Heights*, by Emily Brontë, ed. David Daiches (New York: Penguin, 1988), 39.

17. George Eliot, *The Mill on the Floss*, ed. Gordon S. Haight (Oxford: Clarendon Press, 1980), 91.

18. Winifred Gérin, *Emily Brontë: A Biography* (Oxford: Clarendon Press, 1971), 23.

19. Charlotte Brontë, *Caroline Vernon*, in *Five Novelettes*, ed. Winifred Gérin (London: The Folio Press, 1971), 283.

20. See, for example, Margaret Homans, *Bearing the Word: Language and Female Experience in Nineteenth-Century Women's Writing* (Chicago: University of Chicago Press, 1986), 68–83; Patricia Yaeger, "Violence in the Sitting Room: *Wuthering Heights* and the Woman's Novel," *Genre* 21 (1988): 203–29. Yaeger notes that Catherine's marginal writing "is the prototype of the novel as the site where violence surfaces, where the 'aphoristic energy' of women's writing begins to usurp the encyclopedic grasp of the tradition itself" (211; see also 220–21).

21. Sandra M. Gilbert and Susan Gubar, The Madwoman in the Attic: The Woman Writer and the Nineteenth-Century Literary Imagination (New Haven: Yale University Press, 1979), 281.

22. For a provocative discussion of names and social class in *Wuthering Heights*, see Miles, 56–61.

23. To a twentieth-century reader, Nelly's suggestion that Heathcliff might be the son of the Emperor of China would seem to be visually at odds with the description of him as looking like a gypsy. But that to English eyes in this era these two groups looked far more similar than different is suggested in the account an Oxford country parson, James Woodforde, gave in 1775 of the appearance of the Chinese: they were like "the runabout gypsies," he noted, and "uncommonly ugly." Quoted in Jerome Ch'en, *China and the West: Society and Culture 1815–1937* (London: Hutchinson & Co., 1979), 43.

24. For an example of this triumphant British attitude, see "War with China, and the Opium Question," *Blackwood's Edinburgh Magazine* 47 (1840): 368. "The day may come when the empire boasting its thousands of years shall reach the term of its immortality.... A formidable and outraged power shall press and inflict the first wound.... The cackling of geese once saved an empire; the incident, almost as trivial, of opium-smoking or eating, instead of tobacco—a mere matter of taste—may chance to ruin one." For an overview of the events of the first Opium War, see Sheng Hu, *Imperialism and Chinese Politics* (1955,

rpt. Beijing: Foreign Languages Press, 1981), 1–19; Shouyi Bai, ed., *An Outline History of China* (Beijing: Foreign Languages Press, 1982), 431–36.

25. Heathcliff returns to Wuthering Heights when Catherine and Edgar have been married six months (131). As Hareton is nearly five when they marry (129), and as he was born in the summer of 1778 (103), Catherine and Edgar marry in the spring of 1783. Heathcliff arrives in September of that year (132) and has been absent three years (136).

26. Parkinson, 124.

27. The East India Question, *Blackwood's Edinburgh Magazine* 33 (May 1833): 783.

28. See Parkinson, 125, for an account of the effect of the war on Liverpool.

29. It is perhaps worth noting here that one of Brontë's nineteenth-century biographers, A. Mary F. Robinson, claimed that Hindley's drunken debauchery was modeled on Branwell Brontë's demeanor when, dismissed from his tutoring job for making romantic advances to the (married) mother of his students, he returned home in despair to the parsonage where he drank to excess and smoked opium. A. Mary F. Robinson, *Emily Brontë* (Boston: Roberts, 1883), 217.

30. Compare Harriet Ritvo, *The Animal Estate: The English and Other Creatures in the Victorian Age* (Cambridge: Harvard University Press, 1987), 205–42. Ritvo argues that the creation of menageries and zoos in nineteenth-century Britain, filled with exotic animals from the colonies safely held captive, figured for the British the power of empire.

31. Martin Guenther, "The Changing Western Image of the Bushmen," *Paideuma* 26 (1980): 123–40, cited in Stephen Jay Gould, "The Hottentot Venus," in *The Flamingo's Smile: Reflections in Natural History* (New York: Norton, 1985), 295.

32. Charlotte Brontë, *Jane Eyre*, ed. Jane Jack and Margaret Smith (Oxford: Clarendon Press, 1969), 266–67.

33. Thackeray for example, evokes shudders at a much less startling image of the dissolution of barriers between races, when he expresses disgust at the thought of "Desdemona's golden curls on swart Othello's shoulder." Charles Lamb, like others in this century, felt that *Othello* should not be performed on stage; he found "something extremely revolting in the courtship and wedded caresses of Othello and Desdemona." William Makepeace Thackeray, The Adventures of Philip, vol. 11 of *The Works of William Makepeace Thackeray* (New York: Harper & Brothers, 1899), 185; Charles Lamb, "On the Tragedies of Shakespeare, Considered with Reference to Their Fitness for Stage Representation," in *The Works of Charles Lamb*, ed. William MacDonald (London: J.M. Dent, 1903), 3: 34. For an account of nineteenth–century reactions to performances of Othello, see Ruth Cowhig, "Blacks in English Renaissance Drama," in *The Black Presence in English Literature*, ed. David Dabydeen (Manchester: Manchester University Press, 1985), 1–25.

34. Tania Modleski, Feminism without Women: Culture and Criticism in a "Postfeminist" Age (New York: Routledge, 1991), 126–27.

Chronology

1812	The Reverend Patrick Brontë marries Maria Branwell.
1814	Maria Brontë, their first child, born.
1815	Elizabeth Brontë born.
1816	Charlotte Brontë born.
1817	Patrick Branwell Brontë, the only son, born.
1818	Emily Jane Brontë born.
1820	Anne Brontë born. The Brontë family moves to Haworth, near Bradford, Yorkshire.
1821	Mrs. Brontë dies of cancer in September. Her sister, Elizabeth Branwell, moves in with the family.
1824	Emily Brontë and sisters enroll at the at the infamous Clergy Daughters' School at Cowan Bridge, Lancashire, which is depicted in *Jane Eyre*.
1825	The two oldest girls, Maria and Elizabeth, contract tuberculosis at school. Maria dies on May 6; Elizabeth dies on June 15. Charlotte and Emily are withdrawn from the school on June 1. They do not return to school until they are in their teens; in the meantime they are educated at home.
1826	Mr. Brontë brings home twelve wooden soldiers for Branwell; this is the catalyst for the creation of the Brontës' juvenile fantasy worlds and writings. Charlotte and Branwell begin the "Angrian" stories and magazines; Emily and Anne work on the "Gondal" saga.

1831	Charlotte goes to Miss Wooler's school at Roe Head, but leaves seven months later to tend to her sisters' education.
1835	Charlotte returns to Miss Wooler's school as governess, accompanied by Emily. After three months, Emily leaves school because of homesickness.
1837	Emily becomes a governess at Miss Patchett's school, near Halifax; remains there for about six months.
1838–1842	Over half of Brontë's surviving poems written.
1840	All three sisters live at Haworth.
1842	Charlotte and Emily travel to Brussels to study music and foreign languages at Pensionnat Héger. Upon the death of their aunt, they return to Haworth.
1843	Branwell joins Anne in York as tutor to the Robinson family. Charlotte returns to Brussels. Emily alone at Haworth with her father; a time of creativity and freedom.
1844	Emily begins to arrange her poems into two notebooks, dividing the Gondalan from the non-Gondalan material.
1845	Charlotte discovers Emily's poems and convinces her sister to collaborate on a volume of poems; Emily also begins writing *Wuthering Heights*.
1846	*Poems, by Currer, Ellis, and Acton Bell* published, with the Brontë's paying for costs. Two copies are sold. Charlotte's *The Professor*, Emily's *Wuthering Heights*, and Anne's *Agnes Grey* are all completed. The latter two are accepted by T.C. Newby, but *The Professor* is rejected. Charlotte's *Jane Eyre* is begun and accepted by Smith, Elder & Co. upon its completion in 1847.
1847	*Jane Eyre* published. *Wuthering Heights* and *Agnes Grey* published by T.C. Newby.
1848	Confusion in the literary world over the identity and number of the Bells; Anne publishes *The Tenant of Wildfell Hall*; Emily withdraws more resolutely into herself; September 24, Branwell dies of tuberculosis; October 1, Emily leaves home for the last time to attend Branwell's funeral service—she catches a severe cold which develops into inflammation of the lungs; December 19, Emily Brontë dies of tuberculosis.
1849	Anne dies of tuberculosis, May 28.
1850	*Wuthering Heights* reissued, with a selection of poems, and a biographical notice of her sisters' lives by Charlotte.

Contributors

HAROLD BLOOM is Sterling Professor of the Humanities at Yale University. He is the author of 30 books, including *Shelley's Mythmaking, The Visionary Company, Blake's Apocalypse, Yeats, A Map of Misreading, Kabbalah and Criticism, Agon: Toward a Theory of Revisionism, The American Religion, The Western Canon,* and *Omens of Millennium: The Gnosis of Angels, Dreams, and Resurrection. The Anxiety of Influence* sets forth Professor Bloom's provocative theory of the literary relationships between the great writers and their predecessors. His most recent books include *Shakespeare: The Invention of the Human,* a 1998 National Book Award finalist, *How to Read and Why, Genius: A Mosaic of One Hundred Exemplary Creative Minds, Hamlet: Poem Unlimited, Where Shall Wisdom Be Found?,* and *Jesus and Yahweh: The Names Divine.* In 1999, Professor Bloom received the prestigious American Academy of Arts and Letters Gold Medal for Criticism. He has also received the International Prize of Catalonia, the Alfonso Reyes Prize of Mexico, and the Hans Christian Andersen Bicentennial Prize of Denmark.

VIRGINIA WOOLF was a British author who is considered to be one of the foremost modernist/feminist literary figures of the twentieth century. Between the World Wars, Woolf was a significant figure in London literary society and a member of the Bloomsbury Group. Her most famous novels include *Mrs. Dalloway, To The Lighthouse, Orlando,* and *Jacob's Room.*

DOROTHY VAN GHENT taught at Kansas University and the University of Vermont. Her numerous publications include *The English Novel: Form and Fraction* and *Keats: The Myth of the Hero.*

187

SUSAN GUBAR is Distinguished Professor of English and Women's Studies at Indiana University. She has co-written and edited many books with SANDRA M. GILBERT, professor of English at the University of California. In 1979 they published *The Madwoman in the Attic: The Woman Writer and the 19th-Century Literary Imagination*. They also collaborated on the *Norton Anthology of Literature of Women*; *No Man's Land: The Place of the Woman Writer in the Twentieth Century*; *The War of the Words, Sexchanges, Letters from the Front, MotherSongs*, and *Masterpiece Theatre: An Academic Melodrama*.

NANCY ARMSTRONG is chair of the English department and Nancy Duke Lewis Professor of Comparative Literature, English, Modern Culture and Media, and Gender Studies at Brown University. She is the author of several books including, *Fiction in the Age of Photography: The Legacy of British Realism* and *Desire and Domestic Fiction: A Political History of the Novel*.

Welsh born STEVIE DAVIES is a novelist, literary critic, biographer and historian. She is a Fellow of the Royal Society of Literature, a Fellow of the Academi Gymreig and is Director of Creative Writing at the University of Wales, Swansea. Her nonfiction books include *Images of Kinship in Paradise Lost, Renaissance Views of Man, Emily Brontë: The Artist as Free Woman, Emily Brontë*, and *Unbridled Spirits: Women of the English Revolution*.

JOSEPH ALLEN BOONE is a Professor of English at USC. His interests include Nineteenth-Century; Modern and Contemporary Fiction; Feminist and Gender Studies; and Gay Literature and Theory. He is the author of *Tradition Counter Tradition: Love and the Form of Fiction* and *Libidinal Currents: Sexuality and the Shaping of Modernism*.

REGINA BARRECA is Professor of English Literature and Feminist Theory at the University of Connecticut. She has written and edited a diverse collection of works devoted to feminist explorations of women's humor, gender difference, romance, and the mass media. She is also the author of *Sex and Death in Victorian Literature*.

SUSAN MEYER is the author of *Imperialism at Home: Race and Victorian Women's Fiction*.

Bibliography

Allott, Miriam Farris., ed. *Emily Brontë: Wuthering Heights.* Casebook Series. Houndsmills, Basingstoke: Macmillan, 1992.

———, ed. *The Brontës: The Critical Heritage.* London: Routledge & Kegan Paul, 1974.

Ardholm, Helena. *The Emblem and the Emblematic Habit of Mind in Jane Eyre and Wuthering Heights.* Goteborg, Sweden: Acta Universitatis Gothoburgensis, 1999.

Abraham, Andrew. "Emily Brontë's Gendered Response to Law and Patriarchy." *Brontë Studies: The Journal of the Brontë Society* 29, no 2. (July 2004): 93–103.

Armstrong, Nancy. "Emily Brontë In and Out of Her Time." *Genre* 15 (1982): 243–64.

———. *Desire and Domestic Fiction: A Political History of the Novel.* New York and Oxford: Oxford University Press, 1987.

Barreca, Regina. "The Power of Excommunication: Sex and the Feminine Text in *Wuthering Heights.*" In *Sex and Death in Victorian Literature.* Basingstoke: Macmillan, 1990. 227–240.

Barker, Juliet. *The Brontës.* London: Weidenfeld & Nicolson, 1994.

Beaumont, Matthew. "Heathcliff's Great Hunger: The Cannibal Other in *Wuthering Heights.*" *Journal of Victorian Culture* 9 (Fall 2004): 137–163.

Bloom, Harold, ed. *The Brontë Sisters.* New York: Chelsea House, 2002.

——, ed. *Modern Critical Views: The Brontës*. New Haven: Chelsea House, 1986.

Boone, Joseph Allen. "*Wuthering Heights:* Uneasy Wedlock and Unquiet Slumbers." *Tradition Counter Tradition: Love and the Form of Fiction*. Chicago: U of Chicago P, 1987. 151–172.

Chitham, Edward. *The Birth of Wuthering Heights: Emily Brontë at Work*. New York: St. Martin's Press, 1998.

——. *A Life of Emily Brontë*. Oxford; New York: Basil Blackwell, 1987.

Davies, Stevie. *Emily Brontë*. Plymouth, U.K.: Northcote House, 1998.

——. *Emily Brontë: The Artist as a Free Woman*. Manchester: Carcanet, 1983.

Dawson, Terence. *The Effective Protagonist in the Nineteenth-Century British Novel: Scott, Brontë, Eliot, Wilde*. Aldershot, England; Burlington, VT: Ashgate, 2004.

De Grazia, Emilio. "The Ethical Dimension of *Wuthering Heights*." *Midwest Quarterly* 19 (Winter 1978):178–195.

Delamotte, Eugenia C. *Perils of the Night: A Feminist Study of Nineteenth-Century Gothic*. New York: Oxford University Press, 1990.

Duthie, Enid L. *The Brontës and Nature*. New York: St. Martin's Press, 1986.

Eagleton, Terry. *Heathcliff and the Great Hunger: Studies in Irish Culture*. London: Verso, 1995.

——. *Myths of Power: A Marxist Study of the Brontës*. Anniversary edition. New York: Palgrave Macmillan, 2005.

Frantz, Andrea Breemer. *Redemption and Madness: Three Nineteenth-Century Feminist Views on Motherhood and Childbearing*. Las Colinas, TX: Ide House, 1993.

Goetz, William R. "Genealogy and Incest in *Wuthering Heights*." *Studies in the Novel* 14, no. 4 (Winter 1982): 359–76.

Gilbert, Sandra and Susan Gubar. *The Madwoman in the Attic: The Woman Writer and the Nineteenth-century Literary Imagination*. New Haven: Yale UP, 1979.

Hewish, John. *Emily Brontë: A Critical and Biographical Study*. London: Macmillan, 1969.

Hinton, Laura. "Sentimental Nature in Wuthering Heights; or William Wyler Meets Emily Brontë on the Yorkshire Moors." In *The Perverse Gaze of Sympathy*. Albany, NY: State University of New York Press, 1999.

Holbrook, David. *Wuthering Heights: A Drama of Being*. Sheffield, England: Sheffield Academic Press, 1997.

Homans, Margaret. *Women Writers and Poetic Identity: Dorothy Wordsworth, Emily Brontë, and Emily Dickinson*. Princeton: Princeton UP, 1980.

Kermode, Frank. "Wuthering Heights as Classic." in *The Classic: Literary Images of Performance and Change*. London: Faber & Faber, 1975.

Knoepflmacher, U.C., *Emily Brontë: Wuthering Heights*. Cambridge; New York: Cambridge University Press, 1989.

Leavis, Q. D. "A Fresh Approach to *Wuthering Heights*." In *Lectures in America*, by F. R. Leavis and Q. D. Leavis. New York: Pantheon, 1969.

Lenta, Margaret. "Capitalism or Patriarchy and Immoral Love: A Study of *Wuthering Heights*." *Theoria: A Journal of Studies in the Arts, Humanities and Social Sciences* 62 (1984): 63–76.

Levy, Anita. "Blood, Kinship, and Gender." *Genders* 5 (July 1989): 70–85.

Mengham, Rod. *Emily Brontë: Wuthering Heights*. New York: Penguin Books, 1989.

Meyer, Susan. "'Your Father Was Emperor of China, and Your Mother an Indian Queen': Reverse Imperialism in *Wuthering Heights*." In *Imperialism at Home: Race and Victorian Women's Fiction*. Ithaca and London: Cornell University Press, 1996.

Miller, J. Hillis. *Fiction and Repetition: Seven English Novels*. Cambridge, MA: Harvard UP, 1982.

Mitchell, Hayley R., ed. *Readings on Wuthering Heights*. San Diego: Greenhaven Press, 1999.

Newman, Beth. "The Situation of the Looker-On: Gender, Narration and Gaze in *Wuthering Heights*." *PMLA* 105 (October 1990): 1029–41.

O'Neill, Judith, ed. *Critics on Charlotte and Emily Brontë*. Coral Gables, FL: University of Miami Press, 1968.

Parker, Patricia. "The (Self-) Identity of the Literary Text: Property, Propriety, Proper Place, and Proper Name in *Wuthering Heights*." In *Identity of the Literary Text*. Eds. Mario J. Valdes and Own Miller. Toronto; Buffalo: U of Toronto Press, 1985. 92–116.

Pykett, Lyn. *Emily Brontë*. Savage, MD: Barnes & Noble Books, 1989.

Sale, William, Jr. and Richard Dunn, eds. *Wuthering Heights: Authoritative Text*. Third Edition. New York: W. W. Norton & Company, 1990.

Stewart, Susan. "*The Ballad in Wuthering Heights*." *Representations* 86 (Spring 2004): 175–197.

Stoneman, Patsy. Brontë Transformations: *The Cultural Dissemination of Jane Eyre and Wuthering Heights*. London; New York: Prentice Hall/Harvester Wheatsheaf, 1996.

———, ed. *Wuthering Heights: Emily Brontë*. Houndmills: Macmillan, 1993.

Sutherland, John. *Is Heathcliff a Murderer?: Great Puzzles in Nineteenth-Century Literature*. New York: Oxford University Press, 1996. Thomas, Ronald R. Dreams of Authority: Freud and the Fictions of the Unconscious. Ithaca: Cornell UP, 1990.

Tytler, Graeme. "The Parameters of Reason in *Wuthering Heights*." *Brontë Studies* 30 (November 2005): 232–242.

Van Ghent, Dorothy. "Wuthering Heights." In *The English Novel: Form and Function*. New York: Holt, Rinehart and Winston, 1953. 153–170.

Vine, Steve. *Emily Brontë*. Twayne English Authors Series. New York: Twayne Publishers, 1998.

Vogler, Thomas A., ed. *Twentieth Century Interpretations of Wuthering Heights*. Englewood Cliffs, NJ: Prentice-Hall, 1968.

Winnifrith, Thomas John, ed. *Critical Essays on Emily Brontë*. New York: G. K. Hall & Co., 1997.

Woolf, Virginia. "*Jane Eyre* and *Wuthering Heights*." In *The Common Reader*. London: Hogarth Press, 1925.

Acknowledgments

"'Jane Eyre' and 'Wuthering Heights'" by Virginia Woolf. From *The Common Reader*, pp. 196–204. © 1925 by The Hogarth Press. Reprinted by permission of The Society of Authors.

"On *Wuthering Heights*" by Dorothy Van Ghent. From *The English Novel: Forma and Function*, pp. 153–170. © 1953 by Dorothy Van Ghent. Reprinted by permission of Holt, Rinehart and Winston.

"Looking Oppositely: Emily Brontë's Bible of Hell" by Sandra M. Gilbert and Susan Gubar. From *The Madwoman in the Attic: The Woman Writer and the Nineteenth-Century Literary Imagination*, pp. 248–308. © 1979 by Yale University Press. Reprinted by permission.

"Emily Brontë In and Out of Her Time" by Nancy Armstrong. From *Genre* Vol. 15, No. 3 (Fall 1982), pp. 243–264. © 1982 by The University of Oklahoma. Reprinted by permission.

"Baby-Work: The Myth of Rebirth in *Wuthering Heights*" by Stevie Davies. From *Emily Brontë: The Artist as a Free Woman*, pp. 95–113. ©1983 by Stevie Davies. Reprinted by permission of Carcanet Press, Ltd.

"*Wuthering Heights*: Uneasy Wedlock and Unquiet Slumbers" by Joseph Allen Boone. From *Tradition Counter Tradition: Love and the Form of Fiction*, pp. 151–172. © 1987 by The University of Chicago Press. Reprinted by permission.

"The Power of Excommunication: Sex and the Feminine Text in *Wuthering Heights*" by Regina Barreca. From *Sex and Death in Victorian Literature*, edited by Regina Barreca, pp. 227–240. © 1990 by Regina Barreca. Reproduced with permission of Palgrave Macmillan.

"'Your Father Was Emperor of China, and Your Mother an Indian Queen': Reverse Imperialism in *Wuthering Heights*" by Susan Meyer. From *Imperialism at Home: Race and Victorian Women's Fiction*, pp. 96–125. © 1996 by Cornell University Press. Used by permission of the publisher, Cornell University Press.

Every effort has been made to contact the owners of copyrighted material and secure copyright permission. Articles appearing in this volume generally appear much as they did in their original publication with few or no editorial changes. In some cases foreign language text has been removed from the original essay. Those interested in locating the original source will find bibliographic information in the bibliography and acknowledgments sections of this volume.

Index

Characters in literary works are indexed by first name (if any), followed by the name of the work in parentheses